T0365248

DESTINED FOR GREATNESS

Alex Osorio

authorHOUSE

AuthorHouse™
1663 Liberty Drive
Bloomington, IN 47403
www.authorhouse.com
Phone: 833-262-8899

Published by AuthorHouse 02/10/2022

ISBN: 978-1-6655-5186-1 (sc)
ISBN: 978-1-6655-5185-4 (e)

Print information available on the last page.

Scripture quotations marked KJV are from the Holy Bible, King James Version (Authorized Version). First published in 1611. Quoted from the KJV Classic Reference Bible, Copyright © 1983 by The Zondervan Corporation.

This book is printed on acid-free paper.

CONTENTS

DESTINED FOR GREATNESS

CHAPTER 3

YOUR DESTINY NOW / TU DESTINO AHORA / VOTRE DESTIN MAINTENANT

- Preparation & Discipline / Preparación y disciplina / Préparation et discipline
- Gaining Momentum / Ganando impulso / Prendre de l'élan
- The Final Stretch / La recta final / La dernière ligne droite
- This is Where the NEW You Begins / Aquí es donde comienza tu nuevo yo / C'est ici que le nouveau vous commence
- If not now when? / Si no es ahora, ¿cuándo? / Si ce n'est pas maintenant, quand?

DEDICATION

I want to take this moment and dedicate this book to the Glory of the Father, Son & Holy Ghost. For the fresh revelation and inspiration to write this book, it may be a blessing to all those who may read it.

To my Father & Mother, my dear Apostle and First Lady, for their unwavering and loving support; they have only seen the best in me and for me through my ups and downs. I love you, Dad & Mom.

To my beautiful wife Chrissy, her patience, love and support not only through this project but for doing life with me; thank you, and I love you. Thank you for putting up with the long nights, bright computer screen and the need for silence.

To my firstborn son Elohim, you make being a father a blessing, my pride and joy. The heir to all that I have may your heart and service to God never die but grow ever more to serve your generation.

To my princess Faith, you carry my heart with you daily; my endless love to you, my butterball. Be the woman of God that God has called you to be, and lead your generation into the presence of God, lead and serve; great is your reward in heaven and here on earth.

For the first time, to my youngest son Israel, for he was not born during the last three books, the future is bright for you, my son, for you shall carry my mantle should the Lord tarry. Therefore, serve the Lord with all your heart, my son.

To my Brothers and Sister; Pastor Mayron & Pastor Rachel, Pastor Eve, Pastor Misael & Laura, to Chazak, Alexandra, Victor, Shaddai, Shama, Adonai, Roni, Kadesh Zekiah and of course Zion; THANK YOU for your love, patience and support, as we minister together-thank you!

Thank you to my Fire of God Church family and friends-the best church I could have ever asked for; thank you for your love, prayer, and support. You make being a pastor look easy-The Lord bless you and always keeps you! To the power couple of Erica Morales for the amazing cover photo & Jeremy Sevillano for the outstanding cover design…you guys are the best!

CHAPTER ONE

DESTINED FOR GREATNESS
AND SO IT BEGINS....

This is where it all begins, a self-declaration of who you are because until we don't address the old you, the NEW YOU will never arise. So you must be honest to address the old you, open to addressing your faults, for when you do, you liberate yourself from the shackles and freedom is experienced to begin the process to your destiny.

Weakness? Do I have any faults? It's the first question that sets everything into perspective. Do you have drawbacks? The answer to that question is, I am nothing but weakness. I am not naturally assertive, fast or flexible; I am certainly not the most intelligent man in the world; I get emotional over things that I shouldn't get that emotional over.

I eat the wrong foods, don't sleep enough, procrastinate, and waste time. I care too much about meaningless things and do not care enough about the essential things.

My ego is too big, and my mind is too small to try even to begin to understand God's unlimited plans that he has for my life. So my thoughts are trapped, often inside themselves.

Having said all of this, I have a saying that goes something like this: a person's strength is often their biggest weakness. Yet, their faults can become strengths.

Alex Osorio

You can not accept how the world labels you or defines you. You can not take their conclusion of how you will end up, especially if they declare that you are doomed to fail and doomed to go nowhere.

The world's forecast about you and your goals is dim and not very encouraging. Often, we spend so much time reading that forecast and hearing it that it suddenly becomes what you believe and who you are. It takes hold of your mind and emotions and manifests itself into your vocabulary, shaping you into something outside of God's plan and mould for your life.

We get so caught up in everyone's opinion of you that you forget the path that you should be on. The fight is honest, accurate every day, from the moment you open your eyes to the moment you close them, and it seems like the fight is over then, but it continues in your dreams and thoughts.

I fight every day, I'm fighting, I'm struggling, and I'm scraping, and I'm chipping away at those weaknesses because the battle is real! Your greatest enemy is YOU; your most significant challenge is YOU. The fight to change your weaknesses is real; the struggle to stop your weaknesses from growing is real, and either it defeats you, or you defeat it.

Some days I win, and some days I don't, but every day I get back up, and I move forward, fists clenched, eye on the prize, with everything I got to overcome those weaknesses. So I get back up and run toward the fight, run toward the struggle, run toward the fear that is staring me in the face because the only way to succeed is NEVER to BACK DOWN but always stand up and fight.

Your shortfalls and insecurities will always be yelling at the top of their lungs to try and derail you from your path, but if you can wake up every morning and decide that you will be better today than yesterday, then my dear friend, you have started to win this fight. Many people will decide that you are a threat to them, that your goals are a threat to them, and that is where you decide whether to give in or press in.

2

You are not moulded by what others say; you are set daily by what you say to yourself. The Bible says, **"I can do all things through Christ who strengthens me "Phil 4:13.** That very word is a statement that should be spoken into your life every single day and minute of your life. He starts by saying, **I can!** Think about that for just a minute.....**I CAN!** and he continues to say, **DO ALL THINGS!** It means you can do all things! If that word or phrase does not excite you and motivate you, I don't think anything can.

But here is the key, he says **through Christ that strengthens me!** So you can do all things, but you can not do all things without Christ. **John 15:5 says,'** **"I am the vine, you *are* the branches. He who abides in Me, and I in him, bears much fruit; for without Me you can do nothing.**

Yet again, here he tells us that we can bear much fruit IF we abide in him and that IF is a big one! Our weaknesses often take us outside the path that allows us to bear fruit. Our weaknesses dry up our Faith and Prayer life if you let them. And he finishes the sentence by saying a definitive expression, and that is **FOR WITHOUT ME YOU CAN DO NOTHING!** Not only is it a bold statement, but it's a statement that gives you no room for negotiation; let me explain...

We often want to negotiate with God or play the victim card with Him. But, unfortunately, that does not work! He gave us the key to success, the key to greatness and that key is **HIM!**

In HIM is the power to overcome much of what we try and overcome and fail on our own. I can tell you everything I've done, but the only thing I can not do is grind for you! We read the keys, hear the message, and think that just because we read it or listen to it, all of a sudden, it will manifest itself into something extraordinary in our life. This is when we begin to fail, this state of mind frequently grabs hold of us, and if we don't fight back, we will be defeated before we even start.

I love watching nature shows, primarily where the predators hunt their prey. I love to analyze their thinking, their moves, both the predator and the target. For example, look at the gazelle and the lion for a moment.

What's the difference between the gazelle and the lion other than the obvious? The gazelle is always running in fear; it knows its days are numbered so long as the lion is around. They're running in fear, knowing that the moment they get sloppy, they die.

Their fear is their drive, and many people often are not driven by God, not by their goals and visions; their fear drives them. Fear will always push you to your Death. You have often heard the expression, "**What is your why?** "The lion does not ask why; he does what he does best; they hunt! The problem with that question is that it is often found without any substance. Your **"Why"** is not essential if your **"Why "**does not include HIM. God has to be the centre of everything we do and who we are.

Every opportunity has to be taken like it's the last opportunity you will ever get. But, in reality, it just might be because we don't know when Death will come knocking at our door and call us home. So, the real question should be, what motivates you? What excites you? What makes you want to get up each morning? Every day you must reprove yourself again, still learning, still growing, because the day you become content is the day that you no longer live; you will exist but not live.

The day you stop growing, the day you stop learning, the day you stop reproving yourself is the day you die inside, and it becomes the day that the person that was trying to pass you does.

I'm here to tell you that you can not cry because you gave up, cry because you will keep going, Don't cry to quit! You are already in pain, you are already bruised, you've made it this far, and now you want to stop? You are already hurt might as well get a reward from it.

A woman about to give birth doesn't quit simply because the contractions are too close to each other, or the pain is unbearable? NO! she pushes forward because she's about to give birth to someone incredible. So should you, there is no room to quit, there is no room to stop, there is no room to slow down when the contractions of life hit you one after the other, you don't quit-you push forward and onward.

THE FIGHT IS REAL!

Yes, it is, and they say you must go down swinging, but I tell you more often than none, you won't go down at all; you will win. But you have to make that attitude part of your daily life. Do the things others won't; do those things that make your stomach turn because those things often yield the most significant rewards. In gym terminology, do the extra repetition, run the additional 5 minutes, try an exercise that you don't like because what takes you out of your comfort zone will bring you higher and closer to your goals.

Those things that scare us, those that intimidate us, and those that seem impossible are the things that you must and have to do because what lies behind those mirages of impossibilities are rewards that far exceed our expectations.

I was in my mid 20's, I was staring at my firstborn, just a baby sleeping, and then I looked at myself in the mirror and realized that I had to make changes to my life; otherwise, there was a possibility that my son was never going to see live a long life. I was 25 years old, and I was in the worst shape of my life, physically speaking. I was overweight and felt like a walrus and no offence to the walrus. At that moment, I decided that enough was enough, I was going to impact my health to change the trajectory of my life, and then I was going to do it for my son.

Many people make a mistake because they want to please everyone and make others happy while living miserable. But, unfortunately, you have to do it for you and your first! Psalm 139:14 I will give thanks to you because **I have been so amazingly and miraculously made.** Your works are miraculous, and my soul is fully aware of this.

Ephesians 5:29 For no one has ever hated his own body, **but he nourishes and tenderly cares for it,** as the Lord does the church.

It is vital that you set a goal for yourself and a happy and motivated plan. It's not being selfish; no, in doing so, you are extending the joy you bring to someone else. Hypothetically speaking, I looked at myself in the mirror and decided that I was ok with the way I was and that I should be accepted just the way I am. What a mistake that would have been.

My lack of Action would have brought great pain to myself and my family. Health complications would have cancelled any future activities I might have shared with my son; I would have also brought stress to my wife, all because I decided to do nothing.

THE PRICE OF DOING NOTHING

The price is high and hurts, but a price must be paid. So you see, no matter which road you decide to take, you will pay the price! Guaranteed that the price you will pay for doing nothing will always be higher and more costly than the price of doing something to change your life. So make the right choices, make yourself stronger mentally, physically and spiritually.

When you do nothing, your weakness will do everything to become dominant in your life. When you do nothing, fear grows; problems become more prominent than they are; when you do nothing, chaos erupts; when you do nothing, evil prevails. You see, the cost of doing nothing is exceptionally high and painful. It sets you back days, if not years. Doing nothing sends you down a road filled with depression, sadness, frustrations, and disappointments. When you do nothing, you kill the very essence of what God put inside of you.

Proverbs 19:8 **To acquire wisdom is to love oneself**; people who cherish understanding will prosper. To acquire means action, it requires you do something opposite of nothing. To acquire anything means investing in knowledge of what you will achieve, which means acting and not standing still.

Every day is a fight, fight against fear, fight against weakness, against time, against decay, against the desire to do nothing; every day is a fight that you alone have to fight to achieve that which God has placed inside of you.

When you face a challenge or a situation you know you can not win, remember that you have everything to lose if you do nothing. The cost of doing nothing will not only be felt by you, but it will be felt by everyone around you, even those that may know you from afar.

Stand up, go forward, go out in a blaze of glory, fighting with everything you got, every ounce of energy, every beat of your sweat and every drop of blood till your last breath and then and only then will you have conquered the first step which is overcoming doing nothing!

EXCUSES-WHEN YOU HAVE THEM, YOU NEVER LOSE

It is a powerful weapon that the enemy uses. Excuses seem perfectly legit in their reasoning; they seem justified and fair, but they are a poison that enters your mind and your heart and slowly and indeed begins to eat away your vision, goals, and desire to succeed. When you allow them to join your vocabulary, they dominate your mindset. At this stage, at that moment, your dreams and visions, goals and ambitions begin to spiral out of control into a death spin that very few have been able to overcome and turn around.

Excuses are your licence that you give yourself the right not to do anything and eventually fail. Excuses give you the freedom to blame everything and everyone for your inability or lack thereof to not do anything. They allow you the escape of not saying what you feel or what you want to do or not do. They are so convincing that it becomes "law" to you once you accept it and live by them. They are boundaries that you set on your mind, limitations on your goals and visions, boundaries to your heart that prevent it from growing in Faith.

You can not grow when excuses surround you. You can not excel when excuses are living in your mind and heart. You can not achieve greatness when excuses have become a form of expression and a way of lifestyle.

Life is not easy; nobody said it would be, Jesus himself said in John 16:33 These things I have spoken unto you, that in me ye might have Peace. **In**

the world ye shall have tribulation: but be of good cheer; I have overcome the world. I wish he would have said problems, issues, or dilemmas, but he noted **tribulations!**

One thing is to have problems but to have tribulations is on another level. The pressure and stress that trials can bring on someone can be crushing, and at that moment, excuses are the perfect way to escape the fear and pain that one may experience. Reasonable people can not handle on the level that someone great is. The problem is that we want to be the CEO but not have the CEO problems or stress. We want greatness but not the process of pain to achieve it. We want to be successful, but we want it on a silver platter, but the reality is that nothing great ever comes out of excuses. Nothing worth anything ever comes out of excuses-nothing!

We say we want it, dream and think about it, but then realize that the moment you decide to go after it is when your excuses take life, and you either squash them, or they squash you.

Life is not fair, but excuses are not acceptable on the grand stage to achieve greatness. There is no room for excuses to have a seat at the table of your dreams. If you allow them a chair, then you allow them a voice, you give your excuses a voice, then you have given yourself a "legitimate" reason to fail. Nobody will blame you for it because your reasoning or excuses seem justifiable and must be accepted by everyone.

Yet the next part of that verse is exciting; it says, **"Be of good cheer"** wait a moment, be of good cheer? in the middle of tribulations, be of good cheer? How does that even make any sense? Usually, tribulations are not times of great joy or to be in a cheerful mood. When I think of tribulations, I often think of pain and sorrow, yet in this verse, Jesus says to be of good cheer! Furthermore, he goes on to say, **"For I have overcome the world."**

Read that carefully; Jesus has overcome the world; it never said you. We must understand the following: victory doesn't start with you; success starts with Jesus and only Jesus. If we are in HIM and HE is in us, then that victory that Jesus has claimed is also a victory that we can claim and rejoice over. He overcame the world and all of its tribulations, trials, and fears. Since we are in HIM and HE is in us, that victory claim is also given to those in him.

The longer you wait to put your excuses to rest, the longer your dreams become a reality. Every minute, every hour, and day you wait is a minute, hour and day that prolongs dreams and goals from becoming a living reality in your present. You can not delay in putting those fears to rest; you can not delay in putting those excuses to bed; you must arise with a desire to overcome those fears and excuses, a desire to be a better version of yourself every single day.

The opportunity is before us every single day, and it requires you to give 120% of you, yet you are providing only 70% effort and 50% effort, and we want what those that are paying with sweat, tears and blood have, and that is not going to happen, it is not free!

It takes both emotion and logic to reach your maximum potential; you can not get the top only on either of them; you need both.

THE POWER OF EMOTION

Emotion can propel you to greatness and bring you down to levels so low that you can not begin to imagine. You must give it everything you have to go beyond your limits because emotion and logic will both reach their limits, and when one does, you need to rely on the other. When it doesn't make any logical sense to keep going, you must use emotion to take you to the next step.

It would be best if you learned to use your anger and fears to push you further to say, **I WON'T STOP!**. It is easy to quit, easy to give up and hide behind an excuse; all of that is easy, but easy will never get you to where God wants you to end up. So many believe that God will take them to their destiny, and this is where they make a mistake in assuming that. God has a plan of greatness for your life; he said it clearly in **Jeremiah 29:11 "For I know the thoughts that I think toward you, says the Lord, thoughts of peace and not of evil, to give you a future and a hope."**

9

Paul also states in **2ⁿᵈ Timothy 4:7, "I have fought the good fight, I have finished the race, I have kept the faith."**

Jeremiah spells it out clearly that God's plans for you are GREAT! They are massive, filled with opportunities and filled with Peace, hope and a future. Yet Paul says, I have fought the good fight! he didn't say that someone fought it for him or that it was easy, he said it, I have fought the good FIGHT!

God's plans are great, which translates that the fight will be great, promises a future and hope, but Paul says there is a race to run and finish, and lastly, he says, **I have kept the Faith!** Both of these things work together. I repeat, and you have heard that nobody said it was going to be easy or a walk in the park, and if they did, they either lied to you or don't know what they are talking about.

When your emotions are screaming that they have had enough, and you think that you are going to break emotionally, override that emotion with three key ingredients, Logic, Prayer and Action!

Logic to realize that going back is not an option, Prayer to stimulate your Faith, knowing that with God all things are possible, and Action, because it is not a real prayer if it doesn't boost your Faith into Action. The Bible says in **Hebrews 11:6, And without faith, it is impossible to please God, because anyone who comes to him must believe that he exists and that he rewards those who earnestly seek him.**

You must fight the emotions that cripple your actions, with feelings that give meaning to your fight. It would be best if you found the strength and tenacity to look at yourself in the mirror, and with everything that you have to say to yourself, **I CAN NOT STOP!**

You don't belong at the bottom, and it is time for you to realize this and get yourself up, fight the fight, and begin to walk to where God wants you to be. **Deut 28: 13 says, And the Lord shall make thee THE HEAD, and not the tail, and thou shalt BE ABOVE ONLY, and thou shalt**

not be beneath, if thou hearken unto the commandments of the Lord thy God which I command thee this day, to observe and to do them.

These are powerful words that must be spoken into your daily life each time those emotions begin to whisper in your heart, mind and spirit to give up. It's time for you to get uncomfortable at being at the bottom, and you may ask, is that even possible? But, unfortunately, this is a reality for many these days. Emotions of fear and doubt keep you at the bottom, feeding the sympathy and empathy of others toward you. While all of this is "good," it becomes like a self-virus keeping you from ever getting up and becoming all that you are to be in life.

While it may feel good to have others' sympathy and empathy, it does not give you the strength to get up, and many use that to stay there because there is no pressure being at the bottom. There is no pressure on you to succeed when others give you sympathy; there is no reason to grow when others work so that you may feel better or give you an illusion of getting better. There is no pressure on you to better yourself because your emotions have crippled you, and you feed off the sympathy of others. Eventually, Death comes mentally, spiritually and physically.

The Bible says that the prodigal son was in a pigs pit (**Luke 15**) eating their food, and when he came to himself, he decided to return home to his father's house. Analyze this for a moment; he went from wealth to eating pigs' food; think about the emotional toll this must have taken on this man's life. Then, think about the steps he must have taken to get to that stage in his life. You don't go from wealth to eating pigs' food overnight.

His emotions must have decayed so much to bring him to that state of mind and actions. He lost all hope, motivation, and Faith; instead of immediately returning to his father's house, pride set in and took control of his emotions, which led him to the pig's pit. Pride is a destiny killer; pride is a dream killer; nothing good comes from pride. So the Bible says in **James 4:6, But He gives more grace. Therefore He says: "God resists the proud, But gives grace to the humble."**

God resists the proud! The emotion of pride contradicts everything God wants to do in your life. The prodigal son's pride was so high that he would rather eat pigs' food than go back to his father's house. His pride was so high that he decided that pigs' food was better than returning to his father's house despite losing his money and fortune. Not only did he lose his wealth, but he had also lost all of his so-called "friends" where did they go?

Eventually, when all the sympathy is done, and there is no more empathy to receive, those same people that once gave you those things will turn their backs and say, enough with this person. So this area is critical and very dangerous because once all the support is lost, many find themselves in a very dark space and sadly, many are lying six feet under the ground because they chose never to get up.

Is it possible to get up even if you are alone with nothing and eating pigs food? The answer is a very resounding **YES!**

Again, the Bible says, **I CAN DO ALL THINGS THROUGH CHRIST THAT STRENGTHENS ME! Phil 4:13**

The Bible also says in **Luke 15:17, "But when he came to himself, he said, 'How many of my father's hired servants have bread enough and to spare, and I perish with hunger!**

THE POWER OF LOGIC

The Bible says that **HE CAME TO HIMSELF AND SAID How many of my father's hired servants have bread enough and to spare, and I perish with hunger!**

There comes a moment to each person; through the mercy and grace of God, a "lightbulb" turns on in our mind igniting our spirit to wake up! But, first, he had to acknowledge where he was, had to recognize his surroundings, his condition, and realize what he had left behind.

Realizing where we are is a painful task; accepting that you have made a mistake is where you are because of those mistakes. Accepting that this is on you and no one else is critical. Carrying your cross is yours to bear is just as important as breathing. You will never rise from the ashes by blaming your condition on someone else.

The prodigal son came to himself, but you find that he did not blame anyone for where he was. He took on the responsibility for his actions and did not blame others for his condition. It is elementary to say it's because of this or that, or this person, life is not fair, or whatever you want to bring up, but at the end of the day, **you** must be responsible for where you are at in life and no one else.

Emotions eventually stop, and logic kicks in. Now, it may kick in to blame others and stay where you are, ultimately making things worse, or it kicks in, and you decide to change your status. The Bible says in **1ˢᵗ Peter 2:9, But you *are* a chosen generation, a royal priesthood, a holy nation, His own special people, that you may proclaim the praises of Him who called you out of darkness into His marvellous light;**

You can not quit now; this is the tenth round, you got two more to go, and when you get to a certain level of success and greatness, it has little to do about skill and everything to do about stamina.

The Bible says in **Matthew 24:13 But he that shall endure unto the end, the same shall be saved.** Endure means you must have stamina, not skill. You can have all the power and muscles, but if your opponent can outlast you one more round, then you lose, and he wins!

Your enemy doesn't have to be the strongest or the fastest; he has to last longer in the race than you. The Bible says in **1ˢᵗ Corinthians 9:24-27, "Do you not know that in a race all the runners run, but only one receives the prize? So run that you may obtain it. Every athlete exercises self-control in all things. They do it to receive a perishable wreath, but we an imperishable. So I do not run aimlessly; I do not box as one beating the air. But I discipline my body and keep it under control, lest after preaching to others, I should be disqualified.**

This is a mighty powerful verse; allow me to break this down for you. First, he starts by acknowledging that this is a race and you are not alone trying to obtain the prize. It is a web of intricate parts, all moving simultaneously because even though we are all running this race and only one will receive the "prize," it is symbolic because we all have different goals, visions and plans. Even though maybe some are running after the same prize as yours.

Every athlete exercises self-control in all things; he sees each person as an athlete, an excellent visualization. Self-control is so necessary because it separates you from the rest. Discipline is essential because to reach the end, reach the goal and receive the prize; you will be required to do things that may feel uncomfortable. To achieve the future will require you to pay the price, sacrifices will have to be made, and logic must be exercised. Preparation is necessary to succeed; we are doomed to fail without it.

They do it to receive a perishable wreath, but we an imperishable. So I do not run aimlessly. This is where we must realize that our eternal goal is much more important than our physical goal. We focus so much on natural logic and realistic goals that we forget that we are in this world, but we are not of this world. Our eyes should be set on the real goals, but we can never lose the perspective of our eternal goal.

Therefore, we do not run aimlessly; in other words, our race must be run with purpose and perspective. Stamina gives you the endurance to carry forward relentlessly, with the desire to reach the end and reach it in victory. There is no victory in quitting; there is no joy in giving up; there is no satisfaction in living a life without purpose-we do not run aimlessly!

I do not box as one beating the air. But I discipline my body and keep it under control. He makes it a point here to tell us that our actions must be focused and with purpose. Every step we take must be disciplined and keep our emotions in check. I do not, he says; it is a bold declaration that you must make each day. I do not quit; I do not give up, I do not make excuses, I do not give in to my negative emotions, I do not blame others for my mistakes, I do not become lazy, I do not go backwards-these are the words that you must live by each day.

I discipline my body and keep it under control, which means that greatness requires discipline and self-control. It is too easy to give in to all that negative stuff out there, too easy to hide behind a wall of excuses, but no great athlete ever makes excuses for not continuing.

If you have known me long enough, you will see that I love hockey; I was not born in Canada, but coming here at the early age of 5, Canada is home. I am a true Canadian with a love of hockey and hot chocolate.

In 2017, the Pittsburgh Penguins won their second back-to-back Stanley Cup. A great accomplishment. Hockey is a fast, intense, and fun sport to watch. I remember watching the game, and as the clock wound down to the last second, the excitement on the Penguins bench was electric. The buzzer sounded, and the players leaped onto the ice to congratulate each other. The hugs were deep, the smile on their faces was contagious, and the crowd was on fire!

But little did anyone know that one of their players played and won under circumstances nobody knew. We'll start with Penguins defenceman Ian Cole. The 28-year-old played just over 18 minutes a game for his team, and he did so with a broken hand and broken ribs since early in the Capitals series (second round). Yes, you read that correctly, a broken hand and broken ribs! So how could anyone play under those circumstances?

If I stub my toe on the edge of the bed, I am done; I'm out! Let alone play a high-intensity game with a broken hand or rib, for that matter. He played through his pain; he played through his agony, He played through the adversity-He played on. It would have been easy and justifiable for him to stop playing, and nobody would have faulted him for stopping. Yet what compelled him to keep going was the desire to win!

When your desire to win overcomes your pain, you win; when your passion to excel overcomes your struggle, You win each time. I can not begin to imagine the pain playing through those conditions was, but all we can talk about is that he won! Therefore, your story must speak of how you experienced victory through your pain, through your struggle, and your mess.

People love to tell your story, but they will mostly only say to the level of your pain, fears, struggles, and mess, and rarely about your achievements. Nobody knew he was playing through those conditions only until these things came to light after the series was done. So don't show your pain, don't broadcast your struggle, Don't showcase your weakness, for that will never do any good to you.

His teammates knew, his coaches knew, his family knew, but nobody else did. It must be the same way in your life; only certain people should know your weaknesses, fears, struggles and pain, and out of those specific people, there will only be some standing with you to help you get back up. This man must have had the best doctors advising him and what to do to keep going, not suggesting how to quit.

There are enough people in the world that will go out of their way to try and stop you from achieving anything in life. There will be enough people around to give you a pity party, but only those that are connected to you will understand your fight and help you in that fight to win.

Take a look at this story, Jesus raises the dead girl; the Bible says in **Mark 5:37-40, "He did not let anyone follow him except Peter, James and John the brother of James. When they came to the home of the synagogue leader, Jesus saw a commotion, with people crying and wailing loudly. So he went in and said to them, "Why all this commotion and wailing? The child is not dead but asleep." But they laughed at him.**

After he put them all out, he took the child's father and mother and the disciples who were with him and went in where the child was.

Jesus had an inner circle, but he also had an inner inner circle, shown here in this verse. **He did not let anyone follow him except Peter, James and John, the brother of James.** You must be able to shrink your inner circle to the people close to you, that whether you are going through thick or thin, they will have your back. Out of the 12 disciples, only Peter, James and John were allowed to follow Jesus where the miracle was. What happened to the rest? Where did they go? The Bible does not state their whereabouts but only mentions those that followed Jesus further.

Having many people around is not always a good thing; in this case, many people were taking up space and not making the area valuable. Jesus had shown up, and nobody seemed to care that he had a reputation of doing the miraculous; the Bible says that they laughed at him! How many so-called friends hear your dreams, vision, and goals, and instead of helping you achieve them, they laugh.

Jesus was bothered that there was so much commotion and wailing; he was upset for their lack of faith and belief. But then, those same people creating the ruckus and whaling began to laugh at Jesus suddenly!

Protect your circle, dreams, visions and goals, protect what God has placed inside you, Protect your plans, for they are not to be shared with everyone because not everyone will want to be there to see you succeed.

Protect your words, for they hold power and weight, for it is through them that things get created or things break down. You will have to fight and fight and fight, and many lose the fight not because they are not strong enough, but simply many can not beat the old version of you. You get beaten down by the negative version of you, the version of you that is unwilling to arise from the ashes, which speaks naturally and not by Faith.

You lose to the old you who had no hope or dreams because you don't fight long enough to see the NEW YOU arise. But, I can tell you this, there is a light at the end of the tunnel, it may be a small one, but if you commit to making one good decision after the other, it will pay dividends in ways that you only have dreamed.

Things will get better, maybe not overnight, perhaps not microwave style; it won't be instantaneous as much as we would like it to be; it takes time! But, the process builds character, gives you a thick skin; having character is everything in life; having the word of God in your life is the single most significant thing you can have to obtain the best that God has for you.

17

THE POWER OF YOUR WORDS

Your attitude is going to determine your altitude! Your words create the world you live in. The most challenging thing that I've had to learn over my years was to believe in the power of my words.

No matter your circumstances or situations before you, your words matter here on earth and in heaven. The world will enable you and try to define you through their words, and that is where you accept their terms spoken over you, or you begin to speak into your own life and create a new you.

We rely so much on the words of others; if they are encouraging words, we are lifted, and when they are negative words, they bring us down. Our words are stones. We are nothing but stone-throwers with each word we speak. But, on the other hand, if our words contain beauty, people treasure them. If our words include pain, people toss them aside, but not until after they have dealt with the wound they caused.

Proverbs 15:4 **"Gentle words bring life and health; a deceitful tongue crushes the spirit."** The words you speak or allow them to be said over you is the world you walk in. You will find that two people will be in two different atmospheres while in the same room, simply because they allowed words to change their perspective or mood. Gentle words bring life and health, so therefore your words can bring someone up, give them hope, and bring health to their bodies, mind and soul.

Yet, on the other hand, he says, a deceitful tongue CRUSHES the spirit; it doesn't bring them down; it crushes them. That's how much power our words hold.

Proverbs 16:24 **"Kind words are like honey-sweet to the soul and healthy for the body."** Yes, it is possible to change your future and present through your words. The words you speak over yourself are more important than anybody's other words that they might talk over you, even if they are good words. They come in second to the terms you should talk about over your life.

How many times do people talk themselves out of greatness or success? How often do we talk ourselves out of what God has laid up for us, simply because we don't believe and the words we have spoken into our lives have created a pit of despair and doubt that many never get out of?

It would be best if you made it happen; each day, change your vocabulary that will edify you and build you up. You can not wait for others to speak into your life. So when you see yourself in the mirror each morning, take the opportunity to talk to your new you, and don't let the old you come back, don't stop speaking into your life faith, hope and power, don't stop because if you do stop you allow the old you the come back alive. It will come back with a vengeance.

You must be the most incredible sales agent to yourself. Ask yourself each day, what will I sell to myself today? Would you buy rotten tomatoes at the market? The answer undoubtedly would be no! But how often do you sell to yourself and accept those rotten expressions you have let creep into your mind and heart or have heard someone speak them over you?

How often have you served yourself a dish of rotten words that do nothing to get you closer to your dreams but take you back to ashes of where you are trying to get out of.

For no matter oh bad it is or how bad it gets, your words have the power to change and affect the storm. **Mark 4:39 And he awoke and rebuked the wind and said to the sea, "Peace! Be still!" And the wind ceased, and there was a great calm.**

2ⁿᵈ Corinthians 12:9 But he said to me, "My grace is sufficient for you, for my power is made perfect in weakness." Therefore I will boast all the more gladly of my weaknesses so that the power of Christ may rest upon me.

Feed your mind the word of God, Feed your spirit the word of God, Feed your soul the word of God, **Romans 10:17 For Faith cometh by hearing and hearing by the word of God.** The word you feed yourself the word of God, the more you will see your words change.

When you change your words, you change the trajectory from what the enemy would want to what God has always wanted it to be. So feed your Faith, watch your doubt and fears starve, feed your Faith by digging into the scriptures, and feed your Faith until you begin to see a change in your words.

What you feed your mind is what your mouth will speak. If you only watch the news, the news will be the only thing you speak of, and all of a sudden, you allow the words you hear on the news to begin to influence your comments.

I heard my father once say that if today were the last day of your life, would it be the last thing you would say to yourself about yourself? It made me stop and look at myself in the mirror each day and force myself to change my vocabulary and what I say about myself.

We usually don't think about it; we believe that words are just words, but they have incredible power in reality. For example, God himself spoke everything into existence; with just one word, there was light; things went from nothing to everything with just one word.

***Proverbs 18:4* "A person's words can be life-giving water; words of true wisdom are as refreshing as a bubbling brook."**

The first step to changing your present and impacting your future is to believe that your words matter. There is no plan B because plan B distracts you from plan A. Plan A is to change your comments and believe that what you speak does make a difference in those that hear it and, especially to you, your dream, goals and future.

A person's words can be life-giving water; that's how powerful our words can be, **can be life-changing water!** You can not take your words for granted; you can not take your words as if they do not have any meaning; our words matter. They can produce life or take life in one sentence.

Proverbs 18:21 "Death and life are in the power of the tongue, and those who love it will eat its fruits."

Your tongue has a power that we can not begin to understand. So I had to do a little bit of research on the tongue and found out that, Your tongue is a group of muscles that work without the support of your skeleton. (No other muscle in the human body can do this!) That makes them incredibly flexible, which allows you to form sounds, whistle, move food around your mouth, swallow, and you can even use it to clean your teeth after eating.

Not only can you stick your tongue out, retract it to the back of your mouth, and move it side to side, but you can also completely change its shape! Whenever you roll your tongue, tuck it back, curl it under, or form it into a point, you are changing its shape.

Each person's tongue print is as unique as their fingerprints. Imagine a future in which we use fingerprints, retinal (eye) scans, and tongue scans to confirm our identities. Just picture that!

A swollen tongue is called macroglossia and can indicate other underlying health problems. For example, if you have indentations on the side of your tongue from your teeth, your tongue is probably swollen. It may be caused by hypothyroidism, an infection, allergies, inflammatory diseases, and many other conditions.

How many times do we have a swollen vocabulary or swollen words that cause aches and pains in our everyday life? Swollen words cause pain to the person speaking them but also cause pain to those that hear them. Swollen words can damage relationships, destroy friendships and give long-lasting wounds that often take many years to heal and overcome.

Swollen words can only be healed through prayer and reading the word; the Bible says in **Ephesians 4:29 Let no corrupt word proceed out of your mouth, but what is good for necessary edification, that it may impart grace to the hearers.**

Words are so powerful that not only can they create or destroy your world but also have an effect on those that hear them. For we can not begin to imagine the damage, a sentence can have in the spiritual realm, and if we did, we would change and refrain from the words we speak.

Colossians 3:8 "But now you yourselves are to put off all these: anger, wrath, malice, blasphemy, filthy language out of your mouth."

I always thought that anger, wrath, and malice were actions, but according to Colossians, they were formed from the words we spoke into existence. We create the environment we live in, create the atmosphere we walk in and create a world that impacts every person we encounter.

Don't let the noise of other people's words drown out the voice of God in your life. There will be many voices around you, all speaking to you simultaneously, but you must remember that when you submerge yourself in the word, you are investing in your words.

When you invest time into the word of God, you are making a significant investment into your present and future. An investment will enrich your vocabulary and stimulate your Faith for more significant personal growth. For it is through your Faith that words are spoken, and through those spoken words are mountains removed, giants fall, and walls come crashing down.

My wife is Portuguese, and she speaks it very well. However, we have three great kids, married over 15 years, and to this day, I have yet to learn the language—my apologies. I may hear her speak and pick up on certain words or phrases, but I can not speak them. How many times do we listen to the voice of God speaking to us through his word, and because we hear it and not practice it, we can not speak it when the enemy comes to attack us?

It's time to start working on your dream, not tomorrow, today! Limitations only exist in our minds, and they only exist to bind us and not allow us to grow or push forward. Fear spreads to our vocabulary, silencing our voice of Faith, and we become attached to fear, and we speak it, and once we speak it, we believe it, and once we think it, that thought takes a hold on our life.

Proverbs 12:18 "There is one whose rash words are like sword thrusts, but the tongue of the wise brings healing."

You will encounter many disappointments, setbacks, and defeats in changing your vocabulary. However, in the process of going through that, you will discover many things about yourself that you don't know right now. There is greatness in you, and your words have power. When you realize the magnitude of the power of your comments, you will then quickly begin without hesitation to change those words.

You will realize that you are more significant than your circumstances and that the words you speak directly affect those circumstances. At that moment, you will begin to understand that you are powerful enough to tell that mountain to move out of the way and cast yourself into the sea.

You will realize that heaven pays close attention to what you speak, not only when things are going well but especially when things are going at their worst.

Make a decision today; decide today that you will change the trajectory of your life by changing the way you speak! Just select that today you will change your future by changing the words that come out of your mouth. We don't have to talk about the dark and fear in our present; no, we can in the middle of those dark times and in the middle of that fear, we can choose to stand up and speak light, speak courage, speak the word of God and watch how heaven and God respond to your comments of Faith.

In the process of making that decision, you will be confronted with the old you, speaking the old way, and you can not run from your old self; you must engage yourself and win that battle. Against all odds, you must believe that your words matter and that going back to your old self is not an option. You have been down that road; you know what it feels like and looks like; there is nothing back there for you, just defeat. So when we don't know what to say, speak then the word of God; when we don't know how to say it, say it according to the word of God. For heaven and earth shall pass, but his word shall remain.

You must remain consistent because without consistency, we will never finish this race, if it were easy, then our results would all be great, but because greatness is not easy, only a few reach it. But every day is a battle to be great, not to be compared with someone else, but to challenge yourself to become the best version of yourself possible.

Remember that your competition in life is not anyone else but **you**! Your words give you the edge in that battle or can be your disadvantage. You either win the battle with your words or lose the fight because of your choice of words. We all have a choice in this battle. Your words are the weapons of choice, and only you can select them.

Great words are like swords that are sharpened before each fight; you sharpen your sword through the reading of God's word. The more you dig into HIS Word, the sharper your words become. Now, you are no longer speaking out of your imagination, but not God himself backs up your words because no, you are quoting his word, and he always responds to you repeating his word.

Colossians 4:6 "Let your speech always be gracious, seasoned with salt, so that you may know how you ought to answer each person."

Matthew 12:37 "For by your words you will be justified, and by your words, you will be condemned."

Your words must be forward and not backwards. Rough times will come, but you must remain standing firm on HIS word; tough times come to challenge our resolve, test our words, test our emotions that contribute to our words, but you must remain steadfast in your determination to change your vocabulary!

God gave us his word to overcome when we can not stand on our strength.

CHOOSE YOUR FUTURE

Your future is whatever you make it out to be, it is not what others say it is, not what others want it to be, but rather what you want it to be, it shall be. No matter the issues or the problems that may arise, your future is in your hands. You have the power to change it, affect it, and create it through the power of your words.

Proverb 3:5-6 says, "Trust in the Lord with all your heart and do not lean on your own understanding. In all your ways, acknowledge him, and he will make straight your paths."

No matter how crooked our ways may seem, the moment you acknowledge the Lord with your words, he will make the paths straight. It is no secret that the Lord is watching over you and taking care of you, though he may seem far, and sometimes it may feel like he's not there-he is!

He says **Trust in the Lord with all your heart,** not walking because you understand Him, but rather walking because you believe Him. Trust is also heard and felt through the words that you speak. You are the artist; your words are the paintbrush you use to create your masterpiece. Yet, he sees and knows all; therefore, he will correct our mistakes and make them to our advantage. **Trust** means just that **trust,** blindly, boldly, knowing that he is watching over us.

Our inability to speak life and speak blessing keeps us from receiving them; our lack of seeking the word limits our vocabulary, our declarations are tied up in our unbelief where there is no life at all.

The more the word gets inside of you, the more you become the word, the more you become the word, the better you become at choosing your future. If words are spoken but not believed, then they are just noise that is being made. Comments that are not acted upon become a rattling noise and bear no fruit.

For if you want a new car, you can not just pray for it, you must go and apply for it, but before you apply for it, you must go and see the car; before you see the vehicle, you must be interested in a vehicle, and before you become interested in a vehicle, you must open your mouth and say, I want a new car.

Everything first starts with what comes forth out of our mouths. You can not stop dreaming; you can not stop believing; it is necessary for you to align yourself with folks that will speak the same language as you do, the language of Faith. Align yourself with people that are hungry just like you are, people that will not take no for an answer, people who are relentless in their pursuit of greatness, people who not only will push you further but propel you to your next level.

If you align yourself with people that do not create their future in blessing and hope, then your future will be lost and in the hands of somebody else. Therefore, you must take hold of your future, take hold of your words, submit them to the word of God and watch how the Lord will honour his word and make your dreams a reality.

You may fail early, even fail often but fail forward; it is always a little frustrating to me when people associate a negative connotation with failure. Failure can be used to stay down or can be used to move up in life to achieve your set goals.

Get comfortable with failure because if you take a step backwards and analyze the situation, you will see failure's lessons. Failure is terrible if you let it be a terrible thing, but it can be your most excellent teacher if you let it guide you. It will make you a master, give you the knowledge for your future, and enable you to help others, so yes, failure can be a bad thing if you let it be, or it can be the greatest thing that has ever happened to you.

Successful people fail more than what you think; they fall so much that their stories have more failure than success. So how does that make sense? Successful people know that they will arise again with a vast array of knowledge to help them in their journey if and when they fall. While others will take the failure and stay in failure mode and not learn the lesson to try again and achieve the success they were looking for.

Everything, and I mean everything, starts with the words that come forth out of your mouth; everything! With one sentence, you have the power to make someone's day or week, and yet in one sentence, you can destroy someone's day and week. But, on the other hand, you can bring joy into someone's life, and through simple words, you can get someone's spirits to new lows.

Change your present and create a new future for you and yours today; let nothing stop you or derail you; let the words that come forth out of your mouth be life-changing and fruit-bearing. For when we change our words, we change our very being, and when that is changed, God will do exceedingly and abundantly above all that we could ever ask or dream of, he is able.

Change your words, Change your world!

CHAPTER 2
LESSONS LEARNED
PRIDE THE GREATEST VIRUS

We find a tremendous story in the Bible about King Hezekiah; he was twenty-five years old when he started to reign over Isreal. In 2ⁿᵈ Chronicles 29, we find that the word of God says in verse 2," **He did what was right in the eyes of the Lord, just as his father David had done.**"

A young man opened the temple's doors and repaired them, re-built the temple's altar, brought back the burnt offerings, and restored the levities and high priests.

Everything was going so well in Israel that in Chapter 30 verse 27, the Bible says, **"The priests and the Levites stood to bless the people, and God heard them, for their prayer reached heaven, his holy dwelling place.**

Think about this for a moment; their prayers reached heaven, his holy dwelling place! That's powerful, and it continues from there to say in chapter 31 that the Israelites who were there went out to the towns of Judah, smashed the sacred stones and cut down the Asherah poles. They destroyed the high places and altars throughout Judah and Benjamin, Ephraim, and Manasseh. Then, after they had destroyed all of them, the Israelites returned to their towns and their property.

A mighty move of God took place; a revival of sorts had hit the land. Verse 20 of 2ⁿᵈ Chronicles says, **"This is what Hezekiah did throughout**

Judah, doing what was good and right and faithful before the Lord his God. 21 In everything that he undertook in the service of God's temple and obedience to the law and the commands, he sought his God and worked wholeheartedly. And so he prospered.

There was prosperity in the land; the people fixed their lives and consecrated themselves for the Lord. Everything was going well till we hit chapter 32. Then, we find that Sennacherib, king of Assyria, invaded Judah and laid siege to the fortified cities, thinking of conquering them for himself.

Verse 20, the Bible says, **"King Hezekiah and the prophet Isaiah son of Amoz, cried out in prayer to heaven about this.**

21 And the Lord sent an angel, who annihilated all the fighting men and the commanders and officers in the camp of the Assyrian king. So he withdrew to his own land in disgrace. And when he went into the temple of his God, some of his sons, his flesh and blood, cut him down with the sword.

22 So the Lord saved Hezekiah and the people of Jerusalem from the hand of Sennacherib, king of Assyria, and the hand of all others. He took care of them on every side.

23 Many brought offerings to Jerusalem for the Lord and valuable gifts for Hezekiah, king of Judah. From then on, he was highly regarded by all the nations.

Up to this point, King Hezekiah has led Israel to victory, has done all things well in the eyes of the Lord his God, and suddenly, sickness falls on him to the point of death. But, in his illness, he did what he did best, and that was to seek the face of the Lord his God, he prayer, and God heard his prayer and sent him a sign.

A Sign? he was asking for healing, and God sent him a sign? Stop here for a moment; how many times does God answer our prayers with an answer that we do not expect or ask for? However, the sign was unique, and the answer to his prayer was kindness!

Kindness for a sick and dying person? But the real problem was not the sickness; the problem was not the answer to his prayer; the real problem was that pride had set in his heart!

The Bible says in verse 24 of 2nd Chronicles 32, **"In those days Hezekiah became ill and was at the point of death. So he prayed to the Lord, who answered him and gave him a miraculous sign.**

25 But Hezekiah's heart was proud, and he did not respond to the kindness shown him; therefore, the Lord's wrath was on him and Judah and Jerusalem.

You see, pride is a virus that comes into a person's life not to hurt it but to kill the individual. It is a virus that is so aggressive that it eats down the fibre of your soul. It doesn't allow you to enjoy the present; you complain about your past and destroy your future.

Pride sets in, kills relationships, breaks up partnerships and eventually sucks the very life out of that person. It kills dreams and visions, and any progress you have made up to that point is destroyed in one second; that's how powerful and destructive pride is.

The Bible is clear on its stance of pride,

Proverbs 11:2 "When pride comes, then comes disgrace, but with humility comes wisdom."

Proverbs 16:5 "The LORD detests all the proud of heart. So be sure of this: They will not go unpunished."

Proverbs 16:18 "Pride goes before destruction, a haughty spirit before a fall."

Nothing good can ever come out of pride-nothing! King Hezekiah was sick to death, and in his sickness, he became proud in his heart and brought the wrath of God upon him and the Israelites.

Pride is a dream killer, a destiny destroyer; if you have it and decide not to get rid of it, it will prove to be a mighty stumbling block on your path to greatness. Pride has the power to set you back months if not years and decades because it closes the door to great things for your life.

You look at the rust on a car; it never starts big enough for you to notice. Instead, it starts small and innocent, as if nothing is going on. Meanwhile, it is eating up the paint and the car itself that unless it is taken care of, it will invade the entire vehicle. It doesn't matter where on the car it starts; it is only a matter of time before it spreads and what once was a beautiful car now is a rust bucket that nobody wants.

Pride hurts; it kills, separates you from others, keeps you on an island all to yourself with nobody willing to help you. It isolates you so much that even if people want to help you, they choose not to because of your pride. It is an imaginary stench that comes upon you that others smell and see, but unfortunately, it becomes challenging for you to see it.

If un-treated, pride is like a tornado, it comes in and destroys anything, and everything in its path, leaving a trail of brokeness and despair. King Hezekiah was being shown kindness, the Bible says, and he became proud in his heart, so much so that it offended God and God decided to respond to that pride with anger and judgement.

Your dreams are blocked by pride, and greatness will never be achieved because you chose pride in your heart than being humble. Someone who's prideful **is arrogant and disdainful**. Prideful people don't usually have many friends since they think they're superior to everyone else.

The biblical sin of pride refers **to a high or exalted attitude**—the opposite of the virtue of humility, which is the appropriate posture people ought to have with God.

A prideful heart is **filled with self and loses sight of a leader's true purpose – transforming the lives of others**. But, unfortunately, it's often difficult to see before it's too late. So we charge forward, driven by our prideful heart until the next thing we know – we're transformed into a spirit rock.

Pride is often driven by **poor self-worth and shame**. We feel so badly about ourselves that we compensate by feeling superior. We look for others' flaws as a way to conceal our own. We relish criticizing others as a defence against recognizing our shortcomings.

Proverbs 8:13" The Fear of the LORD is to hate evil: pride, and arrogancy, and the evil way, and the froward mouth, do I hate.

Now, what does it mean to humble yourself before God? To me, it means **coming before Jesus in awe and reverence**, regardless of what people may think of you. It's being willing to say, "I was wrong". ... It's taking the focus off of yourself and focusing on what matters – God! Finally, come to the cross with a clear conscience.

Pride causes us to assess our lives by the standard of our accomplishments rather than our God-given identity. Pride (or, as we say, "ego") severs us from God's design to live in a relationship with others. We are pushed into isolation by our self-confidence, believing the lie that life is better alone.

On your path to greatness, you will have many "opportunities" to accept pride because of your accomplishments, but make the wise choice to reject this opportunity, stay hum, be and be kind, be appreciative of what you have and thankful for the things you don't have. Appreciate and love those in your life, treasure the word of God as a cornerstone and foundation to your progress and watch God turn things in your favour.

1 Peter 5:5 Likewise, younger, be subject to the elders. Clothe yourselves, all of you, with humility toward one another, for "God opposes the proud but gives grace to the humble."

That's powerful, **Grace to the humble!** I have learned that being humble opens doors that money can not. Being humble opens opportunities that otherwise would not be open. So stay humble when you achieve things, and never lend an ear to pride-never!

DON'T PROCRASTINATE

Procrastination is "the act of willfully delaying the doing of something that should be done," In some people, it is a habitual way of handling any task. While the word itself is not found in the Bible, we can find some principles to help guide us.

Sometimes, procrastination results from laziness, and the Bible has plenty to say about that. The Bible commends hard work and industry (**Proverbs 12:24; 13:4**) and warns against sloth and slackness (**Proverbs 15:19; 18:9**).

One cure for procrastination is more diligence, regardless of the task. We should be supremely motivated to be diligent in his work since we ultimately serve the Lord. **"Whatever you do, work at it with all your heart, as working for the Lord, not for men" (Colossians 3:23).**

If we put our hearts into our work, as this verse says to do, we will probably find it challenging to procrastinate too much.

Procrastination is when you keep putting something off that you should be doing now – to another time. There are many reasons people procrastinate: Fear, anxiety, or an unwillingness to face change... Maybe even a fear of success.

The truth is that when we procrastinate, we are setting off a chain reaction of events that can negatively impact others – not just ourselves. And God calls us to do good for one another. But, instead, when we procrastinate, we are doing the opposite of good!

When people think of procrastination, they think of laziness. They may even wonder, **"what does the Bible say about laziness?"** But the truth is those are two very different things.

Laziness means that you're unwilling to work or use energy (Dictionary.com)

On the other hand, procrastination doesn't mean you're unwilling; it means you're putting something off until later.

Dreams can be put on the back burner not because you don't believe in them but because you delay working on your vision. Of course, spending time planning out your dream and the execution of the goal is significant, but it can not be taken over by procrastination.

Procrastination will kill the same drive you might have to fulfill your dreams and goals; it will cripple you and bring you to a halt. If we keep saying, I'll do it tomorrow, and when tomorrow arrives, we still don't start, then we are essentially putting our dreams into a coffin and burying them six feet under the ground.

Procrastination can become very comfortable and quite reasonable.

Because, in the shadow of procrastination, there will be excuses lurking in the darkness, making you believe that doing it tomorrow might be a better decision when in reality doing it tomorrow robs you; of your opportunity to greatness today!

People often procrastinate because of their past failures, and they think about how they felt when they failed and the pain it caused, so to avoid the pain and fears, they procrastinate in giving themselves another shot!

OVERCOMING THE GUILT OF FAILURE

There are two essential words in that title-Guilt & Failure, both of which will be addressed right here. Failure is always associated with defeated emotions and a bad experience. It is never really associated with anything good. We fail all the time; we fail even when we don't want to fail. We fail on purpose, and we fail without wanting to.

Our failures don't necessarily have to be associated with a negative connotation; Failure can also be a good thing that happens to you. You can either see your Failure as a terrible thing that has happened to you and please don't get me wrong, certain events that occur in our life are earth-shattering events.

Some events destroy our emotions and bring us to our knees, shattering any and every thinking that everything will be all right. Events that contain hardships, that test the very fibre of our being. Moments in our life make you wake up in the middle of the night in a cold sweat, frightened because of what you went through or still have to go through.

Failure adds to the stress and pain, the guilt being so significant that we become paralyzed by Failure's guilt that believes hope is long gone. The guilt makes us think that we can not walk another step, and we are sure to die in the pit of that guilt and shame.

We question our Faith; we doubt the word, we take our anger and frustrations on those that don't deserve it, we speak out of line, and our words offend those that are close to us, and most importantly, we often think that it is God's fault for what happened.

The enemy uses the guilt of failing to emphasize that God didn't show up the way he promised he would. Yet, God has an exciting way of making things right. He said in his word **Isaiah 55:8-9, "For My thoughts *are* not your thoughts, Nor *are* your ways My ways," says the Lord. "For *as* the heavens are higher than the earth, So are My ways higher than your ways, And My thoughts than your thoughts.**

His ways are mysterious, and nothing surprises him or catches him off guard. He knows all and sees all, hears all and always has an answer to those things we do not. So your failure did not catch God off guard; it didn't surprise him, he wasn't asleep when it happened to you, and before it happened to you, he had the answer.

If the failure was so great, why did it happen? that is the real question and a perfect one. We don't have the answer to some of the most complex questions at times, yet, there are certain things that I can be assured of, and that is that my failure is not absolute no matter how bad it is or how bad it gets if God before you then who can be against you! **Romans 8:31 says, What shall we then say to these things? If God be for us, who can be against us?**

That **"Who"** can be translated to not only a person, but it is also translated to be a **"something."** For he said **What shall we then say to these THINGS? THINGS!** Things happen, and people happen to us; both are just as deadly and hurtful. So Paul said it well to the Romans, and at this point, things have already happened, something took place, traumatic and all. However, he doesn't offer sympathy at this point, not because he was unsympathetic but because he wanted them to not stay in that emotion of guilt and failure.

Things will happen to us, affect us, and shake us to our core, but he emphasizes that **If God is for us, who can be against us?** He went from things to a who; he addressed both at the same time. If we choose to stay in that emotion of guilt and failure, we will miss out on the real lesson that God wanted to teach us.

Take a look at Job; the Bible says in **Job 1:1 There was a man in the land of Uz, whose name was *Job*; and that man was perfect and upright, and *one* that feared God, and eschewed evil.** You read this man's life from verse 2 through verse 5; you realize that this man is rich, powerful, influence the land, pretty much is set for life. Yet, in one day, his whole world came crashing down before him. In one day, he went from having everything to having nothing! Yet, a man that the Bible says was **perfect** and **upright**. How do you manage to receive an accolade such as Perfect and upright?

Yet, even having these two accolades attached to his name, destruction came to his life in one day. Did he deserve this? What sin did he commit to having all of this happen to him? Maybe, you have asked yourself those same questions, why did this happen? or what did I do to deserve this? I have asked myself those same questions. But, so often, those questions are not answered, it seems as if there is silence, and God has forgotten about you, when it is entirely the opposite, God is in control.

In verse 8, something exciting happens, says, **"And the LORD said unto Satan, Hast thou considered my servant *Job*, that there is none like him in the earth, a perfect and an upright man, *one* that feareth God, and escheweth evil?"**

God offered Job for the test; God offered Job as his star "player," God knew that he could offer up Job, and God was confident that he would pass the test. Wait a moment.....

Could it be that this is God's way of showcasing you and setting you for a more incredible blessing? Could it be that this is God's way of promoting you? Could it be that this is the way that God will use to bring supernatural favour and blessing into your life? Could this be the situation that will turn things around? But, on the other hand, could God you a mess to turn it into a message? And a test into a testimony?

The answer to all of these questions is a resounding **YES!**

Jump forward to the end of Jobs's life, and the Bible says in **Job 42:12, So the LORD blessed the latter end of Job more than his beginning...** it all says in **Job 1:22," In all this Job did not sin nor charge God with wrong."**

His wife left him, friends left him, lost all his cattle, children died, destruction came, was told that it was his fault for all that had happened, blamed for everything, and through it, all he did not sin or blame God, in one word all I can say is WOW!

Today, we stump our baby toe on the corner of the bed, and we declare it is the end of the world as we know it. Even more profound when in the middle of his "failure," he says in **Job 1:21, "Naked came I out of my mother's womb, and naked shall I return thither. The Lord gave, and the Lord hath taken away; blessed be the name of the Lord."**

BLESSED BE THE NAME OF THE LORD-he says this in the middle of his pain and suffering, he blesses the Lord through his guilt of failure, he does what nobody thought would do, he blesses the name of the Lord. This is a lesson to be learned, that, even though the trials and tribulations may come, even though the pain and suffering are complex, the night of sorrow is long, and the storm rages on, you have the POWER to stand up and bless the name of the Lord. You have the POWER to stand up, and with every fibre of your being through it, all acknowledge that you are in the best hands possible and that the Lord will never leave nor forsake you, but will be you all the days of your life!

Your failure is not the end, but acknowledge it as your reset beginning —an opportunity to learn and grow. Your failure is filled with pain and tears. However, you have the power to turn the negative experience into a positive experience, knowing that God has allowed all of the negative things to happen to you so that you may have the experience to share a story that is so powerful in its testimony that all who hear it will know that it was God that was with you.

You have not failed, failure is not your king, and you do not have to be bound by the guilt of that failure; you are the son or daughter of the highest God, and as such, Your latter shall be more significant at the end than at the beginning! It is not over; you are not finished, the race is not over, You have not been knocked out, get yourself up, dust yourself off, you are free from the guilt in Jesus' name.

If Job had the power to stand up and say what he said and sinned not, then you have the ability to do the same; God gives and God takes away, but BLESSED BE THE NAME OF THE LORD!.

There are three fundamental steps to overcoming the guilt of failure; allow me to share them with you.

The First step to being free of that guilt is, putting all your burdens on him; the word says **1ˢᵗ Peter 5:7 "Casting all your care upon Him, for He cares for you."** You will never be free if you are trying to carry this weight over your shoulders each day. An anchor is designed to keep you in place, and if the ship is taking water, it will pull it down. So don't let the guilt be your anchor that brings you down or keeps you from moving forward toward your goal and destiny.

The Second is **Proverbs 3:5 "Trust in the LORD with all your heart, And lean not on your own understanding;"** You have got to believe that God will turn things around. You must believe not just think but believe that God is in control and that everything will turn out for your benefit. Trust that God will make a way where there is no way. **Isaiah 41:10 says Fear not, for I am with you; be not dismayed, for I am your God; I will strengthen you, I will help you, I will uphold you with my righteous right hand.**

Lastly, you can not stay put in that pit of sorrow; you must get up and move forward. The Bible says in **Isaiah 43:18, "Remember not the former things, nor consider the things of old."** You can not stay in that condition; it happened, we can not go back in time to change things, but we can change our tomorrow by our actions of today.

2 Corinthians 5:17 Therefore, if anyone is in Christ, he is a new creation. The old has passed away; behold, the new has come. God wants to mould you into something bigger and better, a new version of you, carrying all the battle scars but with a wealth of knowledge.

John 5:8 "Jesus said to him," Get up, take up your bed, and walk." Those are your marching orders; those are the words for you today; as you read this, no matter what you are going through or went through, God says to you GET UP & WALK! If you follow these three simple yet powerful steps, you will see the power and the mighty hand of God over your life.

Your latter shall be more significant than you beginning-**you are free!**

FREE YOUR HEART FROM FEAR

The brain is complex, and the heart is mysterious; who shall know it? So I had to do a little research and study this, spiritually and physically speaking.

The brain is a complex organ that **controls thought, memory, emotion, touch, motor skills, vision, breathing**, temperature, hunger and every process that regulates our body. The brain and spinal cord that extend from it make up the central nervous system.

In your mind, a battle is brewing each day, decisions must be made, and often decisions that will not only affect you but often affect those around you. This is because your brain (mind) controls your thoughts, emotions, vision and even breathing.

The enemy will fight for control of your mind because battles are won and lost in it. The brain is so complex, but even **more complex is your heart.** The heart is a muscular organ about the size of a fist, located just behind and slightly left of the breastbone. The heart pumps blood through the network of arteries and veins called the cardiovascular system.

The heart has four chambers:

- The right atrium receives blood from the veins and pumps it to the right ventricle.
- The right ventricle receives blood from the right atrium and pumps it to the lungs, loaded with oxygen.
- The left atrium receives oxygenated blood from the lungs and pumps it to the left ventricle.
- The left ventricle (the most robust chamber) pumps oxygen-rich blood to the rest of the body. The left ventricle's vigorous contractions create our blood pressure.

Proverbs 4:23 says, "Above all else, guard your heart, for everything you do flows from it."

Phillippians 4:7 says, "And the peace of God, which transcends all understanding, will guard your hearts and your minds in Christ Jesus.

Your heart is precious, yet people can walk around without a heart, figuratively speaking. A "clean" heart can manifest itself in significant actions by a person; it generates good emotions, puts you in a healthy place; in the same manner, a "dark" heart can translate into evil and harmful actions.

The bible says in Luke 6:45, "A good man out of the good treasure of his heart brings forth good; and an evil man out of the evil treasure of his heart brings forth evil. For out of the abundance of the heart, his mouth speaks."

Fear often creeps into the heart and can cause a spiritual heart attack of sorts. Fear causes pain and anxiety, can cause a person to act or react in a particular manner that otherwise they would not act or react.

Isaiah 41:10 says, "Fear not, for I am with you; be not dismayed, for I am your God; I will strengthen you, I will help you, I will uphold you with my righteous right hand."

As you may well know, the expression "**fear not**" is mentioned in the bible 365 times, coincidence? Absolutely not! Fear in your heart will cause you to go into a state of mind that is very dangerous. It will not allow you to take another step in the direction of your goals and vision.

Fear in the heart will cause you to display emotions that you usually would not reveal, often covered by an illusion of being cautious. Fear rusts the soul and mind of the person. If allowed to linger, it will consume the life of someone, and that person will never be the same.

It will cause your dreams and goals to die, burying them forever in the state of simply that, a dream or goal. It will cause the heart to hurt emotionally and never heal because one of the most challenging things to do is abandon your dreams and goals because you are afraid.

It is painful when you can no longer pursue your dream, not because you are stopped by someone or something, but unable to follow your vision and goals because of fear is one of the most tragic things that can happen. It's hard when you are stopped by things outside of your control, harder to accept when you are the reason why you are not going further.

Fear in your heart will not enable you to do anything; God has not given you a spirit of fear. So the bible says in **2ⁿᵈ Timothy 1:7, "For God has not given us a spirit of fear, but of POWER and of LOVE and of a SOUND MIND.**

This is very powerful because it shows you the areas the fear in the heart will affect. It will weaken you, kill your love, and mess up your mind.

Weaken you not to walk and pursue what God has laid up for you. Weaken your ambition, desire and motivation, essentially killing any drive you had to grow and achieve your dreams. Fear will often weaken your passion for prayer, or seeking the face of God, rendering your spiritual walk to nothing. It will undermine your relationship with God and your relationship with others. You can not let fear weaken you because it will put you in a downward death spiral that you often can not recover.

Only through a relationship with Jesus and the Holy Spirit can you overcome this fear and overcome the weakness that it brings. As you soak in the word, you will gain strength to combat this virus called fear. As you continue to seek His face, you will be able to strengthen your Spirit and your resolve not to give up but continue forward and fight on.

Fear will kill your **LOVE,** for God, your family and friends, and your dreams and goals. If you allow fear to destroy your love for the things of God, you become cold and insensitive to those things of the Spirit. If your passion for the things of God dies, you will experience dryness in your life that can not be filled by anyone or anything.

Fear will also destroy the passion and love for your dreams and goals. Unfortunately, this is where many people often give up. They become frustrated and tend to blame others for their lack of action—a mechanism to hide the genuine emotions that their LOVE for pursuing dreams and goals is abandoned.

When the love dies, frustration enters, and the blame game begins. However, you can not allow fear to kill your passion; you can not allow fear to hinder your love because of a few upsets that you may encounter in life. Difficult moments will come, losses will happen, but they are not enough reason to allow your love for God to wither away into nothing.

You can not allow frustrations to kill your momentum; your race is not a sprint but a marathon, and your love for not only God but God's things and your personal goals and dreams to die. Everything is put in jeopardy when you allow fear to kill your love, and everything will collapse when you allow fear to destroy your love.

Fear will also attack your mind, controlling how you speak, act and react. If your mind is controlled by fear, you will not make correct decisions; it will hamper your ability to generate new ideas and render your actions dead.

If your mind is affected by fear, you will see the results manifest in your talk, and the evidence of fear will be seen in your actions. Fear in your mind will destroy the ability to think straight, putting critical decisions in peril; your anxiety will translate into decisions that will alter the course of your walk. Fear in the mind is dangerous because your mind is a battlefield of a million and one thought that comes across it every day.

Psalms 27:3 "Though an army encamp against me, my heart shall not fear; though war arises against me, yet I will be confident."

It will send signals to the heart that you are afraid, and your ability to function is now put into question. Today, we may not have an army encamped around us physically speaking, but the enemy wages war on you to affect your mind and heart.

The war is ferocious and messy; it will cause you to lose sleep, hunger, and other things. It is a war that you are not exempt from, but it is a war that you must face head-on. A battle that you MUST win, and I emphasize MUST because if you started to walk towards your dream and start building your future, you could not afford yourself the luxury of quitting or giving up.

The bible says in **2nd Corinthians 10:4," For the weapons of our warfare *are* not carnal but mighty in God for pulling down strongholds,"**

It would be best if you acknowledged that your war is not carnal, your fight is not physical, but your battle and war have spiritual implications of epic proportions. But he gave you weapons strong enough to enable you to fight back and win!

He said that your weapons are MIGHTY IN GOD-this is key because they are mighty not because of you or because they are in your hands, but they are mighty in GOD and God alone.

James 4:7 says, "Submit yourselves therefore to God. Resist the devil, and he will flee from you."

Submission to God is your first line of defence. It allows you to submit your dreams and goals to God; it will enable you to kill your pride and will enable you to continue the pursuit of your dreams and goals.

Submission to God will keep your love for Him alive, and it will also keep the desire to walk forward and battle on with new strengthens and determination to succeed. Your submission to God will allow you to fight back and resist the works of the enemy that he has plotted against you.

The word also says, RESIST the enemy; this is where you must activate your Faith, and the word must be active and alive in your mind, heart and mouth. To be able to speak the word of God into your situation, and you will see the power it has to change the atmosphere and alter the course of your walk. If the word is alive in you, you will be able to fend off the attacks on your mind and heart. The word of God enables you to have the spiritual backbone to resist the enemy and his attacks.

When you submit to God your dreams, goals and visions, you are, in essence, including God in them, and if God is included in them, then failure is never an option, but you will achieve tremendous success and victories. The problem with many is that they make plans without including God; they attempt to do BIG things without having God in those talks or projects.

The bible says to not lean on your understanding; in other words, don't try and do things without God because surely it will fail. Now you may say, many people succeed without having God in their plans; they are heathen, and God is far from their conversations, yet they keep on thriving; how is this even possible?

There is always a price to pay; no matter the decision you take, or the road you choose to walk on, you will pay a fee for that decision. To lose weight, you must pay the price, some of which are sacrifice, discipline and self-control. Sacrifice and invest the time at the gym, discipline to stay on course with your workout and diet, and self-control to resist the temptation of not eating what you should not be eating.

The price you pay to be used by God is investing time in prayer, humbleness, patience, and so much more. For everything we choose, we must pay that price. **Nothing comes for free, nothing that matters, at least.**

Isaiah 35:4 "Say to those who have an anxious heart, 'Be strong; fear not! Behold, your God will come with vengeance, with the recompense of God. He will come and save you."

You can not live in a state of fear all of your life; you must be able to be strong and fear not!. It may be said that it is easier said than done, but in reality, when you submit your goals, dreams and visions to the Lord, then that is when your heart will indeed be free from fear.

The most exciting thing about this verse is that Isaiah says **your God will come with vengeance, with the recompense of God. He will come and save you.**

Not only is God coming with a vengeance but also with a recompense! With a vengeance to your enemies but at the same time with compensation for you! When your heart takes the word, believes it and applies it, then your heart will rest and be free from the fear that grips it in a stranglehold.

When you are set free of fear in the heart, you will activate your Faith in a greater dimension. Once your heart is free, then you will be able to release your Spirit to be used of God in a greater capacity, reaching closer to your destiny, and a spirit of excellence takes over you.

THE POWER OF HAVING A SPIRIT OF EXCELLENCE

Anyone can perform any task given to them. Anyone can do things given the proper training and guidance, but what separates those people from achieving their destiny is the Spirit of excellence they possess.

It's what separates average from great, mediocre from impressive, and lame from the wow factor. To achieve your destiny, you must have a spirit of excellence, or rather, commit to a spirit of excellence when doing the things that God has called you to do.

In Matthew 25, the bible tells us of a rather powerful story; it says in verse 14, **"Again, it will be like a man going on a journey, who called his servants and entrusted his wealth to them.**

Verse 15 says, **And to one he gave five talents, to another two, and to another one, to each according to his own ability; and immediately he went on a journey.**

Stop here for a moment.

He gave each one **ACCORDING TO HIS ABILITY!**

God will never give you a burden that you can not carry,

1ˢᵗ Corinthians 10:13 **There hath no temptation taken you but such as is common to man: but God is faithful, who will not suffer you to be tempted above that ye are able; but will with the temptation also make a way to escape, that ye may be able to bear it.**

He will always give you something that t=you can handle; it may seem as if you can't and will be crushed by the load, but God made you strong enough to carry and manage it and persevere no matter what may come your way.

Your destiny is as big as you want it to be and as small as you want it to be. God will be with you no matter the road you choose to walk on; the choice is absolutely all yours. God has a great destiny for everyone, but not everyone accepts that destiny.

Your destiny is dependent on certain factors such as your Faith, your desire to achieve it, your determination to keep going regardless of the circumstances, your drive and lastly, your desire to achieve excellence.

The bible says that he gave each some talents, but what made the difference was not the talent but what each person decided to do.

Matthew 25:16-18 says **Then he who had received the five talents went and traded with them, and made another five talents. And likewise, he who *had received* two gained two more also. But he who had received one went and dug in the ground and hid his lord's money.**

And there lies the problem; he took what his master gave him, paid no attention to the others and buried it. Had no vision, no desire, no drive, no nothing, except for the fact that he buried what his master gave him.

How many times do people, do you, bury what God has given you? Out of fear, or lack of belief, you bury that gift that God has given you and bury your destiny along with it.

The other two had a vision; the other two had grabbed what they were given and produced more. A spirit of excellence will always propel you to do much more for the kingdom; it will never allow you to do nothing with what God gave you.

They took what they were given and achieved greatness with what they were given. The other did nothing, yet he thought he was doing something. You can not make the mistake of taking what God has given you and doing nothing with it.

The bible says in Matthew 7:16, **you shall know them by their fruits!**

What you do with what God gives you will determine the outcome of your life. What you do with the gifts and talents he has entrusted you with will determine your happiness and success rate of achieving your goals and dreams.

He buried the talents that his master had given him; in other words, he was lazy, gave up, didn't want to be bothered with it. How many times are we like this man? We give up because you heard people say we couldn't do it, you quit because you blame your childhood upbringing, and that's not to say that they aren't fair assessments of your life, but as fair as they may seem, they should never be enough to make you quit or stop the pursuit of your dreams.

When I was just a young boy, I remember my parents hearing them talk about giving God the very best of who we were and maximizing the gifts and talents he gave every single one of us. I was young and yet to discover the true meaning of what my dad was saying. I was more interested in playing around and doing what kids do best.

Giving God the absolute best does not mean giving him perfection because that in itself is impossible, but giving God the very best means first and foremost giving him your heart. Then, after you've done so, you give 110% effort into everything he puts before you.

I didn't know how to play the piano back then, but I wanted to become the worship leader at church. My father was a great keyboard player and had recorded some tapes back then, but with his schedule and church responsibilities, seeing him get home and go straight to bed made my heart heavy for him, knowing the pressure he was under. I couldn't find it in myself to go and ask him to teach me how to play when I learned how tired he was.

I know that if I had asked him, I know for a fact that he would have taken 5 minutes and showed me something each night. So I decided to take it upon myself to learn the keyboard. I would stand beside the keyboard player at that time and watch him play, and after every service, while everyone was in fellowship, you would find a young boy in the sanctuary trying to remember what I saw and trying to play it back.

My brother and I would go back home, and in our spare time, we would put a tape on, CDs that didn't exist back then, and follow on a keyboard my dad had bought us. Every day progressed, every day was full of mistakes, and we kept going at it, but we never gave up!

The more we screwed up, the more we would want to try and figure it out and try and perfect what the song was trying to teach us. But we never gave up, didn't give in, didn't stop and didn't quit; that is what it means to have a spirit of excellence-wanting to be better than yesterday!

Are we content with sloppiness and laziness? are we happy that we gave up? It's easy to do so, but are we better off? My dad had a rule, which says, **"be the first one at church, and be the last one to leave."**

You can never achieve your destiny with a lazy attitude and quitter mentality. God deserves the best of you, the best of your time, effort, willingness, drive, passion and skill. So you give God your best and watch his best for you always in action.

Walking by Faith is not supposed to be easy, but it's supposed to make you understand that if you do your part in trusting Him, then God will never disappoint. The flashlight on your phone doesn't give you much more light than two or three feet ahead of you, yet you trust that the light you see, even though it only shines enough for you to walk, will help you navigate the road that you are on.

Faith works in the same manner; Faith only lets you see a couple of steps ahead and nothing more, the purpose of Faith is not to make it easy as I said earlier, the goal of Faith is to create in you a dependency on God, that you may not know what's ahead. However, you trust Him enough to keep on walking.

I repeat you can not bury what God has given you, but you must embrace it with everything you have. It is not a competition with anyone else but instead with yourself. So how can you do better and be better than what you were yesterday? Faith in Action.

A spirit of excellence is born when you realize that you can and should do better for God. A spirit of excellence is reached when you know that the talents and gifts that God has given you can not be buried but activated. A spirit of excellence is born when you decide that what you did for God and the kingdom can be better!

A better husband, father, brother, uncle, preacher, son, daughter, better than yesterday, better than your old version of you.

Matthew 25:19 says, **"After a long time, the lord of those servants came and settled accounts with them."** You can never forget that the Lord will always require a report of the accounts of your life and what you did with what he gave while here on earth.

Verse 20 says, **"So he who had received five talents came and brought five other talents, saying, 'Lord, you delivered to me five talents; look, I have gained five more talents besides them."** He was rewarded with a double to the one who invested and activated that Spirit of excellence!

There is always a reward for your effort and work in the kingdom-always! Never in vain, but it will always yield a reward.

Verse 21 says, **"His lord said to him, 'Well *done,* good and faithful servant; you were faithful over a few things, I will make you ruler over many things. Enter into the joy of your lord."**

Good & Faithful servant those words are trustworthy and powerful, Good not because of who he was, but good because of his work ethic, discipline and intelligence. He didn't only receive a reward, but he was labelled with a label that could not be taken away from him for life. He went from a servant to a **RULER over many things!**

All because he chose to do something, he had that spirit of excellence that caused him to act to better the kingdom and his master. He reached his destiny by simply taking the initiative and outworking everyone else, and suddenly he was a servant no more but rather a ruler.

Matthew 25:22-23 says, **"He also that had received two talents came and said, Lord, thou deliveredst unto me two talents: behold, I have gained two other talents beside them. His lord said to him, 'Well *done*, good and faithful servant; you have been faithful over a few things, I will make you ruler over many things. Enter into the joy of your lord."**

This servant, too, was intelligent and he had doubled what he was given, and because of that, he was rewarded, and his life changed at that very moment. Now, this servant didn't complain because he only received two talents, and the first five, no, he maximized what he was given.

Stop looking around at who has more than you, who is better than you, who has more talents and skills than you; what matters is what you do with what God has given you at that moment. So he didn't whine because the other got more than he did, he blocked all of that out and ran his race, stayed in his lane and did the very best with what God had given him, and in the end, it proved to be a winner.

Let's look ahead; verses 24-25 says, **"Then he who had received the one talent came and said, 'Lord, I knew you to be a hard man, reaping where you have not sown, and gathering where you have not scattered seed. And I was AFRAID and went and hid your talent in the ground. Look, *there* you have *what is* yours.'**

His response seemed full of knowledge and reason, but it was shallow and hallow on the inside in reality. So, first, you find that he was disabled with fear, rendering him useless. Then, you discover that he did what no one else did and tried to justify it with his reasoning.

He went and buried it; then he had to unearth it and give it back to his master—this required work to be done. It took time, energy, willingness, and drive for someone to take his talent and bury it. But, imagine if he had used those same principles in the right direction? Imagine what would have been the results he would have had?

How often do we use the energy God has given us, the talent, skill, passion, and so much more, in the right direction? Or are we using all of those things and making our lives worse?

Verse 26 of Matthew 25 says, **"But his lord answered and said to him, 'You wicked and lazy servant, you knew that I reap where I have not sown, and gather where I have not scattered seed."**

Two words jump out at me in this text: they are **Wicked and lazy.** According to the dictionary, wicked is **Evil or morally wrong.** Evil for burying the talent? a bit harsh, would you say so? Quite the opposite, he who does nothing about anything is evil and morally wrong.

You must do something; you must act, and you can not stay quiet or lazy; you must try and not quit—lazy means unwilling to work or use energy.

There is nothing more horrendous than a lazy person in life. I don't know about you, but being around a lazy person is so frustrating and infuriating that it boils me on the inside. A lazy person can quickly infect others, and it will ruin others very fast if not promptly dealt with it.

Look at what the scripture says next; verse 30 of Matthew 25 says, **"And cast the unprofitable servant into the outer darkness. There will be weeping and gnashing of teeth."**

What an end to this servant; not only what he had was taken away and given to the one who had ten talents, but he was cast into the outer darkness! A sad ending to a man that had started on the same page as the others.

We all start at the same level in this life, but our choices quickly begin to create a division and separation between you and others, and that is where you see some succeed and some don't. We all face adversity in life; all of us do, but what we do in the face of adversity is what matters.

Please don't get me wrong, yes, certain things happen that are beyond our control, certain things come to shatter us and beat us down to a pulp, but one thing is for sure that the bible says in 1st John 4:4 **"Ye are of God, little children, and have overcome them: because *greater is he* that is in you than he that is in the world."**

When you realize the magnitude of the God that we serve and his power, then at that moment, you will begin to change your words and change your actions. Of course, as I said earlier, challenges will come, but that is the opportunity for you to grab hold of the truth in God's word and apply it to your life.

Let nothing defeat you, and if someone does beat you, then let it be you that defeats you! Defeat you're old you, filled with excuses and complaints. Defeat your old you full of fear and insecurities, beat you're old you by getting closer to God and deciding that a setback doesn't mean you have failed, but instead use it as a stepping stone to go higher.

A spirit of excellence doesn't settle for the ordinary; it is not conformed with average or settle for the minimum. Instead, it means giving God the very best "product" or sacrifice possible. It doesn't mean competing with someone else's drive or passion, but running your race and staying in your lane.

The mistake that you can quickly make is comparing your race and sacrifice with others; you can not allow the enemy to draw you into that arena. It is an arena that you will permanently lose the fight in. So you must stay focused on your calling, and if others pass you, so be it, and if others do better than you, so be it, but you must focus on yourself, and YOU must be able to give God the very best of YOU.

Your success is not dependent on others and what they might think of you; no, somewhat reliant on you activating your Faith, trusting God, running your race, climbing your mountain, defeating your giants and finishing the task at hand.

Mount Everest is the largest mountain on earth, standing at 29,032 feet. People who climb that mountain is considered unique, and to do it, you indeed are fantastic for doing so. But let me tell you about a bit of hill close to where I live that in the summer, I challenge myself each time to run up that hill as fast as I can three times. That tiny hill is my mount Everest; that small hill presents a challenge each year; that little hill must be conquered each time I decide to run up it.

I say this because we each must face our little mount Everest, now my Mount Everest might be different from yours, and just because my hill is more prominent or vice versa doesn't make it any less significant.

You must decide to challenge yourself with a spirit of determination, with a heart of excellence and resolve, that you will not be denied or deterred; you will not quit and give up. First, however, you must rise to the occasion, run up that hill and when you do, run up the mountain and reach for the top-celebrate it and don't look at other people's peak or their celebrations.

Celebrate your accomplishments, celebrate your achievements, and **never** compare your victory to someone else's victories. Paul said it well in 2nd Timothy 4:7-8 **"I have fought the good fight, I have finished the race, I have kept the Faith. Finally, there is laid up for me the crown of righteousness, which the Lord, the righteous Judge, will give to me on that day, and not to me only but also to all who have loved His appearing.**

With a spirit of excellence, decide once and for all that you will arise, you will be better, and above all, give God the very best of who you are.

CHAPTER 3

YOUR DESTINY NOW
PREPARATION & DISCIPLINE

For anything to be great, it must be prepared right; one must prepare to accomplish that goal to achieve greatness. Therefore, preparation and discipline are critical to your futures excellence. As devoted as you can be, without preparation and discipline execution of said goals and dreams will never come to pass.

Jeremiah 29:11 I know the thoughts that I think toward you, says the Lord, thoughts of peace and not of evil, to give you a future and a hope.

For every thought, there must be a plan that must follow, for if there is no plan that follows, that thought will die and not come to pass. So every dream needs a plan of action; every project requires discipline to execute it. There will be giants and adversities that will come and challenge your dreams and goals. They will come to kill your Faith and ensure that your vision never sees the light of day.

Your enemies will try and smear you and your Faith; you will be presented with many opportunities to quit and give up. You will be encouraged to stop building towards your dream, urged to stop running towards the finish line, but when their shout for you to stop grow louder, that is when you must push harder, run fast and above all, don't you quit!

You better thank God cause your enemies have done more for you than any of your friends have ever done. If you see it from the perspective of Faith, you will know that they will cause you to press in; if your enemy ever knew what they were doing for you when they were doing it to you, they would have left you alone.

They would have never messed with you; that's why the Bible says to pray for your enemies. **Matthew 5:44** says, **"But I say unto you, Love your enemies, bless them that curse you, do good to them that hate you, and pray for them which despitefully use you, and persecute you; ... For example, the New International Version reads: "But I tell you, love your enemies and pray for those who persecute you."**

My enemies cause me to fall on my face; they cause me to say, God, I need you now more than ever before. They force me to fast, pray, believe and keep on walking. You can either let your enemies bring you down and keep you sidelined, or you can allow your enemies to push you closer to God and closer to your dreams and visions.

There is one thing fascinating about funerals: when they carry the coffin out, you usually have six people carrying out the casket. Yet, in life, when you are working towards your dreams and goals, you often find yourself alone. Where are those six people when it is the darkest before the light comes? Where are those six people when you find yourself all feeling defeated?

In those moments, you need to lean on the everlasting God that never fails to be there when no one else is. So he said in his word in **Hebrews 13:5, "...For He hath said, "I will never leave thee, nor forsake thee."**

You must be a trouble maker to laziness; you must be a trouble maker to conformity; you must be trouble make to your doubt, give more headaches to the enemy than the enemy gives you headaches. Let's take a look at this story;

Acts 17:6 says, But when they did not find them, they dragged Jason and some other believers before the city officials, shouting: "These men who have caused trouble all over the world have now come here,

I firmly believe that to be a trouble maker, spiritually and prophetically, is to flip the script and to stir it up; you must rise and declare a war to your unbelief and your doubt. But, to obtain victory, there must be a price to pay. Maybe the pain you feel is the price you must pay to give birth to your miracle.

Maybe the pain you feel is the price you must pay to give birth to what God wants to do THROUGH you, there is always a price to pay, and in your distress, God will enlarge you.

When you realize that God does everything, God does it on purpose with purpose and for purpose. And you are left wondering why is that nobody has thought of this? Maybe it is a handful of purposes only for you.

There is a reason why God does what he does, and there is a reason why God allows things to happen and take place; the Bible says in

Isaiah 55: 8-9, "For My thoughts *are* not your thoughts, Nor *are* your ways My ways," says the Lord. For *as* the heavens are higher than the earth, So are My ways higher than your ways, And My thoughts than your thoughts.

We may never, and we will never understand God's ways and his thoughts, we will never be able to understand his reasoning, we will never be able to under how God thinks. Yet, in the world of Faith, understanding is not required, comprehension is not needed, true Faith is not when you understand it all; you know nothing and still choose to walk forward.

True Faith is when you are surrounded by doubt and unbelief yet still choose to believe in God's word. Feelings follow focus; if I focus on the peace and focus on the cure and the process, I feel confident.

When I am confident, I feel peaceful and joyful, but if I am focused on the problem, I feel anxious, and I feel fearful. I may feel nervous about what's going on if I focus on what's wrong. If I focus on what I've lost instead of what I got left, my dreams are in trouble.

When I realize that if God ever creates a miracle in your life, it will often never be with what you have lost; instead, he will use what you have left.

Jesus took the leftover fish and bread and fed the five thousand, let me remind you that God can take whatever you've got left and turn it into a supernatural miracle.

You can be broken because nobody believed or believes in you and your dreams, but God will take what you have left and bless you with it. He will bless you with what the world thinks and believes is insignificant; he will use that to "show off" his power and glory through your acts of Faith.

God will never do what you have to do; your preparation is critical, your discipline is crucial, and your Faith must be relentless.

The real question you must ask yourself is, do you see what you have left? Do you value it? Do you believe that God can use that to turn things around? Of course, the answer to all these questions must be a resounding Yes!

2 Kings 4 tells us about an amazing woman and her acts of trust and faith in the word that came from the prophet's mouth.

Her husband had died, and she was in outstanding debt, so much that they were coming to take her two boys as servants to pay off the debt. Just when she thought it was all over, just when she thought there was nothing more that could be done, then God showed up through the prophet.

All she had left was a jar of oil; Elisha said to her, **"What can I do for you? Tell me, what do you have in the house?" And she said, "Your woman servant has nothing in the house except a jar of oil." 2 Kings 4:3**

Out of a jar of oil was going to come a great miracle; out of something so small and insignificant was going to come a breakthrough for her and her family. So he didn't ask her what she had lost, even though he knew that she had lost everything, he asked her **what she had in her house?**

Faith will always look at what you have left and never at what you have lost. Faith will never see the cup half empty rather; it will see it half full. To obtain the strength to take the next step, you will require a great deal of patience and discipline for things to begin to happen in your life.

The prophet then proceeds to ask her to do something very unusual; he asks her to gather many pots and fill the empty jars with her left oil. That order may have seemed without any rationale to the natural mind, but an explanation was not needed to the people of Faith; only Faith was required. True Faith does not require understanding; it does not require a reason, but it does require unconventional patience and discipline.

In the middle of a moment of crisis, she was ordered to work for her miracle. In the middle of her trials, she was called to grab her two sons and get herself to work. The man of God could have easily prayed, and the miracle could have taken place right there and then, but instead, she was ordered to get to work.

Why didn't he pray? Because prayer without action is void. A miracle without work performed will create in you a spoiled child mentality. Notice that the woman didn't complain or question what she was being told to do; she didn't throw her hands up in the air and give up; she rolled up her sleeves with her two boys and got to work.

Your dreams, visions, and goals will **always** cause you to work for them. She and her boys were prepared to work, and that required discipline. They bought into the plan; they were determined to get out of the mess that they were in. You must be prepared and disciplined to go the extra mile, no matter what God may ask of you.

I have often said at church that if God were to say, "I will give you a million dollars, and all you have to do is run around the block ten times, how many of you would remain in your seats? I can almost guarantee that very few people would remain sitting in their seats.

Those that remain would be the ones who refused to do what was being asked of them and would complain by saying, why run? Why doesn't God give me the million without running around the block?

As I stated earlier, true miracles will never be done for you while you are in a lazy state of mind. If you genuinely want a blessing, then you must be willing to get up, dress up, and do what is being asked of you. If the woman decides to stay in her negative state of mind, she would have lost her boys and never seen the miracles before her very eyes.

If she had complained or asked for an explanation, her miracle would have died, and the story would have ended differently. Yet, she chose not to question the instruction, but she showed her preparation and determination to do whatever it takes to get the job done. If she decides to walk away, so would have her miracle.

If you decide to abandon the pursuit of your dreams and goals just because you don't like the instructions given to you, disagree with the method, or think what was being asked of you is unreasonable. Then, you can kiss your dreams and goals goodbye because the moment you decide to take on that attitude, you will never reach your destiny.

It would help if you were prepared and disciplined to be mentally, emotionally and spiritually ready to receive the word or instruction, then find it in yourself to get up and proceed on the road to achieving greatness.

You must, and I emphasize, **must** be ready to do what God has called you to do at a moment's notice. If you sit and complain, then don't complain when things die, you are called to greatness, and therefore you must, at all costs, keep going and never stop. With preparation and discipline, you will unlock great things for yourself and activate your Faith. When that happens, you will begin to see supernatural miracles take place, not just blessings but supernatural gifts.

GAINING MOMENTUM

When launching a slingshot, you must first pull back to release the stone; the further you pull back, the further the stone will travel.

In our pursuit of achieving our dreams and goals, we often go through the process of being pulled back. That feeling may not always seem pleasant and accepted, but it is needed. When you are pulled back, it looks as if you are being stopped from going further.

You take a step forward and three steps backwards; it is a depressing feeling, and unless you are willing to deposit your goals and dreams in the hands of God, you will never understand this process. Finally, you arch backwards to get momentum as you throw your arm forward to get the maximum distance, even to throw a stone with your bare hand.

You can not get discouraged.

The slingshot is the process God will often use to propel you forward at a maximum rate of speed. Though we may not understand what is happening when pulled back, it may feel like we are going backwards and not forward; we must know that we will gain momentum through this process, launching us ahead to our destiny.

Here in Canada, we know a thing or two about getting stuck in the snow, and we know the headache of getting stuck. You spin the tires by stepping down on the accelerator but going nowhere. You twist the tires left and right, and nothing is even more complicated if you are yourself.

But blessed we are to be Canadian, that sooner or later someone will come by and offer to give you a hand. So I've been on both sides of this scenario, and both are great because on one side, you get to help someone in distress, and on the other, you are being supported in your time of grief.

Now, this holds to be accurate; you first start trying to shovel your way out; after that, you begin the process of rocking the car back and forth to give yourself some traction. When you start rocking the car back and forth, you are creating some momentum to get out of the mess you are in.

You rock back and forth till finally, you are free, and you have traction to go forward. But, again, going backwards was necessary to your opportunity to go forward.

Don't ever be discouraged by the notion that you must go "backwards" or the idea that you are being pulled back. God manifests his most extraordinary power on an idea that may not make sense to you at that moment.

Daniel's story is interesting; everything was going great until he was condemned to the lion's den. It is not till verse 25 of Daniel chapter 6 that we find the redemption power.

The Bible says in Daniel 6:25, **"Then King Darius wrote to all the nations and peoples of every language in all the earth: "May you prosper greatly! "I issue a decree that in every part of my kingdom, people must fear and reverence the God of Daniel. "For he is the living God, and he endures forever; his kingdom will not be destroyed, his dominion will never end. He rescues, and he saves; he performs signs and wonders.**

He was sent to his death, but God had a different plan; you may find yourself in a moment of crisis, going backwards instead of forward. You must trust God and his all-knowing, perfect plan for your life. Often, being pulled back is the best thing that could happen to you because God sees what you can not, and his pull-back of you is to propel you forward and give you the momentum you are looking for.

When we fail to understand that God is in control, we become frustrated and angry at the notion of going backwards. We can not control what happens to us, but we can control how we react to those things. Momentum often goes backwards, but only to propel you forward.

Daniel faced imminent death by being sent to the lion's den; his future was certain, death was assured, but they forgot that Daniel had a God he prayed to consistently. It looked like he had to go backwards, and he looked that way in specific ways, but God was about to show up powerfully.

It would be best if you never forgot that the God of the Bible is a living God, and he has yet to lose a battle. Therefore, gaining momentum can only be attributed to God, for he is the one that allows you to excel, grow and expand.

The Bible says in **1st Corinthians 3:6, "I planted, Apollos watered, but God gave the increase."**

The key here is **that God gives the increase!** At this point, we can not forget that God is the one who gives you growth and momentum. The Bible also says in **Revelation 3:8, "I know your works. See, I have set before you an open door, and no one can shut it; for you have a little strength, have kept My word, and have not denied My name."**

When God gives you momentum, it will accelerate you to places you thought were only a dream. Things that should take months and years to achieve are achieved in days and hours. Momentum in God increases favour in your life; it causes blessings to be set before you, causes a shift in the pursuit of your dreams and goals.

Psalms 23:5 says, "You prepare a table before me in the presence of my enemies; You anoint my head with oil; My cup runs over."

This is a powerful verse to consider; One, **You prepare a table before me in the presence of my enemies.** This brings me back to the grace and favour that God puts on your life, things that shouldn't happen-happen, and your enemies cause you to be at peace, and they can only witness what God is doing for you and through you.

It means that when your enemies want to fight you, God says NO-and he begins to bless you in the presence of those that may not like you or be for you.

Secondly, he says, **You anoint my head with oil.** The oil that keeps mosquitos away, oil that makes you a repellent to those things that might come and harm you. He anoints you with precious oil, giving you a sweet aroma that attracts people and blessing to your life. Don't get me wrong; I am not saying that the enemy won't come and attack you, but what I am saying is that they will go against you but shall not prevail against you.

The Bible says **Psalms 91:7 "A thousand may fall at your side and ten thousand at your right hand,** *But* **it shall not come against you."**

That is what the oil does; it gives you a covering around you in which your enemies can not penetrate. That oil only comes through your seeking of God; the more you seek Him, the more oil he anoints you with.

Thirdly and lastly, he says, **My cup runs over.** Here he talks about abundance and what I like to refer to as momentum. Here in Canada, we have a great place that I like to visit: Niagra falls.

Niagra Falls, Ontario, is a Canadian city at the famous waterfall of the same name, linked with the U.S by the Rainbow Bridge. It is said that Niagra Falls has the world's highest flow rate. About twenty-eight million litres or about 700,000 gallons of water travel down Niagra Falls every second.

That is much water flowing, and the Bible says that your cup runs over! Suddenly, you have so much blessing coming your way that you can not explain it with human explanation, only to give God the glory.

Your cup runs over, which means you have so much momentum, and you are on such a roll that you expand in ways you thought you never would. You start making huge strides, leaps and bounds, to the point that you can not explain what is happening at that moment, only to say that God is behind what is taking place.

Your first place of gaining is on your keens in prayer; this is where it all starts, on your knees. Prayer causes you to have not only a relationship with

God, but it allows you to fly high and gain much distance in the pursuit of the vision and goals that you may have.

Prayer causes you to run faster, fly higher, climb more and never give up in the pursuit of what you are trying to achieve.

THE FINAL STRETCH

I love seeing relay races online because I constantly analyze why they put that runner in that race position. Yet the most exhilarating experience is that final stretch that leads towards the finish line. Every runner is carefully picked and strategically placed to give the team an advantage during the race.

In 2015 at the Beijing Olympics, the Jamaicans won the 4x100m relay final race. Watching Usain Bolt take off on the last 100 meters was so exciting that you have to watch it time and time again. Every position matters; every second counts, the handoffs must be perfect for the team to succeed.

On your journey towards the finish line, you must remember that every association you have matters; every time you invest time into someone or something matters, and that investment will produce negatively or positively in your life.

You see the finish line, the end is near, but the most challenging part has just begun; getting yourself across the finish line is critical, and usually, the most complex battles are left right up to the very end.

I have often spoken about the power of association, and when you see the finish line, this becomes even more important than ever before. I am a firm believer that you have to be nice to everyone, regardless of how they are towards you. I know that may seem easier said than done but it is the truth, be nice to everyone.

Be nice to people on every level because a relationship or association can change overnight. That relationship or association can often make the difference between you crossing the line of victory or not crossing that line at all.

Success is always connected to motion; you must get moving; these are true principles of greatness; **work, have a great attitude, love & kindness.**

You have to be the most challenging working individual in the room; there can not be anybody that outworks you. The drive you must have should be copied from everybody else; you must be the first one in and the last out. Your work ethic must be top-notch; second-rate work ethic will never achieve greatness.

People must feed off your passion and drive, but they can not inspire you to greatness; when it is your dream, you must be at the steering wheel and in command of your ship.

Your attitude must be confident in God, not arrogant, and there is a difference between both. The Bible says in **James 4:6," But He gives more grace. Therefore He says: "God resists the proud, But gives grace to the humble."**

Grace gives you confidence and posture; it is a silent enforcer that powerfully surrounds your life. Grace is what others see in you, but you don't see it yourself. Grace opens doors that money can often can not; it puts you in front of people who would not be able to in other circumstances.

Grace covers your errors, makes your flaws un-noticeable, gives you a glow when you speak and makes your enemies be at peace with you.

On the other hand, pride is the opposite of you having grace; it is an excellent divider, shutting doors everywhere you go. Pride is offensive and comes across unpleasant. If God himself resists the proud and can not stand a proud person, this also happens naturally.

Pride will kill the goodwill others may feel towards you; it kills the willingness to help someone, it offends others, hurts, cuts and often burns bridges that can never be repaired. But, on the other hand, pride can come through achievements and or progress that you make, and this is where you must be careful not to destroy everything you have been working hard on because, in one moment, everything can be ruined.

Proverbs 11:12 "When pride comes, then comes disgrace, but with the humble is wisdom."

1 Peter 5:5: Likewise, you who are younger, be subject to the elders. Clothe yourselves, all of you, with humility toward one another, for "God opposes the proud but gives grace to the humble."

Humility is often characterized as genuine gratitude and a lack of arrogance, a modest view of oneself. However, the biblical definition of humility goes beyond this. Humility is a critical and continuous emphasis of godliness in the Bible, as we are called upon to be humble followers of Christ and trust in the wisdom and salvation of God. Therefore, let us be humble before our creator for the gift of life we have been given.

Biblical humility is grounded in God. The Father descends to help the poor and afflicted; the incarnate Son manifests humility from birth until His crucifixion. The coupled usage of "meek" and "humble in heart" in **Matthew 11:29** emphasizes Christ's humility before humankind, whom he came to serve, and His submission before God. Humility and meekness are often interrelated as both are righteous traits for doing the will of God.

"Trust in the LORD with all your heart and lean not on your understanding;" **Proverbs 3:5**

The importance of humility is directly related to the deadly consequences of pride. Pride separates us from God as we do not acknowledge and appreciate the eternal sovereignty of our Lord. Therefore, the importance of humility is seen in the deep gratitude we hold in proper recognition of God's divinity and love for us. Humility's significance is also found in recognizing our flawed nature as humans on earth and our susceptibility to sin if not vigilant against temptation.

"Be sober-minded; be watchful. Your adversary, the devil, prowls around like a roaring lion, seeking someone to devour." ~ 1 Peter 5:8

During the final stretch, you must be careful not to allow pride to cloud your judgment and not let the accomplishments or accolades you may receive ruin everything you have achieved so far.

Staying humble means acknowledging that God was the one who gave you the power to make it up to this point and realizing that without Him, nothing would be possible, and because of Him, all things are possible.

John 15:5 says, "I am the vine, you *are* the branches. He who abides in Me, and I in him, bears much fruit; for without Me you can do nothing."

2nd Timothy 4:7-8 says, "I have fought the good fight, I have finished the race, I have kept the Faith. Finally, there is laid up for me the crown of righteousness, which the Lord, the righteous Judge, will give to me on that day, and not to me only but also to all who have loved His appearing."

The race is not over till you make it until you must continue to work hard, keep your head down, acknowledge God in all your ways and press through, press in, for you are too close to have everything come tumbling down.

It will be very tempting to steer, of course, because of your accomplishments, effortless to lose your focus because of the accolades you receive, and all this happens just when you are close to reaching your goals.

There is a battle to get to where you are going, but never forget that there will be a battle to stay where you are going. The struggle does not end because you made it; you must recognize that you made it but that the war has just begun. During that final stretch, where you see the end in sight is not the end; it is the beginning of something new. A new chapter in your life is about to begin, and this is where you do not slow down and get complacent; this is where you gear up, find that new strength and push even harder.

Everything right that you have done has led you to this point in your life, and now is not the time to cave in. I remember the winter of 1997, as I walked through the doors of 212 Murray St for the very first time and said to my dad, "this is the place, dad."

We had made it, I thought; this was the pinnacle moment in the church; we were about to but our very first building. It was empty, but I could already see the people, dirty, but all I could see was a beauty; this was a masterpiece waiting to happen.

As we toured the building, I was like a bit of a kid in the candy store, excited for what was about to happen, excited for this new chapter to begin. I remember telling my Mom how exciting this was how great it would be; my Mom just smiled and agreed with keeping her joy inside while the realtor gave us the grand tour of the place.

We had made it, I thought, what my Father had preached on, for so many years, it was finally coming to light; what was talked about and dreamed about was finally seeing the light of day. All that was needed now was to cross the T's and dot the I's, and the dream was fulfilled. Was it, though?

My mind had jumped from the dirty to the beauty and skipped everything in between. I had gone from empty to full and bypassed everything needed to get there. I thought that my result would manifest instantly in a snap of my fingers, and boy was I wrong.

We often get caught up in the images of the finished product that we forget there is a process to get there, and it is not always pretty.

The building was upside down and inside out, yet my present didn't see any of that; all I saw was the polished finished product. So it would be best to get excited about the finished product but never get down when you stare at the process to get there.

Purchasing the building was just the start, but to me, it was the end, not realizing that the road to greatness in achieving your goals and dreams is never done; it is constantly growing and expanding.

We are about to celebrate 25 years of ministry at 212 Murray St, right here in the nation's capital, and I can genuinely say that we have not reached the end goal, far from it. We have gone through multiple renovations, extensive repair and modifications, and there is still more to be done.

Thousands of dollars have been spent improving and adapting to the times throughout the years, and we're still not done. Things that once were great have become obsolete, but we do not get bottled down at the thought of how much money has gone out the door; we realize that was the price to pay on this road we call ministry.

You can not look back and beat yourself down at the decisions you should have made or the road you should have crossed; no matter what decision you made or what route you decided to go on, it has brought you to this point right here and now. We can not change the past, but we can affect our future.

If we stop for a moment and realize that we ought to be grateful that we are not dead or worse in hell, then thankful we should be at having an opportunity to change our future now while in the present. Looking back with regret does no good to anybody; what could you have been? And so many other questions are nonsense and a complete waste of time and energy.

During that moment when you think you made it, and you have reached the finish line, take a step back, breath, and realize that you have reached the end of a milestone, but another one is about to begin.

The final stretch is often the most difficult because it is filled with excitement and delusion. Excitement because you have genuinely believed that you made it, but delusion because the road keeps going. So why then is it called the final stretch?

Every milestone has a "final stretch" every time you reach the end of the growth step in your life; you enter this zone that many fail. Then, finally, you get to that point where you think and believe that you've made it, and suddenly you throw your hands up in the air and celebrate, but only to realize that the next step is about to begin.

Many get discouraged because, like me, they jump to the end result when we fail to see that getting to our goal is ever-changing and evolving, and we are never done. I repeat you can not get discouraged at the fact that what you thought was the "it" is only the beginning to your dreams and goals being fulfilled.

When an aircraft travels from point A to point B, specific "markers" must go through on their route to their destination. These markers let the pilots know that they are on the right path to their destination. The pilot doesn't celebrate the marker; they celebrate till they've reached their destination.

Each marker must be celebrated in life because they represent our growth in maturity, knowledge, confidence, obedience, and relationship with God. We observe that each day we learn and grow through the experiences we may go through. Each adversity and trial we face are an opportunity if we let them improve ourselves and become a better person as we strive for the goal.

Once you accept the fact that our real goal is heaven and the earthly goals are needed but come secondary to our eternal goal, we will then be at peace when we reach those milestones that looked like the end but, in reality, are only the birthing place of your next level.

The birthing of the NEW YOU!

THIS IS WHERE THE NEW YOU BEGINS

2nd Corinthians 5:17 "Therefore, if anyone *is* in Christ, *he is* a new creation; old things have passed away; behold, all things have become new."

71

There is always a greater level, and each greater level requires a greater you. You have come this far not to go back, but you have reached and crossed the point of no return.

Multiple signs tell you what you can and can not take across the security checkpoint when you travel and are about to go through security. No matter where you are going, or the reason for going, everyone must go through this security checkpoint. If you are carrying something you are not supposed to have, you will be denied entry.

The higher your pursuit of greatness will require specific changes in your life that will not go well with where God wants to take you. Certain things that may have worked for you in the past may not work with you going forward. Methods, plans & strategies that may have helped you previously do not mean that it will work in this new season or level you are about to embark on.

One of the greatest mistakes you can make is living a new season with an old mentality. The word says, **"all things are made new."** not some, but all things are made new.

Every person will pursue their own goals and dreams, and not one is better than the other, but rather, you must not look at what your friend or family members' vision is and compare yours to theirs; you must reach for your dreams and goals.

Reach for that dream, pray for that dream, fast and sow for it, for in doing so, you will activate your Faith, and God will respond. Don't stop till you reach the goal, and when you do, find it in you to excel and move into the next season.

Since there is a new you, there will be new challenges, new giants to face, new adversities will come your way, but remember that the Bible says, in **1st John 4:4, "Ye are of God, little children, and have overcome them: because greater is he that is in you than he that is in the world."**

God will always be greater than those things, including people that will rise against you. You must believe that you are worthy of that blessing you are chasing. You can not allow anyone to tell you that you are unworthy of your goals and dreams because of your past.

Your past does not disqualify you all good things, but through the blood of Jesus, we are a new creation, the old you is washed away and again, all things are made fresh, including you.

Often people quit the pursuit of their dreams and goals because others tell them that they are crazy or far-fetched. Those are indirect phrases telling you that you are not worthy. That negativity is so poisonous that it cripples the person into believing that they do not deserve such a crazy dream or goal.

Your dreams, goals, aspirations, and visions should be huge. However, it would be best to remember that smaller dreams, goals, aspirations, and ideas must be completed beforehand to get to the finished product. Achieving these things at the end will enable you to reach that finished product.

When they build a car, it always starts with a rendering of the car, modifications are made, 3D designs are brought out, and after various renditions, the manufacturer then decides on the finished product.

Following the approval of the renditions, the car then proceeds to get built; first, the shell of the vehicle is made, followed by all the other components, and after several weeks the car rolls out and onto the car dealership ready for their new owners to take possession.

There was a process to creating the car; now, the designer doesn't get discouraged because the vehicle didn't instantly appear or didn't get frustrated because he had to make revisions; no, he knew there was a process. When you understand the process, frustration has no place in your life.

I repeat, every new level requires a new you, a new way of thinking, talking, engaging and adapting. They say you can not teach an old dog new tricks, oh, but you can!

When you have a dream, it often whispers to you; God does not shout; he whispers to you. The closer you are to God, the softer is voice becomes. God must be your source of inspiration; when he becomes your source of inspiration, you will begin to receive wisdom and understanding in all the things you do and want to do.

Never give up; without commitment, you will never start anything; without consistency, you will never finish; it is not easy; if it were, then the story would be different. So instead, you must keep working on the new you, fall seven times but get up eight times, beat yourself up into acknowledging that the old you can not carry you past specific points of your life.

1st Corinthians 13:11 says, **"When I was a child, I spoke as a child, I understood as a child, I thought as a child; but when I became a man, I put away childish things."**

You must grow each day, seek God, grow in maturity, knowledge, obedience, submission and respect. Grow in appreciation for others, grow in your love for the word of God, Grow in the desire to be close to God and to hear his voice.

One of my most significant motivating factors for continuing this journey is the doubt, and unbelief others may have in me or my dreams. Their doubt of me motivates me to push harder, serve better, reach for the highest, and outwork everyone in the room.

The new you will have to leave many things behind, adapt to new environments, and above all, continue to pursue the greatness that God has called you for. Of course, the old you will cling on and fight not to let go, but it is imperative that you resign your old new and accept the new you God has called you for.

The new you must accept that more significant challenges will arise, and therefore your vocabulary must change, the words that come forth out of your mouth must be aligned with the word of God. Therefore, it is crucial for the new you to get into the word of God, memorize it, study it, declare it and live by it.

The Bible says in **2ⁿᵈ Corinthians 5:7, "For we walk by faith, not by sight."**

Your old you wants to walk based on what you see and hear, based on an experience to help you keep walking. The old you needs evidence to believe, needs things that are felt to walk. The new you needs nothing of the natural; it doesn't require that which is heard, felt and seen to walk; our trust is in the Lord God, and that is the energy we need to walk.

The new you doesn't need motivation or encouragement to come from someone else; you find that in the Lord. So **1ˢᵗ Samuel 30:6 says, "...but David encouraged himself in the Lord his God.**

Find the encouragement and motivation in knowing that all things are possible with God, and nothing is possible without God. For if you do not accept this fact, then when will you ever see the Glory of God manifested in your life?

Now is the time for the new you to arise from the ashes and bury your old you. Letting go of those things that have served you only to block you, releasing yourself from guilt, shame and your past, and accepting that today God has called you for something greater.

Every day, month, year, hour and second that goes by living in the old you, full of disappointments and failures, guilt and shame, is a moment that will never come back to us. Of course, it never comes back to us when time passes, but the seed that we planted at that moment will yield fruit in our tomorrow. Whether they be good or bad, those seeds will either help you grow or keep you down in the pits of despair.

For this is the time, this is the moment you must decide to arise and take charge first and foremost of yourself. Become a new version of yourself, redefine who you are, challenge yourself to be better; this is that time. The Bible says, in **Ecclesiastes 3:1, "There is a time for everything and a season for every activity under the heavens."**

For this is the season that God wants to do great things with you, through you and for you!

IF NOT NOW, WHEN?

When is the right time to do anything? Are we to wait till we have no problems? Or till we have all the money needed? When is the right time to act?

If we wait until everything aligns, we might be here some time. If Peter had waited for the waters to calm down, he might have then never walked on water; if Daniel had waited for there not to be a decree, it would have never seen God's wonders in the lion's den.

If David had waited till he got bigger and stronger, Goliath would not have been defeated. If these men, among others, would have waited to act, then we would have a different story to read about in the Bible.

If we wait for things to be perfect to act, we will never work because nothing will ever be perfect. The Bible says, **Proverbs 3:5-6, "There is a time for everything, and a season for every activity under the heavens."**

Peter had to trust God, and he walked on water; Daniel had to be faithful in his prayer, and God sent deliverance, David had to believe in himself, and his God and Goliath came down.

You can not sit around and hope for things to work themselves out, sometimes they do, but you must roll up your sleeves and get to work when they don't. Hoping for God to do everything is a complete waste of your time and energy. God will never do what you are supposed to do, he does what you can not do, but he waits for you to do what he has given you the ability to do.

There is no perfect time to do anything; there is no correct scenario to begin in, you must decide that and it is up to you to say to yourself, this is my time! Faith does not wait for the right time; Faith creates the time to act. Faith doesn't wait for the stars to align; Faith is bold and active, Faith causes movement.

Excuses tell you that you must wait for the right time, and yes, as I stated earlier, there is a time and season for everything under the sun, but you must act when it comes to your Faith.

The Bible says, **James 2:14, "What *does it* profit, my brethren if someone says he has faith but does not have works? Can faith save him?** verse 18 says, **"But someone will say, "You have faith, and I have works." Show me your faith without your works, and I will show you my faith by my works**

This is a powerful verse, especially at the end, when he says, **"I will show you my faith by my works!"**

Your works directly result from your Faith and vice versa; your lack of works directly results from your lack of confidence. So to say you are waiting for the "right" time is simply masking around the fact that you have reasons why you don't want to start.

They may be justifiable reasons or valid points of view, but the reality is that if you never decide to start, you never will. When will it ever be a good time? No matter of good of a time, it may seem there will always be things that may not be perfect, and if you focus on the things that are not right, they will serve to block you before you even begin.

Excuses often mask themselves as legitimate things, and please understand me, they may very well be. However, I am trying to convey that if you always let those things stop you, when will you ever get things done?

Esther was a bold woman, confident in her calling, of a sound mind, but her timing was not the best. You couldn't just approach the king without being called in; to do so would mean certain death. She had her back against the wall; the enemy was all around, restrictions out of her control, yet she knew what she had to do.

Knowing what the law and penalty were concerning approaching the king unannounced, she decided to do the unthinkable. With one sentence, she sealed her fate and left it up to God when she said in **Esther 4:16, "Go, gather together all the Jews who are present in Shushan, and fast ye for me; and neither eat nor drink three days, night or day. So I also and my maidens will fast likewise. And so will I go in unto the king, which is not according to the law; and if I perish, I perish."**

She could not wait for the right time or be called by the king; she needed to activate her Faith and act according to her Faith and what needed to be done. There are moments when you must wait for certain things to happen for you to work, but then there are times when you must act before the right time is right.

Both points of view are essential, but if you get stuck on always waiting for the right time, moment or circumstance to act, then the moment may never come to you. During your pursuit to accomplish what God has called you to do, you will encounter moments that will require you to wait for a window to open up; those moments need patience, counsel and guidance.

Patience to see the window open wide enough for you to take your opportunity, receive counsel on whether you should act or not, and guidance from those that have been through it so that similar mistakes may not happen again.

Then there are those moments that Faith in action is required. Again, Peter to walk on the waters did not take a vote from the other disciples; he didn't check to see how they felt about him walking on water. Peter also didn't wait until there was no storm and the seas were calm. Peter reacted in Faith, took in the moment, and walked on the waters.

There will be days for you to take a step back and analyze the situation, but then there will be days in which you must act and see the wonders God has for you.

Esther said, it well, **if I perish, I perish!** Nevertheless, she was willing to risk her own life to see a miracle happen.

Daniel 3:16-18 says, Shadrach, Meshach, and Abednego answered and said to the king, O Nebuchadnezzar, we are not careful to answer thee in this matter. If it be so, our God whom we serve is able to deliver us from the burning fiery furnace, and he will deliver us out of thine hand, O king. But if not, be it known unto thee, O king, that we will not serve thy gods, nor worship the golden image which thou hast set up.

But if not, be it known unto thee, O king, that we will not serve thy gods, nor worship the golden image which thou hast set up. As they say, they drew a line in the sand, and they stood their ground.

In the face of a fiery furnace, in front of death, they stood their ground, and they boldly declared their faith in God. That bold declaration caused them to act "defiantly" before the king, but it was the only way out.

Faced with the prospect of death, they chose to boldly stand for what they believed in instead of caving to save their own life. What are you willing to do now? Are you ready to yield or stand?

You and only you can make that decision; you must own the decision and stand by it no matter what may come your way. You must push fear out of your mind, heart, and words. You must be able to stand up and say,

"What shall we then say to these things? If God be for us, who can be against us? Romans 8:31

That **"who"** can symbolize a person or a thing, that **"who"** must be defeated in your life, even if that **"who"** is yourself.

We are in a season that is so unpredictable, so many variables are happening around us, and things are changing by the minute. So the word of God says, in **2nd Timothy 1:7, "For God has not given us a spirit of fear, but of power and of love and of a sound mind."**

Fear can not have a place in your thoughts and or words. Fear can not have a place to live in your mind; fear can not have a place in how you live; you must be free from all free.

The only way you are set free of fear is by surrounding yourself and submerging yourself in the presence of God. Then, you are free from that fear when you do, and you can make clear and direct decisions regarding your future.

You will make mistakes in your decision-making, get it wrong, make the wrong turn, and sometimes make horrible decisions that you may later regret. But remember, *"But as for you, you meant evil against me; but God meant it for good to bring it about as it is this day, to save many people alive. Genesis 50:20"*

You will get it wrong sometimes, but God, in His infinite wisdom, in his great grace, will turn things around for you in ways that He only knows how to do so.

Peter could have easily thought when he was drowning, "this was a wrong move on my part" how many times have you said those words? I can tell you that I have said those words many times during my life. Yet throughout all of my mistakes, I have concluded that God's mercy is so immense and very special that he gives us grace and compassion even when we should be receiving judgment.

Moments when we are guilty, he gives us a pardon, that this the great love of God. We may never be able to understand it or comprehend it, but the reality is that if we trust the Lord with all our hearts, then we can be guaranteed that his mercy will never fail us.

You may be correct, but God is absolute, you may have a perspective, God sees it all, we may have an idea, God has the way; For without God, we can do nothing.

It is my sincere prayer that your life was edified and challenged to do the unthinkable through this book. I pray that you will arise today and pursue the dream, goal and or vision that God has placed on your heart and that you will see it come to fruition.

For this is the season, which is the moment that God has been waiting for, the moment you decide to arise, dust yourself off, and be what God has called you to be.

Your problems are only as big as you give them credit for, and God can be as big as your faith lets him be. So then, you can arise today and accomplish what you set yourself to.

Be the Daniel that was relentless in prayer, be the fearless Deborah, be the David that brought down a giant and saved a nation, be the Esther and stand up to the face of uncertainty, be the Peter that walked on water.

The Bible is full of heroes of the faith and none other than our Lord and Saviour Jesus Christ.

Again, the world is full of heroes, but now is the time for a new chapter to be written and a new hero to emerge, and that hero needs to be **you**!

Be the hero to your family, the hero to your friends, be the hero to yourself. Acknowledge that God is on your side, and he will never leave you nor forsake you.

This is your moment and your time, grab it, conquer the moment, arise, stand up and shout it from the mountain top;

I HAVE BEEN DESTINED FOR GREATNESS!

DESTINADO A LA GRANDEZA
Y ASÍ COMIENZA....

Aquí es donde todo comienza, una auto-declaración de quién eres porque hasta que no nos dirigimos al viejo tú, el NUEVO TÚ nunca surgirá. Así que debes ser honesto para abordar el viejo tú, abierto a abordar tus defectos, porque cuando lo haces, te liberas de los grilletes y se experimenta la libertad para comenzar el proceso hacia tu destino.

¿Débil? ¿Tengo algún defecto? Es la primera pregunta que pone todo en perspectiva. ¿Tienes defectos? La respuesta a esta pregunta es que no tengo más que debilidades. No soy naturalmente asertivo, rápido o flexible; ciertamente no soy el hombre más inteligente del mundo; me emociono por cosas que no debería emocionarme tanto.

Como los alimentos equivocados, no duermo lo suficiente, dejo las cosas para después y pierdo el tiempo. Me preocupo demasiado por las cosas sin sentido y no me preocupo lo suficiente por las cosas esenciales.

Mi ego es demasiado grande, y mi mente es demasiado pequeña para intentar siquiera empezar a entender los planes ilimitados que Dios tiene para mi vida. Así que mis pensamientos están atrapados, a menudo dentro de sí mismos.

Dicho todo esto, tengo un dicho que dice algo así: la fuerza de una persona es a menudo su mayor debilidad. Sin embargo, sus defectos pueden convertirse en fortalezas.

No puedes aceptar cómo el mundo te etiqueta o te define. No puedes aceptar su conclusión de cómo acabarás, sobre todo declaran que estás condenado a fracasar y a no ir a ninguna parte.

El pronóstico del mundo sobre ti y tus objetivos es sombrío y poco alentador. A menudo, pasamos tanto tiempo leyendo ese pronóstico y escuchándolo que de repente se convierte en lo que crees y en lo que eres. Se apodera de tu mente y tus emociones y se manifiesta en tu vocabulario, moldeándote en algo fuera del plan y el molde de Dios para tu vida.

Nos quedamos tan atrapados en la opinión de todo el mundo sobre ti que te olvidas del camino que deberías seguir. La lucha es honesta, precisa cada día, desde que abres los ojos hasta que los cierras, y parece que entonces la lucha ha terminado, pero continúa en tus sueños y pensamientos.

Yo lucho todos los días, lucho, lucho y raspo, y voy picando esas debilidades porque la batalla es real. Tu mayor enemigo eres TÚ; tu reto más importante eres TÚ. La lucha para cambiar tus debilidades es real; la lucha para evitar que tus debilidades crezcan es real, y o te vence, o la vences.

Algunos días gano, y otros no, pero cada día me vuelvo a levantar, y avanzo, con los puños cerrados, con la vista puesta en el premio, con todo lo que tengo para superar esas debilidades. Así que me vuelvo a levantar y corro hacia la pelea, corro hacia la lucha, corro hacia el miedo que me está mirando a la cara porque la única manera de tener éxito es NUNCA RETIRARSE sino siempre levantarse y luchar.

Tus carencias e inseguridades siempre estarán gritando a todo pulmón para intentar desviarte de tu camino, pero si puedes levantarte cada mañana y decidir que hoy serás mejor que ayer, entonces mi querido amigo, has empezado a ganar esta lucha. Muchas personas decidirán que eres una amenaza para ellos, que tus objetivos son una amenaza para ellos, y ahí es donde tú decides si ceder o presionar.

No te moldea lo que digan los demás; te marca cada día lo que te dices a ti mismo. La Biblia dice: "Todo lo puedo en Cristo que me fortalece"-Fil 4:13. Esa misma palabra es una declaración que debería ser pronunciada en tu vida cada día y minuto de tu vida. Comienza diciendo, ¡puedo! Piensa en eso por un minuto ..... ¡Puedo! y continúa diciendo, ¡Haz todas las cosas! ¡Significa que puedes hacer todas las cosas! Si esa palabra o frase no te emociona y te motiva, no creo que nada pueda hacerlo.

Pero aquí está la clave, él dice ¡por medio de Cristo que me fortalece! Así que puedes hacer todas las cosas, pero no puedes hacer todas las cosas sin Cristo. Juan 15:5 dice,' "Yo soy la vid, vosotros los pámpanos. El que permanece en mí, y yo en él, da mucho fruto; porque sin mí no podéis hacer nada".

Una vez más, aquí nos dice que podemos dar mucho fruto SI permanecemos en él y ese SI es grande. Nuestras debilidades a menudo nos sacan del camino que nos permite dar fruto. Nuestras debilidades secan nuestra fe y nuestra vida de oración si las dejamos. Y termina la frase diciendo una expresión definitiva, y es que ¡SIN MÍ NO PUEDES HACER NADA! No sólo es una afirmación audaz, sino que es una afirmación que no da lugar a la negociación; me explico...

A menudo queremos negociar con Dios o jugar la carta de la víctima con Él. Pero, desafortunadamente, ¡eso no funciona! Él nos dio la llave del éxito, la llave de la grandeza y esa llave es ÉL.

En ÉL está el poder de superar mucho de lo que intentamos y fallamos por nuestra cuenta. Yo puedo decirte todo lo que he hecho, pero lo único que no puedo hacer es moler por ti. Leemos las claves, escuchamos el mensaje, y pensamos que solo por leerlo o escucharlo, de repente, se manifestará en algo extraordinario en nuestra vida. Es entonces cuando empezamos a fracasar, este estado mental se apodera frecuentemente de nosotros, y si no nos defendemos, seremos derrotados incluso antes de empezar.

Me encanta ver programas sobre la naturaleza, principalmente cuando los depredadores cazan a sus presas. Me encanta analizar su pensamiento, sus movimientos, tanto del depredador como del objetivo. Por ejemplo, mira la gacela y el león por un momento. ¿Cuál es la diferencia entre la gacela y el león, aparte de la obvia? La gacela siempre corre con miedo; sabe que sus días están contados mientras el león esté cerca. Corren con miedo, sabiendo que en el momento en que se descuidan, mueren.

Su miedo es su impulso, y muchas personas a menudo no son impulsadas por Dios, ni por sus metas y visiones; su miedo las impulsa. El miedo siempre te empujará a tu muerte. A menudo has escuchado la expresión: "¿Cuál es tu por qué? "El león no pregunta por qué; hace lo que mejor sabe hacer; ¡caza! El problema con esa pregunta es que a menudo se encuentra sin ninguna sustancia. Tu "Porqué" no es esencial si tu "Porqué" no lo incluye a ÉL. Dios tiene que ser el centro de todo lo que hacemos y de lo que somos.

Cada oportunidad tiene que ser tomada como si fuera la última oportunidad que tendrás. Pero, en realidad, podría ser porque no sabemos cuándo la Muerte vendrá a llamar a nuestra puerta y nos llamará a casa. Así que la verdadera pregunta debería ser: ¿qué te motiva? ¿Qué te entusiasma? ¿Qué te hace querer levantarte cada mañana? Cada día debes volver a reprenderte, seguir aprendiendo, seguir creciendo, porque el día en que te conformes es el día en que ya no vivirás; existirás pero no vivirás.

El día que dejas de crecer, el día que dejas de aprender, el día que dejas de reprenderte es el día en que mueres por dentro, y se convierte en el día en que la persona que intentaba pasarte lo hace.

Estoy aquí para decirte que no puedes llorar porque te has rendido, llora porque vas a seguir adelante, ¡No llores para abandonar! Ya te duele, ya estás magullado, has llegado hasta aquí, ¿y ahora quieres parar? Ya estás herido, más vale que obtengas una recompensa por ello.

Una mujer que está a punto de dar a luz no abandona simplemente porque las contracciones están demasiado cerca unas de otras, o porque el dolor es insoportable? NO! ella sigue adelante porque está a punto de dar a luz a alguien increíble. Tú también deberías hacerlo, no hay espacio para renunciar, no hay espacio para detenerse, no hay espacio para bajar el ritmo cuando las contracciones de la vida te golpean una tras otra, no te rindes- empujas hacia adelante y hacia delante.

¡LA LUCHA ES REAL!

Sí, lo es, y dicen que hay que bajar balanceándose, pero yo te digo más que nada que no vas a bajar, vas a ganar. Pero tienes que hacer que esa actitud forme parte de tu vida diaria. Haz las cosas que otros no hacen; haz las cosas que te revuelven el estómago porque esas cosas a menudo producen las recompensas más significativas. En la terminología del gimnasio, haz la repetición extra, corre los 5 minutos adicionales, prueba un ejercicio que no te gusta porque lo que te saca de tu zona de confort te llevará más alto y más cerca de tus objetivos.

Esas cosas que nos asustan, las que nos intimidan y las que parecen imposibles son las que debes y tienes que hacer porque lo que hay detrás de esos espejismos de imposibilidad son recompensas que superan con creces nuestras expectativas.

Estaba a mediados de mis 20 años, miraba a mi primogénito, apenas un bebé durmiendo, y entonces me miré en el espejo y me di cuenta de que tenía que hacer cambios en mi vida; de lo contrario, existía la posibilidad de que mi hijo nunca viera vivir una larga vida. Tenía 25 años y estaba en la peor forma de mi vida, físicamente hablando. Tenía sobrepeso y me sentía como una morsa, sin ofender a la morsa. En ese momento, decidí que ya era suficiente, que iba a incidir en mi salud para cambiar la trayectoria de mi vida, y que lo iba a hacer por mi hijo.

Muchas personas se equivocan porque quieren complacer a todo el mundo y hacer felices a los demás mientras viven miserablemente. Pero, lamentablemente, ¡tienes que hacerlo por ti y por tu primero! Salmo 139:14 Te daré gracias porque he sido hecho de manera tan asombrosa y milagrosa. Tus obras son milagrosas, y mi alma es plenamente consciente de ello.

Efesios 5:29 Porque nadie ha odiado jamás su propio cuerpo, sino que lo nutre y lo cuida con ternura, como el Señor hace con la iglesia.

Es fundamental que te fijes un objetivo y un plan de felicidad y motivación. No es ser egoísta; no, al hacerlo, estás extendiendo la alegría que aportas a otra persona. Hipotéticamente hablando, me miré en el espejo y decidí que estaba bien con mi forma de ser y que debía aceptarme tal y como soy. Qué error habría sido eso.

Mi falta de acción habría supuesto un gran dolor para mí y para mi familia. Las complicaciones de salud habrían cancelado cualquier actividad futura que pudiera compartir con mi hijo; también habría provocado estrés a mi mujer, todo porque decidí no hacer nada.

EL PRECIO DE NO HACER NADA

El precio es alto y duele, pero hay que pagarlo. Así que ya ves, no importa el camino que decidas tomar, ¡pagarás el precio! Está garantizado que el precio que pagarás por no hacer nada siempre será más alto y costoso que el precio de hacer algo para cambiar tu vida. Así que toma las decisiones correctas, hazte más fuerte mental, física y espiritualmente.

Cuando no haces nada, tu debilidad hará todo lo posible para ser dominante en tu vida. Cuando no haces nada, el miedo crece; los problemas se vuelven más prominentes de lo que son; cuando no haces nada, el caos estalla; cuando no haces nada, el mal prevalece. Como ves, el coste de no hacer nada es excepcionalmente alto y doloroso. Te hace retroceder días, si no años. No hacer nada te envía por un camino lleno de depresión, tristeza, frustraciones y decepciones. Cuando no haces nada, matas la esencia misma de lo que Dios puso dentro de ti.

Proverbios 19:8 Adquirir sabiduría es amarse a sí mismo; la gente que aprecia el entendimiento prosperará. Adquirir significa acción, requiere que hagas algo en vez de nada. Adquirir algo significa invertir en el conocimiento de lo que vas a lograr, lo que significa actuar y no quedarse quieto.

Cada día es una lucha, lucha contra el miedo, lucha contra la debilidad, contra el tiempo, contra la decadencia, contra el deseo de no hacer nada;

cada día es una lucha que sólo tú tienes que librar para lograr lo que Dios ha puesto dentro de ti.

Cuando te enfrentes a un reto o a una situación que sabes que no puedes ganar, recuerda que tienes todas las de perder si no haces nada. El coste de no hacer nada no sólo lo sentirás tú, sino que lo sentirán todos los que te rodean, incluso los que te conocen de lejos.

Levántate, avanza, sal con un resplandor de gloria, luchando con todo lo que tienes, con cada gramo de energía, con cada latido de tu sudor y con cada gota de sangre hasta tu último aliento, y entonces, y sólo entonces, habrás conquistado el primer paso que es superar el no hacer nada.

EXCUSAS-CUANDO LAS TIENES, NUNCA PIERDES

Es un arma poderosa que utiliza el enemigo. Las excusas parecen perfectamente legítimas en su razonamiento; parecen justificadas y justas, pero son un veneno que entra en tu mente y en tu corazón y lentamente y de hecho comienza a carcomer tu visión, tus objetivos y tu deseo de tener éxito. Cuando permites que se unan a tu vocabulario, dominan tu mentalidad. En esta etapa, en ese momento, tus sueños y visiones, metas y ambiciones comienzan a salirse de control en una espiral de muerte que muy pocos han podido superar y dar vuelta.

Las excusas son la licencia que te das a ti mismo para no hacer nada y acabar fracasando. Las excusas te dan la libertad de culpar a todo y a todos por tu incapacidad o falta de ella para no hacer nada. Te permiten la escapatoria de no decir lo que sientes o lo que quieres hacer o no hacer. Son tan convincentes que se convierten en "ley" para ti una vez que las aceptas y vives según ellas. Son límites que pones a tu mente, limitaciones a tus metas y visiones, límites a tu corazón que le impiden crecer en la Fe.

No puedes crecer cuando las excusas te rodean. No puedes sobresalir cuando las excusas viven en tu mente y en tu corazón. No puedes alcanzar la grandeza cuando las excusas se han convertido en una forma de expresión y un estilo de vida.

La vida no es fácil, nadie dijo que lo sería, el mismo Jesús dijo en Juan 16:33 Estas cosas os he hablado para que en mí tengáis Paz. En el mundo tendréis tribulación; pero tened buen ánimo; yo he vencido al mundo. Me hubiera gustado que dijera problemas, cuestiones o dilemas, ¡pero señaló tribulaciones!

Una cosa es tener problemas, pero tener tribulaciones está en otro nivel. La presión y el estrés que las pruebas pueden traer a alguien pueden ser aplastantes, y en ese momento, las excusas son la manera perfecta de escapar del miedo y el dolor que uno puede experimentar. Las personas razonables no pueden manejarse al nivel que lo hace alguien grande. El problema es que queremos ser el CEO pero no tener los problemas o el estrés del CEO. Queremos la grandeza pero no el proceso de dolor para lograrla. Queremos tener éxito, pero lo queremos en bandeja de plata, pero la realidad es que nada grande sale de las excusas. Nada que valga la pena sale de las excusas, ¡nada!

Decimos que lo queremos, soñamos y pensamos en ello, pero luego nos damos cuenta de que en el momento en que decides ir a por ello es cuando tus excusas cobran vida, y las aplastas, o te aplastan a ti.

La vida no es justa, pero las excusas no son aceptables en el gran escenario para alcanzar la grandeza. No hay lugar para que las excusas tengan un asiento en la mesa de tus sueños. Si les permites una silla, entonces les permites una voz, le das voz a tus excusas, entonces te has dado una razón "legítima" para fracasar. Nadie te culpará por ello porque tus razonamientos o excusas parecen justificables y deben ser aceptados por todos.

Sin embargo, la siguiente parte de ese versículo es emocionante; dice: "Tened buen ánimo" espera un momento, tened buen ánimo? en medio de las tribulaciones, tened buen ánimo? ¿Cómo puede tener eso algún sentido? Normalmente, las tribulaciones no son momentos de gran alegría o para estar de buen humor. Cuando pienso en las tribulaciones, a menudo pienso en el dolor y la tristeza, sin embargo, en este versículo, Jesús dice que hay que tener buen ánimo. Además, continúa diciendo: "Porque yo he vencido al mundo".

Lee eso cuidadosamente; Jesús ha vencido al mundo; nunca dijo tú. Debemos entender lo siguiente: la victoria no comienza con usted; el éxito comienza con Jesús y sólo con Jesús. Si estamos en ÉL y ÉL está en nosotros, entonces esa victoria que Jesús ha reclamado es también una victoria que podemos reclamar y regocijarnos. Él venció al mundo y todas sus tribulaciones, pruebas y temores. Ya que estamos en ÉL y ÉL está en nosotros, ese reclamo de victoria también se le da a los que están en él.

Cuanto más tiempo esperes para poner tus excusas a descansar, más tiempo tus sueños se harán realidad. Cada minuto, cada hora y día que esperas es un minuto, una hora y un día que prolonga los sueños y las metas para que se conviertan en una realidad viva en tu presente. No puedes retrasar el descanso de esos miedos; no puedes retrasar el descanso de esas excusas; debes levantarte con el deseo de superar esos miedos y excusas, el deseo de ser una mejor versión de ti mismo cada día.

La oportunidad está ante nosotros cada día, y requiere que des el 120% de ti, sin embargo, sólo estás aportando un 70% de esfuerzo y un 50% de esfuerzo, y queremos lo que tienen los que están pagando con sudor, lágrimas y sangre, y eso no va a suceder, ¡no es gratis!

Se necesita tanto la emoción como la lógica para alcanzar tu máximo potencial, no puedes llegar a la cima sólo con una de las dos, necesitas las dos.

EL PODER DE LA EMOCIÓN

La emoción puede impulsarte a la grandeza y llevarte a niveles tan bajos que no puedes ni empezar a imaginar. Debes darlo todo para ir más allá de tus límites, porque tanto la emoción como la lógica llegarán a sus límites, y cuando una lo haga, deberás apoyarte en la otra. Cuando no tenga ningún sentido lógico seguir adelante, deberás utilizar la emoción para dar el siguiente paso.

Lo mejor sería que aprendieras a utilizar tu rabia y tus miedos para que te empujen a decir: ¡NO ME PARO! Es fácil renunciar, fácil rendirse y esconderse detrás de una excusa; todo eso es fácil, pero lo fácil nunca te llevará a donde Dios quiere que termines. Muchos creen que Dios los llevará a su destino, y aquí es donde cometen un error al asumirlo. Dios tiene un plan de grandeza para tu vida; lo dijo claramente en Jeremías 29:11 "Porque yo sé los pensamientos que tengo para ti, dice el Señor, pensamientos de paz y no de mal, para darte un futuro y una esperanza."

Pablo también afirma en 2ª Timoteo 4:7, "He peleado la buena batalla, he terminado la carrera, he guardado la fe."

Jeremías explica claramente que los planes de Dios para ti son GRANDES. Son enormes, llenos de oportunidades y llenos de Paz, esperanza y futuro. Sin embargo, Pablo dice: "¡He peleado la buena batalla!" No dijo que alguien la peleara por él o que fuera fácil, lo dijo, ¡he peleado la buena batalla!

Los planes de Dios son grandes, lo que se traduce en que la lucha será grande, promete un futuro y esperanza, pero Pablo dice que hay una carrera que correr y terminar, y por último, dice, ¡he guardado la Fe! Ambas cosas van juntas. Repito, y has escuchado que nadie dijo que iba a ser fácil o un paseo en el parque, y si lo hicieron, o te mintieron o no saben de lo que están hablando.

Cuando tus emociones están gritando que han tenido suficiente, y crees que vas a romperte emocionalmente, anula esa emoción con tres ingredientes clave, ¡Lógica, Oración y Acción!

Lógica para darte cuenta de que volver atrás no es una opción, Oración para estimular tu Fe, sabiendo que con Dios todo es posible, y Acción, porque no es una verdadera oración si no impulsa tu Fe a la Acción. La Biblia dice en Hebreos 11:6: "Y sin fe es imposible agradar a Dios, porque todo el que se acerca a él debe creer que existe y que recompensa a los que lo buscan fervientemente".

Debes combatir las emociones que paralizan tus acciones, con sentimientos que den sentido a tu lucha. Lo mejor sería que encontraras la fuerza y la tenacidad para mirarte al espejo, y con todo lo que tienes decirte: ¡NO PUEDO PARAR!

Tu no perteneces al fondo, y es hora de que te des cuenta de esto y te levantes, luches la pelea, y comiences a caminar hacia donde Dios quiere que estés. Deut 28: 13 dice, Y el Señor te hará la CABEZA, y no la cola, y estarás por encima solamente, y no estarás por debajo, si oyes los mandamientos del Señor tu Dios que yo te mando hoy, para que los observes y los cumplas.

Estas son palabras poderosas que deben ser pronunciadas en tu vida diaria cada vez que esas emociones comienzan a susurrar en tu corazón, mente y espíritu para que te rindas. Es hora de que te sientas incómodo por estar en el fondo, y te preguntarás, ¿es eso posible? Pero, por desgracia, esto es una realidad para muchos en estos días. Las emociones de miedo y duda te mantienen en el fondo, alimentando la simpatía y la empatía de los demás hacia ti. Aunque todo esto es "bueno", se convierte en un autovirus que te impide levantarte y convertirte en todo lo que debes ser en la vida.

Aunque se sienta bien tener la simpatía y la empatía de los demás, no te da la fuerza para levantarte, y muchos lo utilizan para quedarse ahí porque no hay presión estando en el fondo. No hay presión para que tengas éxito cuando los demás te dan su simpatía; no hay razón para crecer cuando los demás trabajan para que te sientas mejor o te den la ilusión de mejorar. No hay presión para que te superes porque tus emociones te han paralizado y te alimentas de la simpatía de los demás. Finalmente, la muerte llega mental, espiritual y físicamente.

La Biblia dice que el hijo pródigo estaba en un pozo de cerdos (Lucas 15) comiendo su comida, y cuando volvió en sí, decidió regresar a la casa de su padre. Analiza esto por un momento; pasó de la riqueza a comer la comida de los cerdos; piensa en la carga emocional que esto debe haber tenido en la vida de este hombre. Luego, piensa en los pasos que debió dar para llegar a esa etapa de su vida. No se pasa de la riqueza a comer comida para cerdos de la noche a la mañana.

Sus emociones deben haber decaído tanto para llevarlo a ese estado de ánimo y acciones. Perdió toda la esperanza, la motivación y la Fe; en lugar de regresar inmediatamente a la casa de su padre, el orgullo se impuso y tomó el control de sus emociones, lo que le llevó al pozo del cerdo. El orgullo es un asesino del destino; el orgullo es un asesino de sueños; nada bueno viene del orgullo. Por eso la Biblia dice en Santiago 4:6, Pero Él da más gracia. Por eso dice: "Dios resiste a los soberbios, Pero da gracia a los humildes".

¡Dios resiste a los orgullosos! La emoción del orgullo contradice todo lo que Dios quiere hacer en tu vida. El orgullo del hijo pródigo era tan alto que prefería comer comida de cerdos que volver a la casa de su padre. Su orgullo era tan alto que decidió que la comida de los cerdos era mejor que volver a la casa de su padre a pesar de perder su dinero y su fortuna. No sólo perdió su riqueza, sino que también perdió a todos sus supuestos "amigos", ¿a dónde fueron a parar?

Eventualmente, cuando toda la simpatía está hecha, y no hay más empatía que recibir, esas mismas personas que una vez te dieron esas cosas te darán la espalda y dirán, basta con esta persona. Así que esta área es crítica y muy peligrosa porque una vez que se pierde todo el apoyo, muchos se encuentran en un espacio muy oscuro y tristemente, muchos están tirados a dos metros bajo tierra porque eligieron no levantarse nunca.

¿Es posible levantarse aunque se esté solo sin nada y comiendo cerdos? ¡La respuesta es un SÍ muy rotundo!

Una vez más, la Biblia dice: ¡Puedo hacer todas las cosas por medio de Cristo que me fortalece! Fil 4:13

La Biblia también dice en Lucas 15:17, "Pero cuando volvió en sí, dijo: ¡Cuántos jornaleros de mi padre tienen pan de sobra y yo perezco de hambre!

EL PODER DE LA LÓGICA

La Biblia dice que "Cuando vino a sí mismo, dijo: ¡Cuántos jornaleros de mi padre tienen pan de sobra, y yo perezco de hambre!

A cada persona le llega un momento en el que, por la misericordia y la gracia de Dios, se le enciende una "bombilla" en la mente que hace que nuestro espíritu se despierte. Pero, primero, tuvo que reconocer dónde estaba, tuvo que reconocer su entorno, su condición, y darse cuenta de lo que había dejado atrás.

Darse cuenta de dónde estamos es una tarea dolorosa; aceptar que te has equivocado es el lugar donde estás por culpa de esos errores. Aceptar que esto depende de ti y de nadie más es fundamental. Llevar tu cruz es tan importante como respirar. Nunca resurgirás de las cenizas culpando de tu condición a otra persona.

El hijo pródigo volvió en sí mismo, pero se da cuenta de que no culpó a nadie de dónde estaba. Asumió la responsabilidad de sus actos y no culpó a otros de su condición. Es elemental decir que es por culpa de esto o aquello, o de esta persona, que la vida no es justa, o lo que quieras sacar a relucir, pero al final del día, tú debes ser el responsable de dónde estás en la vida y nadie más.

Las emociones acaban por detenerse y la lógica entra en acción. Ahora bien, puede entrar en juego el culpar a los demás y quedarse donde está, empeorando en última instancia las cosas, o entra en juego y decide cambiar su situación. La Biblia dice en 1 Pedro 2:9, Pero ustedes son una generación elegida, un sacerdocio real, una nación santa, su propio pueblo especial, para que proclamen las alabanzas de aquel que los llamó de las tinieblas a su luz maravillosa;

No puedes abandonar ahora; este es el décimo asalto, te quedan dos más, y cuando llegas a cierto nivel de éxito y grandeza, tiene poco que ver con la habilidad y todo con la resistencia.

La Biblia dice en Mateo 24:13 "Pero el que resista hasta el fin, ése se salvará". Aguantar significa que debes tener resistencia, no habilidad. Puedes tener todo el poder y los músculos, pero si tu oponente puede superar un asalto más, entonces tú pierdes, ¡y él gana!

Tu enemigo no tiene que ser el más fuerte o el más rápido; tiene que durar más en la carrera que tú. La Biblia dice en 1 Corintios 9:24-27, "¿No sabéis que en una carrera todos los corredores corren, pero sólo uno recibe el premio? Así que corran para obtenerlo. Todo atleta ejerce el autocontrol en todas las cosas. Ellos lo hacen para recibir una corona perecedera, pero nosotros una imperecedera. Así que no corro sin rumbo; no boxeo como quien golpea el aire. Sino que disciplino mi cuerpo y lo mantengo bajo control, no sea que después de predicar a los demás, quede descalificado.

Este es un verso muy poderoso; permítanme desglosarlo para ustedes. Primero, comienza reconociendo que esta es una carrera y que no estás solo tratando de obtener el premio. Es una red de partes intrincadas, todas moviéndose simultáneamente porque aunque todos estamos corriendo esta carrera y sólo uno recibirá el "premio", es simbólico porque todos tenemos diferentes metas, visiones y planes. Aunque tal vez algunos corran tras el mismo premio que los suyos.

Todo atleta ejerce el autocontrol en todas las cosas; ve a cada persona como un atleta, una excelente visualización. El autocontrol es tan necesario porque te separa del resto. La disciplina es esencial porque para llegar al final, alcanzar la meta y recibir el premio; se te exigirá hacer cosas que pueden resultar incómodas. Para alcanzar el futuro tendrás que pagar el precio, habrá que hacer sacrificios y ejercitar la lógica. La preparación es necesaria para tener éxito; estamos condenados a fracasar sin ella.

Ellos lo hacen para recibir una corona perecedera, pero nosotros una imperecedera. Por lo tanto, no hay que correr sin rumbo. Aquí es donde debemos darnos cuenta de que nuestro objetivo eterno es mucho más importante que nuestro objetivo físico. Nos centramos tanto en la lógica natural y en las metas realistas que olvidamos que estamos en este mundo, pero no somos de este mundo. Nuestros ojos deben estar puestos en las metas reales, pero nunca podemos perder la perspectiva de nuestra meta eterna.

Por lo tanto, no corremos sin rumbo; en otras palabras, nuestra carrera debe correr con propósito y perspectiva. La resistencia te da el aguante para seguir adelante sin descanso, con el deseo de llegar al final y alcanzarlo con victoria. No hay victoria en el abandono; no hay alegría en la renuncia; no hay satisfacción en vivir una vida sin propósito-¡no corremos sin rumbo!

No boxeo como quien golpea el aire. Pero disciplino mi cuerpo y lo mantengo bajo control. Aquí nos dice que nuestras acciones deben ser enfocadas y con propósito. Cada paso que damos debe ser disciplinado y mantener nuestras emociones bajo control. No lo hago, dice; es una declaración audaz que debes hacer cada día. No renuncio; no me rindo, no pongo excusas, no cedo a mis emociones negativas, no culpo a los demás por mis errores, no me vuelvo perezoso, no retrocedo-estas son las palabras con las que debes vivir cada día.

Disciplino mi cuerpo y lo mantengo bajo control, lo que significa que la grandeza requiere disciplina y autocontrol. Es demasiado fácil ceder a todas esas cosas negativas que hay por ahí, demasiado fácil esconderse detrás de un muro de excusas, pero ningún gran atleta pone nunca excusas para no continuar.

Si me conocen lo suficiente, verán que amo el hockey; no nací en Canadá, pero al venir aquí a la temprana edad de 5 años, Canadá es mi hogar. Soy un verdadero canadiense con amor por el hockey y el chocolate caliente.

En 2017, los Pittsburgh Penguins ganaron su segunda Copa Stanley consecutiva. Un gran logro. El hockey es un deporte rápido, intenso y divertido de ver. Recuerdo haber visto el partido, y mientras el reloj se acercaba al último segundo, la emoción en el banquillo de los Penguins era eléctrica. Sonó el timbre y los jugadores saltaron al hielo para felicitarse mutuamente. Los abrazos eran profundos, la sonrisa en sus rostros era contagiosa y el público ardía.

Pero nadie sabía que uno de sus jugadores jugó y ganó en circunstancias que nadie conocía. Empezaremos por el defensa de los Penguins Ian Cole. El jugador de 28 años jugó poco más de 18 minutos por partido para su equipo, y lo hizo con una mano rota y costillas rotas desde principios de la serie de los Capitals (segunda ronda). Sí, has leído bien, ¡una mano y unas costillas rotas! ¿Cómo puede jugar alguien en esas circunstancias?

Si me golpeo el dedo del pie con el borde de la cama, estoy acabado; ¡estoy fuera! Y mucho menos jugar un partido de alta intensidad con una mano o una costilla rota. Jugó a pesar de su dolor; jugó a pesar de su agonía, jugó a pesar de la adversidad-siguió jugando. Habría sido fácil y justificable para él dejar de jugar, y nadie le habría culpado por dejar de hacerlo. Sin embargo, lo que le impulsó a seguir adelante fue el deseo de ganar.

Cuando tu deseo de ganar supera el dolor, ganas; cuando tu pasión por sobresalir supera la lucha, ganas siempre. No puedo empezar a imaginar el dolor que supuso jugar en esas condiciones, pero lo único que podemos decir es que ¡ganó! Por lo tanto, tu historia debe hablar de cómo experimentaste la victoria a través de tu dolor, a través de tu lucha y tu desorden.

A la gente le encanta contar su historia, pero la mayoría de las veces sólo dirá al nivel de su dolor, sus miedos, sus luchas y su desorden, y raramente sobre sus logros. Nadie sabía que jugaba en esas condiciones hasta que estas cosas salieron a la luz después de la serie. Así que no muestres tu dolor, no transmitas tu lucha, no muestres tu debilidad, porque eso nunca te hará ningún bien.

Sus compañeros de equipo lo sabían, sus entrenadores lo sabían, su familia lo sabía, pero nadie más lo sabía. Lo mismo debe ocurrir en tu vida; sólo ciertas personas deben conocer tus debilidades, tus miedos, tus luchas y tu dolor, y de entre esas personas concretas, sólo habrá algunas que estén a tu lado para ayudarte a levantarte. Este hombre debe haber tenido a los mejores médicos aconsejándole lo que debe hacer para seguir adelante, no sugiriéndole cómo dejarlo.

Hay suficiente gente en el mundo que se desvivirá por intentar que no consigas nada en la vida. Habrá suficiente gente alrededor para darte una fiesta de lástima, pero sólo aquellos que están conectados a ti entenderán tu lucha y te ayudarán en esa lucha para ganar.

Mira esta historia, Jesús resucita a la chica muerta; la Biblia dice en Marcos 5:37-40, "No dejó que nadie le siguiera sino Pedro, Santiago y Juan el hermano de Santiago. Cuando llegaron a la casa del jefe de la sinagoga, Jesús vio una conmoción, con gente llorando y lamentándose fuertemente. Entró y les dijo: "¿Por qué tanto alboroto y tanto lamento? El niño no está muerto, sino dormido". Pero se rieron de él.

Después de echarlos a todos, tomó al padre y a la madre del niño y a los discípulos que estaban con él y entró donde estaba el niño.

Jesús tenía un círculo interno, pero también tenía un círculo interno, mostrado aquí en este versículo. No dejó que nadie le siguiera, excepto Pedro, Santiago y Juan, el hermano de Santiago. Debes ser capaz de reducir tu círculo íntimo a las personas cercanas a ti, que ya sea en las buenas o en las malas, te cubrirán las espaldas. De los 12 discípulos, sólo a Pedro, Santiago y Juan se les permitió seguir a Jesús donde estaba el milagro. ¿Qué pasó con el resto? ¿A dónde fueron? La Biblia no indica su paradero, sino que sólo menciona a los que siguieron a Jesús más allá.

Tener mucha gente alrededor no siempre es algo bueno; en este caso, mucha gente estaba ocupando espacio y no hacía valer el área. Jesús se había presentado, y a nadie parecía importarle que tuviera fama de hacer lo milagroso; la Biblia dice que se reían de él. Cuántos supuestos amigos escuchan tus sueños, tu visión y tus objetivos, y en lugar de ayudarte a conseguirlos, se ríen.

A Jesús le molestó que hubiera tanta conmoción y lamentos; estaba molesto por su falta de fe y creencia. Pero entonces, esas mismas personas que creaban el alboroto y los lamentos comenzaron a reírse de Jesús de repente.

Protege tu círculo, tus sueños, tus visiones y tus metas, protege lo que Dios ha puesto dentro de ti, Protege tus planes, pues no deben ser compartidos con todo el mundo porque no todos querrán estar ahí para verte triunfar.

Protege tus palabras, porque tienen poder y peso, porque es a través de ellas que las cosas se crean o se rompen. Tendrás que luchar y luchar y luchar, y muchos pierden la lucha no porque no sean lo suficientemente fuertes, sino que simplemente muchos no pueden vencer a la vieja versión de ti. Te vence la versión negativa de ti, la versión de ti que no está dispuesta a surgir de las cenizas, que habla naturalmente y no por Fe.

Pierdes ante el viejo tú que no tenía esperanza ni sueños porque no luchas lo suficiente para ver surgir al NUEVO TÚ. Pero, puedo decirte esto, hay una luz al final del túnel, puede ser una pequeña, pero si te comprometes a tomar una buena decisión tras otra, pagará dividendos en formas que sólo has soñado.

Las cosas mejorarán, tal vez no de la noche a la mañana, tal vez no al estilo microondas; no será instantáneo tanto como quisiéramos; ¡toma tiempo! Pero, el proceso construye carácter, te da una piel gruesa; tener carácter es todo en la vida; tener la palabra de Dios en tu vida es lo más significativo que puedes tener para obtener lo mejor que Dios tiene para ti.

EL PODER DE TUS PALABRAS

¡Tu actitud va a determinar tu altitud! Tus palabras crean el mundo en el que vives. La cosa más desafiante que he tenido que aprender a lo largo de mis años fue creer en el poder de mis palabras.

No importa las circunstancias o situaciones que tengas delante, tus palabras importan aquí en la tierra y en el cielo. El mundo te habilitará y tratará de definirte a través de sus palabras, y ahí es donde aceptas sus términos hablados sobre ti, o empiezas a hablar en tu propia vida y creas un nuevo tú.

Confiamos mucho en las palabras de los demás; si son palabras alentadoras, nos levantan, y cuando son palabras negativas, nos hunden. Nuestras palabras son piedras. No somos más que lanzadores de piedras con cada palabra que pronunciamos. Pero, por otro lado, si nuestras palabras contienen belleza, la gente las atesora. Si nuestras palabras incluyen dolor, la gente las tira a un lado, pero no hasta después de haber lidiado con la herida que causaron.

Proverbios 15:4 "Las palabras suaves dan vida y salud; la lengua engañosa aplasta el espíritu". Las palabras que hablas o permites que se digan sobre ti es el mundo en el que caminas. Usted encontrará que dos personas estarán en dos atmósferas diferentes mientras están en el mismo cuarto, simplemente porque permitieron que las palabras cambiaran su perspectiva o estado de ánimo. Las palabras amables traen vida y salud, por lo que tus palabras pueden levantar a alguien, darle esperanza y traer salud a sus cuerpos, mente y alma.

Sin embargo, por otro lado, dice, una lengua engañosa Aplasta el espíritu; no los baja, los aplasta. Ese es el poder que tienen nuestras palabras.

Proverbios 16:24 "Las palabras amables son como la miel: dulces para el alma y saludables para el cuerpo". Sí, es posible cambiar tu futuro y tu presente a través de tus palabras. Las palabras que dices sobre ti mismo son más importantes que las otras palabras que cualquiera pueda decir sobre ti, aunque sean buenas palabras. Vienen en segundo lugar a los términos que debes hablar sobre tu vida.

¿Cuántas veces la gente habla de sí misma para evitar la grandeza o el éxito? ¿Cuántas veces hablamos con nosotros mismos fuera de lo que Dios ha puesto para nosotros, simplemente porque no creemos y las palabras que hemos hablado en nuestras vidas han creado un pozo de desesperación y duda del que muchos nunca salen?

Lo mejor sería que lo hicieras; cada día, cambia tu vocabulario que te edificará y te construirá. No puedes esperar a que otros hablen en tu vida. Así que cuando te veas en el espejo cada mañana, aprovecha la oportunidad para hablar con tu nuevo yo, y no dejes que el viejo tú regrese, no dejes de hablar en tu vida de fe, esperanza y poder, no te detengas porque si te detienes permites que el viejo tú regrese vivo. Volverá con una venganza.

Debes ser el más increíble agente de ventas para ti mismo. Pregúntate cada día, ¿qué me voy a vender hoy a mí mismo? ¿Comprarías tomates podridos en el mercado? La respuesta sería, sin duda, ¡no! Pero, ¿con qué frecuencia te vendes a ti mismo y aceptas esas expresiones podridas que has dejado que se cuelen en tu mente y en tu corazón o que has oído que alguien las diga sobre ti?

¿Cuántas veces te has servido un plato de palabras podridas que no te acercan a tus sueños sino que te devuelven a las cenizas de donde estás intentando salir?

Porque no importa qué tan malo sea o qué tan mal se ponga, tus palabras tienen el poder de cambiar y afectar la tormenta. Marcos 4:39 Y despertando, reprendió al viento y dijo al mar: "¡Paz! Cállate!" Y el viento cesó, y se produjo una gran calma.

2ª Corintios 12:9 Pero me dijo: "Te basta mi gracia, porque mi poder se perfecciona en la debilidad". Por lo tanto, me gloriaré aún más de mis debilidades, para que el poder de Cristo descanse sobre mí.

Alimenta tu mente con la palabra de Dios, Alimenta tu espíritu con la palabra de Dios, Alimenta tu alma con la palabra de Dios, Romanos 10:17 Porque la fe viene por el oír y el oír por la palabra de Dios. Cuanto más te alimentes de la palabra de Dios, más verás que tus palabras cambian.

Cuando cambias tus palabras, cambias la trayectoria de lo que el enemigo querría a lo que Dios siempre ha querido que sea. Así que alimenta tu Fe, mira como tus dudas y miedos mueren de hambre, alimenta tu Fe escarbando en las escrituras, y alimenta tu Fe hasta que empieces a ver un cambio en tus palabras.

Lo que alimenta su mente es lo que su boca hablará. Si sólo ves las noticias, las noticias serán lo único de lo que hables, y de repente, permites que las palabras que escuchas en las noticias empiecen a influir en tus comentarios.

Una vez escuché a mi padre decir que si hoy fuera el último día de tu vida, ¿sería lo último que te dirías de ti mismo? Me hizo detenerme y mirarme en el espejo cada día y obligarme a cambiar mi vocabulario y lo que digo de mí.

Normalmente no pensamos en ello; creemos que las palabras son sólo palabras, pero en realidad tienen un poder increíble. Por ejemplo, Dios mismo habló de la existencia de todo; con una sola palabra, hubo luz; las cosas pasaron de la nada al todo con una sola palabra.

Proverbios 18:4 "Las palabras de una persona pueden ser agua que da vida; las palabras de verdadera sabiduría son refrescantes como un arroyo burbujeante".

El primer paso para cambiar tu presente e impactar tu futuro es creer que tus palabras importan. No hay plan B porque el plan B te distrae del plan A. El plan A es cambiar tus comentarios y creer que lo que hablas sí hace la diferencia en los que lo escuchan y, sobre todo para ti, tu sueño, tus metas y tu futuro.

Las palabras de una persona pueden ser agua que da vida; así de poderosas pueden ser nuestras palabras, ¡pueden ser agua que cambia la vida! No puedes dar por sentado tus palabras; no puedes tomar tus palabras como si no tuvieran ningún significado; nuestras palabras importan. Pueden producir vida o quitarla en una sola frase.

Proverbios 18:21 "La muerte y la vida están en poder de la lengua, y los que la aman comerán sus frutos."

Tu lengua tiene un poder que no podemos empezar a comprender. Así que tuve que investigar un poco sobre la lengua y descubrí que, Tu lengua es un grupo de músculos que trabajan sin el apoyo de tu esqueleto. (¡Ningún otro músculo del cuerpo humano puede hacer esto!) Eso hace que sean increíblemente flexibles, lo que te permite formar sonidos, silbar, mover la comida por la boca, tragar, e incluso puedes usarla para limpiarte los dientes después de comer.

No sólo puedes sacar la lengua, retraerla a la parte posterior de la boca y moverla de lado a lado, sino que también puedes cambiar completamente su forma. Cada vez que enrollas la lengua, la metes hacia atrás, la enroscas o la formas en punta, estás cambiando su forma.

La huella lingual de cada persona es tan única como sus huellas dactilares. Imagina un futuro en el que utilicemos huellas dactilares, escáneres de retina (ojos) y escáneres de lengua para confirmar nuestra identidad. Imagíneselo.

Una lengua hinchada se llama macroglosia y puede indicar otros problemas de salud subyacentes. Por ejemplo, si tiene hendiduras en el lado de la lengua a causa de los dientes, es probable que su lengua esté hinchada. La causa puede ser el hipotiroidismo, una infección, alergias, enfermedades inflamatorias y muchas otras afecciones.

¿Cuántas veces tenemos el vocabulario hinchado o las palabras hinchadas que provocan dolores en nuestra vida cotidiana? Las palabras hinchadas causan dolor a la persona que las dice, pero también causan dolor a los que las escuchan. Las palabras hinchadas pueden dañar las relaciones, destruir las amistades y provocar heridas duraderas que a menudo tardan muchos años en curarse y superarse.

Las palabras hinchadas sólo pueden ser sanadas a través de la oración y la lectura de la palabra; la Biblia dice en Efesios 4:29 Ninguna palabra corrompida salga de vuestra boca, sino la que sea buena para la necesaria edificación, a fin de dar gracia a los oyentes.

Las palabras son tan poderosas que no sólo pueden crear o destruir tu mundo, sino que también tienen un efecto en aquellos que las escuchan. Porque no podemos empezar a imaginar el daño que una frase puede tener en el reino espiritual, y si lo hiciéramos, cambiaríamos y nos abstendríamos de las palabras que decimos.

Colosenses 3:8 "Pero ahora, vosotros mismos debéis despojaros de todo esto: de la ira, del enojo, de la malicia, de la blasfemia, de las palabras obscenas de vuestra boca."

Siempre pensé que la ira, el enojo y la malicia eran acciones, pero según Colosenses, se formaron a partir de las palabras que pronunciamos para existir. Nosotros creamos el ambiente en el que vivimos, creamos la atmósfera en la que caminamos y creamos un mundo que impacta a cada persona que encontramos.

No dejes que el ruido de las palabras de otras personas ahogue la voz de Dios en tu vida. Habrá muchas voces a tu alrededor, todas hablándote simultáneamente, pero debes recordar que cuando te sumerges en la palabra, estás invirtiendo en tus palabras.

Cuando inviertes tiempo en la palabra de Dios, estás haciendo una importante inversión en tu presente y futuro. Una inversión que enriquecerá tu vocabulario y estimulará tu Fe para un crecimiento personal más significativo. Porque es a través de tu Fe que las palabras son habladas, y a través de esas palabras habladas las montañas son removidas, los gigantes caen, y los muros se derrumban.

Mi esposa es portuguesa, y lo habla muy bien. Sin embargo, tenemos tres grandes hijos, casados desde hace más de 15 años, y hasta el día de hoy, todavía no he aprendido el idioma-mis disculpas. Puedo oírla hablar y captar ciertas palabras o frases, pero no puedo hablarlas. ¿Cuántas veces escuchamos la voz de Dios hablándonos a través de su palabra, y por escucharla y no practicarla, no podemos hablarla cuando el enemigo viene a atacarnos?

Es hora de empezar a trabajar en tu sueño, no mañana, ¡hoy! Las limitaciones solo existen en nuestra mente, y solo existen para atarnos y no permitirnos crecer o avanzar. El miedo se extiende a nuestro vocabulario, silenciando nuestra voz de Fe, y nos apegamos al miedo, y lo hablamos, y una vez que lo hablamos, lo creemos, y una vez que lo pensamos, ese pensamiento se apodera de nuestra vida.

Proverbios 12:18 "Hay uno cuyas palabras imprudentes son como golpes de espada, pero la lengua del sabio trae sanación."

Encontrarás muchas decepciones, contratiempos y derrotas al cambiar tu vocabulario. Sin embargo, en el proceso de pasar por eso, descubrirás muchas cosas sobre ti mismo que ahora no conoces. Hay grandeza en ti, y tus palabras tienen poder. Cuando te des cuenta de la magnitud del poder de tus comentarios, entonces comenzarás rápidamente y sin dudar a cambiar esas palabras.

Te darás cuenta de que eres más importante que tus circunstancias y que las palabras que dices afectan directamente a esas circunstancias. En ese momento, empezarás a comprender que eres lo suficientemente poderoso como para decirle a esa montaña que se aparte del camino y se arroje al mar.

Te darás cuenta de que el cielo presta mucha atención a lo que hablas, no sólo cuando las cosas van bien, sino especialmente cuando las cosas van peor.

Toma una decisión hoy; decide hoy que vas a cambiar la trayectoria de tu vida cambiando tu forma de hablar. Selecciona que hoy cambiarás tu futuro cambiando las palabras que salen de tu boca. No tenemos que hablar sobre la oscuridad y el miedo en nuestro presente; no, podemos en medio de esos tiempos oscuros y en medio de ese miedo, podemos elegir levantarnos y hablar luz, hablar coraje, hablar la palabra de Dios y ver como el cielo y Dios responden a tus comentarios de Fe.

En el proceso de tomar esa decisión, serás confrontado con tu viejo yo, hablando de la vieja manera, y no puedes huir de tu viejo yo; debes comprometerte y ganar esa batalla. Contra todo pronóstico, debes creer que tus palabras importan y que volver a tu viejo yo no es una opción. Ya has pasado por ese camino; sabes lo que se siente y lo que parece; no hay nada ahí atrás para ti, sólo la derrota. Así que cuando no sepamos qué decir, hablemos entonces la palabra de Dios; cuando no sepamos cómo decirlo, digámoslo según la palabra de Dios. Porque el cielo y la tierra pasarán, pero su palabra permanecerá.

Debes ser constante porque sin constancia, nunca terminaremos esta carrera, si fuera fácil, entonces nuestros resultados serían todos grandes, pero como la grandeza no es fácil, sólo unos pocos la alcanzan. Pero cada día es una batalla para ser grande, no para ser comparado con alguien más, sino para desafiarte a ti mismo a ser la mejor versión de ti mismo posible.

Recuerda que tu competencia en la vida no es nadie más que tú. Tus palabras te dan la ventaja en esa batalla o pueden ser tu desventaja. O ganas la batalla con tus palabras o pierdes la lucha por tu elección de palabras. Todos tenemos una opción en esta batalla. Tus palabras son las armas que eliges, y sólo tú puedes seleccionarlas.

Las grandes palabras son como espadas que se afilan antes de cada pelea; tú afilas tu espada a través de la lectura de la palabra de Dios. Cuanto más profundizas en SU Palabra, más afiladas se vuelven tus palabras. Ahora, ya no estás hablando por tu imaginación, sino que no es Dios mismo quien respalda tus palabras porque no, estás citando su palabra, y él siempre responde a que repitas su palabra.

Colosenses 4:6 "Que tu discurso sea siempre amable, sazonado con sal, para que sepas cómo debes responder a cada persona."

Mateo 12:37 "Porque por tus palabras serás justificado, y por tus palabras serás condenado".

Tus palabras deben ir hacia adelante y no hacia atrás. Vendrán tiempos difíciles, pero debes permanecer firme en SU palabra; los tiempos difíciles vienen a desafiar nuestra determinación, a probar nuestras palabras, a probar nuestras emociones que contribuyen a nuestras palabras, pero debes permanecer firme en tu determinación de cambiar tu vocabulario.

Dios nos dio su palabra para vencer cuando no podemos mantenernos en nuestras fuerzas.

ELIGE TU FUTURO

Tu futuro es lo que tú haces que sea, no es lo que otros dicen que es, no es lo que otros quieren que sea, sino que lo que tú quieres que sea, será. No importa las cuestiones o los problemas que puedan surgir, tu futuro está en tus manos. Tienes el poder de cambiarlo, afectarlo y crearlo a través del poder de tus palabras.

Proverbio 3:5-6 dice: "Confía en el Señor con todo tu corazón y no te apoyes en tu propio entendimiento. Reconócelo en todos tus caminos, y él enderezará tus sendas".

No importa lo torcidos que parezcan nuestros caminos, en el momento en que reconozcas al Señor con tus palabras, él enderezará las sendas. No es un secreto que el Señor te está cuidando y velando por ti, aunque pueda parecer que está lejos, y a veces puede parecer que no está ahí-¡lo está!

Dice Confía en el Señor con todo tu corazón, no caminando porque lo entiendes, sino caminando porque lo crees. La confianza también se escucha y se siente a través de las palabras que dices. Tú eres el artista; tus palabras son el pincel que utilizas para crear tu obra maestra. Sin embargo, Él lo ve y lo sabe todo; por lo tanto, corregirá nuestros errores y los pondrá a nuestro favor. La confianza significa precisamente eso, confiar ciegamente, con valentía, sabiendo que él vela por nosotros.

Nuestra incapacidad para hablar de vida y hablar de bendición nos impide recibirlas; nuestra falta de búsqueda de la palabra limita nuestro vocabulario, nuestras declaraciones están atadas a nuestra incredulidad donde no hay vida alguna.

Cuanto más entra la palabra en ti, más te conviertes en la palabra, más te conviertes en la palabra, mejor te vuelves en la elección de tu futuro. Si las palabras se pronuncian pero no se creen, entonces no son más que ruido que se hace. Los comentarios que no se ponen en práctica se convierten en un ruido que no da frutos.

Porque si quieres un coche nuevo, no puedes limitarte a rezar por él, debes ir a solicitarlo, pero antes de solicitarlo, debes ir a ver el coche; antes de ver el vehículo, debes interesarte por un vehículo, y antes de interesarte por un vehículo, debes abrir la boca y decir: quiero un coche nuevo.

Todo comienza con lo que sale de nuestra boca. No puedes dejar de soñar; no puedes dejar de creer; es necesario que te alinees con gente que hable el mismo lenguaje que tú, el lenguaje de la Fe. Alinéate con gente que tenga el mismo hambre que tú, gente que no acepte un no por respuesta, gente que sea implacable en su búsqueda de la grandeza, gente que no sólo te empuje más allá sino que te impulse a tu siguiente nivel.

Si te alineas con personas que no crean su futuro en la bendición y la esperanza, entonces tu futuro estará perdido y en manos de otra persona. Por lo tanto, debes apoderarte de tu futuro, apoderarte de tus palabras, someterlas a la palabra de Dios y ver cómo el Señor honrará su palabra y hará realidad tus sueños.

Puedes fracasar pronto, incluso fracasar a menudo, pero fracasar hacia adelante; siempre me resulta un poco frustrante cuando la gente asocia una connotación negativa al fracaso. El fracaso puede servir para quedarse abajo o puede servir para ascender en la vida y conseguir los objetivos que te propongas.

Acomódate al fracaso porque si das un paso atrás y analizas la situación, verás las lecciones del fracaso. El fracaso es terrible si dejas que sea algo terrible, pero puede ser tu mejor maestro si dejas que te guíe. Te convertirá en un maestro, te dará los conocimientos para tu futuro y te permitirá ayudar a los demás, así que sí, el fracaso puede ser algo malo si lo dejas ser, o puede ser lo mejor que te haya pasado nunca.

Las personas de éxito fracasan más de lo que crees; caen tanto que sus historias tienen más fracasos que éxitos. ¿Y eso qué sentido tiene? Las personas de éxito saben que se levantarán de nuevo con una gran cantidad de conocimientos que les ayudarán en su camino si se caen. Mientras que otros tomarán el fracaso y se quedarán en el modo de fracaso y no aprenderán la lección para intentar de nuevo y lograr el éxito que estaban buscando.

Todo, y quiero decir todo, empieza con las palabras que salen de tu boca; ¡todo! Con una frase, tienes el poder de hacer el día o la semana de alguien, y sin embargo, en una frase, puedes destruir el día y la semana de alguien.

Pero, por otro lado, puedes llevar la alegría a la vida de alguien, y a través de simples palabras, puedes llevar el ánimo de alguien a nuevos mínimos.

Cambia tu presente y crea hoy un nuevo futuro para ti y los tuyos; que nada te detenga ni te haga descarrilar; que las palabras que salgan de tu boca cambien la vida y den fruto. Porque cuando cambiamos nuestras palabras, cambiamos nuestro propio ser, y cuando eso cambia, Dios hará mucho y abundantemente todo lo que podamos pedir o soñar, él es capaz.

Cambia tus palabras, cambia tu mundo.

CAPÍTULO 2

LECCIONES APRENDIDAS
EL ORGULLO ES EL MAYOR VIRUS

Encontramos una tremenda historia en la Biblia sobre el rey Ezequías; tenía veinticinco años cuando comenzó a reinar sobre Isreal. En 2da de Crónicas 29, encontramos que la palabra de Dios dice en el verso 2," El hizo lo que era correcto a los ojos del Señor, tal como su padre David había hecho."

El joven abrió las puertas del templo y las reparó, reconstruyó el altar del templo, devolvió los holocaustos y restauró las levitas y los sumos sacerdotes.

Todo iba tan bien en Israel que en el capítulo 30, versículo 27, la Biblia dice: "Los sacerdotes y los levitas se pusieron de pie para bendecir al pueblo, y Dios los escuchó, porque su oración llegó al cielo, su santa morada".

Piensa en esto por un momento; ¡sus oraciones llegaron al cielo, su santa morada! Eso es poderoso, y continúa desde allí para decir en el capítulo 31 que los israelitas que estaban allí salieron a las ciudades de Judá, rompieron las piedras sagradas y cortaron los postes de Asera. Destruyeron los lugares altos y los altares en todo Judá y Benjamín, Efraín y Manasés. Luego, después de haberlos destruido todos, los israelitas regresaron a sus ciudades y a sus propiedades.

Un poderoso movimiento de Dios tuvo lugar; una especie de avivamiento había golpeado la tierra. El versículo 20 de la segunda edición de Crónicas dice: "Esto es lo que hizo Ezequías en todo Judá, haciendo lo que era bueno y correcto y fiel ante el Señor su Dios. 21 En todo lo que emprendió en el servicio del templo de Dios y en la obediencia a la ley y a los mandatos, buscó a su Dios y trabajó de todo corazón. Y así prosperó.

Hubo prosperidad en la tierra; el pueblo arregló su vida y se consagró al Señor. Todo iba bien hasta que llegamos al capítulo 32. Entonces, encontramos que Senaquerib, rey de Asiria, invadió Judá y sitió las ciudades fortificadas, pensando en conquistarlas para sí.

En el versículo 20, la Biblia dice: "El rey Ezequías y el profeta Isaías hijo de Amoz, clamaron en oración al cielo sobre esto.

21 Y el Señor envió un ángel que aniquiló a todos los combatientes y a los comandantes y oficiales del campamento del rey asirio. Entonces éste se retiró a su tierra en desgracia. Y cuando entró en el templo de su Dios, algunos de sus hijos, su carne y su sangre, lo mataron a espada.

22 Así el Señor salvó a Ezequías y al pueblo de Jerusalén de la mano de Senaquerib, rey de Asiria, y de la mano de todos los demás. Los cuidó por todos lados.

23 Muchos trajeron a Jerusalén ofrendas para el Señor y regalos valiosos para Ezequías, rey de Judá. Desde entonces, fue muy apreciado por todas las naciones.

Hasta este momento, el rey Ezequías ha llevado a Israel a la victoria, ha hecho todo bien a los ojos del Señor, su Dios, y de repente, la enfermedad cae sobre él hasta el punto de morir. Pero, en su enfermedad, hizo lo que mejor sabía hacer, y eso fue buscar el rostro del Señor su Dios, orar, y Dios escuchó su oración y le envió una señal.

¿Una señal? ¿Él pedía la curación y Dios le envió una señal? Deténgase aquí por un momento; ¿cuántas veces Dios responde a nuestras oraciones con una respuesta que no esperamos o pedimos? Sin embargo, la señal fue única, y la respuesta a su oración fue la bondad.

¿Bondad para un enfermo y moribundo? Pero el verdadero problema no era la enfermedad; el problema no era la respuesta a su oración; ¡el verdadero problema era que el orgullo se había instalado en su corazón!

La Biblia dice en el versículo 24 de 2ª Crónicas 32: "En aquellos días Ezequías enfermó y estuvo a punto de morir. Entonces oró al Señor, quien le respondió y le dio una señal milagrosa.

25 Pero el corazón de Ezequías era orgulloso, y no respondió a la bondad que se le había mostrado; por lo tanto, la ira del Señor cayó sobre él y sobre Judá y Jerusalén.

Verás, el orgullo es un virus que llega a la vida de una persona no para dañarla sino para matarla. Es un virus que es tan agresivo que carcome la fibra de tu alma. No te permite disfrutar del presente; te quejas de tu pasado y destruyes tu futuro.

El orgullo se instala, mata las relaciones, rompe las asociaciones y finalmente chupa la vida misma de esa persona. Mata los sueños y las visiones, y cualquier progreso que hayas hecho hasta ese momento se destruye en un segundo; así de poderoso y destructivo es el orgullo.

La Biblia es clara en su postura sobre el orgullo,

Proverbios 11:2 "Cuando viene el orgullo, entonces viene la desgracia, pero con la humildad viene la sabiduría".

Proverbios 16:5 "El Señor detesta a todos los soberbios de corazón. Así que estén seguros de esto: No quedarán impunes".

Proverbios 16:18 "La soberbia va delante de la destrucción, el espíritu altivo antes de la caída".

Nada bueno puede salir del orgullo-¡nada! El rey Ezequías estaba enfermo de muerte, y en su enfermedad, se volvió orgulloso en su corazón y trajo la ira de Dios sobre él y los israelitas.

El orgullo es un asesino de sueños, un destructor del destino; si lo tienes y decides no deshacerte de él, resultará ser un poderoso obstáculo en tu camino hacia la grandeza. El orgullo tiene el poder de hacerte retroceder meses si no años y décadas porque cierra la puerta a grandes cosas para tu vida.

Si miras el óxido de un coche, nunca empieza lo suficientemente grande como para que lo notes. Por el contrario, empieza de forma pequeña e inocente, como si no pasara nada. Mientras tanto, se va comiendo la pintura y el propio coche que, a menos que se cuide, invadirá todo el vehículo.

No importa en qué parte del coche empiece; es sólo cuestión de tiempo que se extienda y lo que antes era un coche precioso ahora sea un cubo de óxido que nadie quiere.

El orgullo duele; mata, te separa de los demás, te mantiene en una isla para ti solo sin que nadie esté dispuesto a ayudarte. Te aísla tanto que, aunque la gente quiera ayudarte, decide no hacerlo debido a tu orgullo. Es un hedor imaginario que llega a ti y que los demás huelen y ven, pero desgraciadamente, se convierte en un reto para ti verlo.

Si no se trata, el orgullo es como un tornado, viene y destruye cualquier cosa, y todo a su paso, dejando un rastro de ruptura y desesperación. La Biblia dice que al rey Ezequías se le mostró bondad, y se volvió orgulloso en su corazón, tanto que ofendió a Dios y éste decidió responder a ese orgullo con ira y juicio.

Sus sueños están bloqueados por el orgullo, y la grandeza nunca se alcanzará porque eligió el orgullo en su corazón en lugar de ser humilde. Alguien que es orgulloso es arrogante y desdeñoso. Las personas orgullosas no suelen tener muchos amigos ya que se creen superiores a los demás.

El pecado bíblico de la soberbia se refiere a una actitud elevada o exaltada-lo contrario de la virtud de la humildad, que es la postura apropiada que las personas deben tener con Dios.

Un corazón orgulloso se llena de sí mismo y pierde de vista el verdadero propósito de un líder: transformar la vida de los demás. Pero, por desgracia, a menudo es difícil verlo antes de que sea demasiado tarde. Así que cargamos hacia adelante, impulsados por nuestro corazón orgulloso hasta que lo siguiente que sabemos es que nos transformamos en una roca espiritual.

El orgullo es a menudo impulsado por la baja autoestima y la vergüenza. Nos sentimos tan mal con nosotros mismos que compensamos sintiéndonos superiores. Buscamos los defectos de los demás como una forma de ocultar los nuestros. Nos gusta criticar a los demás como defensa contra el reconocimiento de nuestros defectos.

Proverbios 8:13 "El temor de Jehová es aborrecer el mal; la soberbia, la arrogancia, el mal camino y la boca perversa, aborrezco."

Ahora, ¿qué significa humillarse ante Dios? Para mí, significa venir ante Jesús con temor y reverencia, sin importar lo que la gente pueda pensar de ti. Es estar dispuesto a decir: "Me equivoqué". ... Es dejar de centrarte en ti mismo y centrarte en lo que importa: ¡Dios! Por último, llegar a la cruz con la conciencia tranquila.

El orgullo hace que evaluemos nuestras vidas por el estándar de nuestros logros en lugar de nuestra identidad dada por Dios. El orgullo (o, como decimos, el "ego") nos separa del diseño de Dios para vivir en relación con los demás. Nuestra confianza en nosotros mismos nos empuja al aislamiento, creyendo la mentira de que la vida es mejor sola.

En tu camino hacia la grandeza, tendrás muchas "oportunidades" de aceptar el orgullo por tus logros, pero toma la sabia decisión de rechazar esta oportunidad, mantente humilde, sé y sé amable, aprecia lo que tienes y agradece las cosas que no tienes. Aprecia y ama a los que están en tu vida, atesora la palabra de Dios como piedra angular y fundamento de tu progreso y observa cómo Dios pone las cosas a tu favor.

1 Pedro 5:5 Así mismo, jóvenes, estad sujetos a los mayores. Revestíos todos de humildad unos con otros, porque "Dios se opone a los soberbios, pero da gracia a los humildes".

Eso es poderoso, ¡Gracia a los humildes! He aprendido que ser humilde abre puertas que el dinero no puede. Ser humilde abre oportunidades que de otro modo no se abrirían. Así que mantén la humildad cuando consigas cosas, y nunca prestes oídos al orgullo, ¡nunca!

NO PROCRASTINES

La procrastinación es "el acto de retrasar voluntariamente la realización de algo que debería hacerse". Aunque la palabra en sí no se encuentra en la Biblia, podemos encontrar algunos principios que nos ayuden a guiarnos.

A veces, la procrastinación es el resultado de la pereza, y la Biblia tiene mucho que decir al respecto. La Biblia elogia el trabajo duro y la laboriosidad (Proverbios 12:24; 13:4) y advierte contra la pereza y la holgazanería (Proverbios 15:19; 18:9).

Una cura para la procrastinación es más diligencia, independientemente de la tarea. Deberíamos estar supremamente motivados para ser diligentes en su trabajo, ya que en última instancia servimos al Señor. "Todo lo que hagáis, trabajadlo con todo vuestro corazón, como quien trabaja para el Señor, no para los hombres" (Colosenses 3:23).

Si ponemos nuestro corazón en nuestro trabajo, como dice este versículo que hagamos, probablemente nos resultará difícil procrastinar demasiado.

La procrastinación es cuando uno sigue posponiendo para otro momento algo que debería estar haciendo ahora. Hay muchas razones por las que la gente procrastina: El miedo, la ansiedad, la falta de voluntad para afrontar el cambio... Tal vez incluso el miedo al éxito.

La verdad es que cuando procrastinamos, estamos desencadenando una reacción en cadena de eventos que pueden impactar negativamente a otros-no sólo a nosotros mismos. Y Dios nos llama a hacer el bien a los demás. Pero, en cambio, cuando procrastinamos, ¡estamos haciendo lo contrario del bien!

Cuando la gente piensa en la procrastinación, piensa en la pereza. Incluso pueden preguntarse: "¿Qué dice la Biblia sobre la pereza?". Pero la verdad es que son dos cosas muy diferentes.

La pereza significa que uno no está dispuesto a trabajar o a emplear energía (Dictionary.com)

Por otro lado, la procrastinación no significa que no estés dispuesto; significa que estás dejando algo para más tarde.

Los sueños pueden quedar relegados no porque no creas en ellos, sino porque retrasas el trabajo en tu visión. Por supuesto, dedicar tiempo a la planificación de tu sueño y a la ejecución del objetivo es importante, pero no puede ser asumido por la procrastinación.

La procrastinación matará el mismo impulso que puedas tener para cumplir tus sueños y metas; te paralizará y te llevará a un punto muerto. Si seguimos diciendo "lo haré mañana" y, cuando llega el día siguiente, seguimos sin empezar, entonces estamos metiendo nuestros sueños en un ataúd y enterrándolos a dos metros bajo tierra.

La procrastinación puede llegar a ser muy cómoda y bastante razonable.

Porque, a la sombra de la procrastinación, habrá excusas acechando en la oscuridad, haciéndote creer que hacerlo mañana podría ser una mejor decisión, cuando en realidad hacerlo mañana te roba; ¡tu oportunidad de grandeza hoy!

Las personas a menudo procrastinan debido a sus fracasos pasados, y piensan en cómo se sintieron cuando fracasaron y el dolor que les causó, así que para evitar el dolor y los temores, ¡procrastinan en darse otra oportunidad!

Alex Osorio

SUPERAR LA CULPA DEL FRACASO

Hay dos palabras esenciales en ese título-Culpa y Fracaso, las cuales serán tratadas aquí mismo. El fracaso siempre se asocia con emociones de derrota y una mala experiencia. Nunca se asocia realmente con algo bueno. Fallamos todo el tiempo; fallamos incluso cuando no queremos fallar. Fracasamos a propósito y fracasamos sin quererlo.

Nuestros fracasos no tienen por qué estar asociados a una connotación negativa; el fracaso también puede ser algo bueno que te ocurra. Puedes ver tu Fracaso como algo terrible que te ha sucedido y, por favor, no me malinterpretes, ciertos eventos que ocurren en nuestra vida son eventos demoledores.

Algunos eventos destruyen nuestras emociones y nos ponen de rodillas, destrozando cualquier pensamiento de que todo estará bien. Acontecimientos que contienen dificultades, que ponen a prueba la fibra de nuestro ser. Momentos de nuestra vida que hacen que te despiertes en mitad de la noche con un sudor frío, asustado por lo que has pasado o tienes que pasar.

El fracaso se suma al estrés y al dolor, la culpa es tan importante que nos paraliza la culpa del fracaso que cree que la esperanza ha desaparecido. La culpa nos hace pensar que no podemos caminar un paso más, y estamos seguros de morir en el pozo de esa culpa y vergüenza.

Cuestionamos nuestra Fe, dudamos de la palabra, descargamos nuestra rabia y frustraciones en aquellos que no lo merecen, hablamos fuera de lugar, y nuestras palabras ofenden a los que están cerca de nosotros, y lo más importante, muchas veces pensamos que es culpa de Dios lo que ha pasado.

El enemigo utiliza la culpa de fallar para enfatizar que Dios no se presentó de la manera que prometió que lo haría. Sin embargo, Dios tiene una forma emocionante de arreglar las cosas. Dijo en su palabra Isaías 55:8-9: "Porque mis pensamientos no son vuestros pensamientos, ni vuestros caminos son mis caminos, dice el Señor. "Porque como los cielos son más altos que la tierra, así mis caminos son más altos que los vuestros, y mis pensamientos más que los vuestros.

Sus caminos son misteriosos, y nada le sorprende ni le coge desprevenido. Él lo sabe todo y lo ve todo, lo escucha todo y siempre tiene una respuesta para aquellas cosas que nosotros no tenemos. Así que tu fracaso no cogió a Dios desprevenido; no le sorprendió, no estaba dormido cuando te ocurrió, y antes de que te ocurriera, tenía la respuesta.

Si el fracaso fue tan grande, ¿por qué sucedió? esa es la verdadera pregunta y una pregunta perfecta. ¡No tenemos la respuesta a algunas de las preguntas más complejas a veces, sin embargo, hay ciertas cosas de las que puedo estar seguro, y es que mi fracaso no es absoluto no importa lo malo que sea o lo mal que se ponga si Dios delante de ti entonces quién puede estar en contra de ti! Romanos 8:31 dice: ¿Qué diremos, pues, a estas cosas? Si Dios está a favor de nosotros, ¿quién puede estar en contra de nosotros?

Ese "Quién" puede traducirse no sólo a una persona, sino que también se traduce en un "algo". "Porque dijo ¿Qué diremos entonces a estas COSAS? ¡COSAS! Las cosas suceden, y las personas nos suceden; ambas son igual de mortales e hirientes. Así que Pablo lo dijo bien a los romanos, y en este punto, las cosas ya han sucedido, algo tuvo lugar, traumático y todo. Sin embargo, no ofrece simpatía en este punto, no porque sea antipático sino porque quería que no se quedaran en esa emoción de culpa y fracaso.

Las cosas nos sucederán, nos afectarán y nos sacudirán hasta el fondo, pero él subraya que si Dios está a favor de nosotros, ¿quién puede estar en contra? Pasó de las cosas a un quién; se dirigió a ambos al mismo tiempo. Si elegimos quedarnos en esa emoción de culpa y fracaso, nos perderemos la verdadera lección que Dios quería enseñarnos.

Mira a Job; la Biblia dice en Job 1:1 Había un hombre en la tierra de Uz, cuyo nombre era Job; y ese hombre era perfecto y recto, y uno que temía a Dios, y evitaba el mal. Lees la vida de este hombre desde el verso 2 hasta el verso 5; te das cuenta de que este hombre es rico, poderoso, influye en la tierra, más o menos está preparado para la vida. Sin embargo, en un día, todo su mundo se derrumbó ante él. En un día, pasó de tenerlo todo a no tener nada. Sin embargo, un hombre que la Biblia dice que era perfecto y recto. ¿Cómo se puede recibir un elogio como perfecto y recto?

Sin embargo, aun teniendo estos dos elogios unidos a su nombre, la destrucción llegó a su vida en un día. ¿Merecía esto? ¿Qué pecado cometió para que le sucediera todo esto? Tal vez, usted se ha hecho esas mismas preguntas, ¿por qué sucedió esto? o ¿qué hice para merecer esto? Yo me he hecho esas mismas preguntas. Pero, muchas veces, esas preguntas no tienen respuesta, parece como si hubiera silencio, y Dios se hubiera olvidado de ti, cuando es todo lo contrario, Dios tiene el control.

En el versículo 8, sucede algo emocionante, dice: "Y Jehová dijo a Satanás: ¿Has considerado a mi siervo Job, que no hay otro como él en la tierra, hombre perfecto y recto, temeroso de Dios y apartado del mal?"

Dios ofreció a Job para la prueba; Dios ofreció a Job como su jugador "estrella," Dios sabía que podía ofrecer a Job, y Dios estaba seguro de que pasaría la prueba. Espera un momento.....

¿Podría ser que esta sea la manera en que Dios te exhibe y te prepara para una bendición más increíble? ¿Podría ser que esta es la manera en que Dios te promueve? ¿Podría ser que esta es la forma que Dios utilizará para traer el favor y la bendición sobrenatural a tu vida? ¿Podría ser esta la situación que dará un giro a las cosas? Pero, por otro lado, ¿podría Dios que un lío para convertirlo en un mensaje? ¿Y una prueba en un testimonio?

La respuesta a todas estas preguntas es un rotundo ¡SÍ!

Salte hacia adelante hasta el final de la vida de Job, y la Biblia dice en Job 42:12, Así que el SEÑOR bendijo el último final de Job más que su principio... todo dice en Job 1:22," En todo esto Job no pecó ni acusó a Dios de mal."

Su esposa lo dejó, los amigos lo dejaron, perdió todo su ganado, los niños murieron, la destrucción vino, se le dijo que era su culpa por todo lo que había sucedido, se le culpó por todo, y a través de todo esto, no pecó ni culpó a Dios, en una palabra todo lo que puedo decir es ¡WOW!

Hoy en día, nos tropezamos con el dedo del pie del bebé en la esquina de la cama, y declaramos que es el fin del mundo tal como lo conocemos. Aún más profundo cuando en medio de su "fracaso", dice en Job 1:21, "Desnudo salí del vientre de mi madre, y desnudo volveré a él. El Señor dio, y el Señor quitó; bendito sea el nombre del Señor".

BENDITO SEA EL NOMBRE DEL SEÑOR-dice esto en medio de su dolor y sufrimiento, bendice al Señor a través de su culpa por el fracaso, hace lo que nadie pensó que haría, bendice el nombre del Señor. Esta es una lección que hay que aprender, que, aunque las pruebas y tribulaciones vengan, aunque el dolor y el sufrimiento sean complejos, la noche de dolor sea larga, y la tormenta arrecie, tienes el PODER de levantarte y bendecir el nombre del Señor. Tienes el PODER de ponerte de pie, y con cada fibra de tu ser a través de ella, reconocer que estás en las mejores manos posibles y que el Señor nunca te dejará ni te abandonará, sino que estará contigo todos los días de tu vida.

Tu fracaso no es el final, sino que lo reconoces como un nuevo comienzo, una oportunidad para aprender y crecer. Tu fracaso está lleno de dolor y lágrimas. Sin embargo, tienes el poder de convertir la experiencia negativa en una experiencia positiva, sabiendo que Dios ha permitido que todas las cosas negativas te sucedan para que puedas tener la experiencia de compartir una historia tan poderosa en su testimonio que todos los que la escuchen sabrán que fue Dios quien estuvo contigo.

No has fracasado, el fracaso no es tu rey, y no tienes que estar atado por la culpa de ese fracaso; eres hijo o hija del Dios más alto, y como tal, ¡tu último será más significativo al final que al principio! No ha terminado; no estás acabado, la carrera no ha terminado, No has sido noqueado, levántate, desempolva, estás libre de la culpa en el nombre de Jesús.

Si Job tuvo el poder de levantarse y decir lo que dijo y no pecó, entonces tú tienes la capacidad de hacer lo mismo; Dios da y Dios quita, pero ¡BENDITO SEA EL NOMBRE DEL SEÑOR!

Hay tres pasos fundamentales para superar la culpa del fracaso; permíteme compartirlos contigo.

El primer paso para ser libre de esa culpa es, poner todas tus cargas sobre él; la palabra dice 1 Pedro 5:7 "Echando toda vuestra carga sobre él, porque él tiene cuidado de vosotros. "Nunca serás libre si tratas de llevar este peso sobre tus hombros cada día. Un ancla está diseñada para mantenerte en tu lugar, y si el barco está haciendo agua, la tirará hacia abajo. Así que no dejes que la culpa sea tu ancla que te haga caer o te impida avanzar hacia tu meta y destino.

La segunda es Proverbios 3:5 "Confía en el Señor con todo tu corazón, Y no te apoyes en tu propia inteligencia;" Tienes que creer que Dios cambiará las cosas. Tienes que creer, no solo pensar, sino creer que Dios está en control y que todo saldrá para tu beneficio. Confía en que Dios hará un camino donde no hay camino. Isaías 41:10 dice: "No temas, porque yo estoy contigo; no desmayes, porque yo soy tu Dios; te fortaleceré, te ayudaré, te sostendré con mi justa diestra".

Por último, no puedes quedarte en ese pozo de tristeza; debes levantarte y seguir adelante. La Biblia dice en Isaías 43:18: "No te acuerdes de las cosas pasadas, ni consideres las cosas antiguas". No puedes quedarte en esa condición; ya pasó, no podemos retroceder en el tiempo para cambiar las cosas, pero podemos cambiar nuestro mañana por nuestras acciones de hoy.

2 Corintios 5:17 Por lo tanto, si alguien está en Cristo, es una nueva creación. Lo viejo ha pasado; he aquí que lo nuevo ha llegado. Dios quiere moldearte en algo más grande y mejor, una nueva versión de ti, llevando todas las cicatrices de la batalla pero con una riqueza de conocimiento.

Juan 5:8 "Jesús le dijo: "Levántate, toma tu cama y anda". Esas son tus órdenes de marcha; esas son las palabras para ti hoy; mientras lees esto, no importa lo que estés pasando o hayas pasado, Dios te dice ¡Levántate y camina! Si sigues estos tres simples pero poderosos pasos, verás el poder y la poderosa mano de Dios sobre tu vida.

Tu último será más significativo de lo que empiezas-¡eres libre!

LIBERA TU CORAZÓN DEL MIEDO

El cerebro es complejo, y el corazón es misterioso; ¿quién lo conocerá? Así que tuve que investigar un poco y estudiar esto, espiritual y físicamente hablando.

El cerebro es un órgano complejo que controla el pensamiento, la memoria, la emoción, el tacto, la motricidad, la visión, la respiración, la temperatura, el hambre y todos los procesos que regulan nuestro cuerpo. El cerebro y la médula espinal que se extienden desde él constituyen el sistema nervioso central.

En tu mente se está gestando una batalla cada día, hay que tomar decisiones, y a menudo decisiones que no sólo te afectarán a ti, sino que a menudo afectan a los que te rodean. Esto se debe a que tu cerebro (mente) controla tus pensamientos, emociones, visión e incluso la respiración.

El enemigo luchará por el control de tu mente porque las batallas se ganan y se pierden en ella. El cerebro es muy complejo, pero aún más complejo es tu corazón. El corazón es un órgano muscular del tamaño de un puño, situado justo detrás y ligeramente a la izquierda del esternón. El corazón bombea la sangre a través de la red de arterias y venas llamada sistema cardiovascular.

El corazón tiene cuatro cámaras:

-La aurícula derecha recibe la sangre de las venas y la bombea al ventrículo derecho.

-El ventrículo derecho recibe la sangre de la aurícula derecha y la bombea a los pulmones, cargada de oxígeno.

-La aurícula izquierda recibe la sangre oxigenada de los pulmones y la bombea al ventrículo izquierdo.

-El ventrículo izquierdo (la cámara más robusta) bombea la sangre oxigenada al resto del cuerpo. Las vigorosas contracciones del ventrículo izquierdo crean nuestra presión arterial.

Proverbios 4:23 dice: "Sobre todo, guarda tu corazón, porque todo lo que haces fluye de él".

Filipenses 4:7 dice: "Y la paz de Dios, que sobrepasa todo entendimiento, guardará vuestros corazones y vuestras mentes en Cristo Jesús.

Tu corazón es precioso, sin embargo, la gente puede andar sin corazón, figurativamente hablando. Un corazón "limpio" puede manifestarse en acciones significativas por parte de una persona; genera buenas emociones, te pone en un lugar saludable; de la misma manera, un corazón "oscuro" puede traducirse en acciones malas y dañinas.

La biblia dice en Lucas 6:45, "El hombre bueno del buen tesoro de su corazón saca el bien; y el hombre malo del mal tesoro de su corazón saca el mal. Porque de la abundancia del corazón habla su boca".

El miedo a menudo se cuela en el corazón y puede causar una especie de ataque espiritual al corazón. El miedo causa dolor y ansiedad, puede hacer que una persona actúe o reaccione de una manera particular que de otra manera no actuaría o reaccionaría.

Isaías 41:10 dice: "No temas, porque yo estoy contigo; no desmayes, porque yo soy tu Dios; te fortaleceré, te ayudaré, te sostendré con mi justa diestra".

Como bien sabes, la expresión "no temas" se menciona en la Biblia 365 veces, ¿coincidencia? En absoluto. El miedo en tu corazón te hará entrar en un estado mental que es muy peligroso. No te permitirá dar un paso más en la dirección de tus objetivos y visión.

El miedo en el corazón te hará mostrar emociones que normalmente no revelarías, a menudo cubiertas por una ilusión de ser cauteloso. El miedo oxida el alma y la mente de la persona. Si se permite que perdure, consumirá la vida de alguien, y esa persona nunca será la misma.

Hará que sus sueños y metas mueran, enterrándolos para siempre en el estado de simplemente eso, un sueño o una meta. Hará que el corazón duela emocionalmente y nunca sane porque una de las cosas más difíciles de hacer es abandonar tus sueños y metas porque tienes miedo.

Es doloroso cuando ya no puedes perseguir tu sueño, no porque te detenga alguien o algo, pero no poder seguir tu visión y metas por miedo es una de las cosas más trágicas que pueden suceder. Es difícil cuando te detienen cosas que están fuera de tu control, más difícil de aceptar cuando tú eres la razón por la que no vas más allá.

El miedo en tu corazón no te permitirá hacer nada; Dios no te ha dado un espíritu de miedo. Así que la biblia dice en 2 Timoteo 1:7, "Porque Dios no nos ha dado un espíritu de temor, sino de PODER y de AMOR y de una MENTE SANA.

Esto es muy poderoso porque te muestra las áreas que el miedo en el corazón afectará. Te debilitará, matará tu amor, y desordenará tu mente.

Te debilitará para no caminar y perseguir lo que Dios ha dispuesto para ti. Debilitará tu ambición, deseo y motivación, esencialmente matando cualquier impulso que tuvieras para crecer y alcanzar tus sueños. El miedo a menudo debilitará tu pasión por la oración, o por buscar el rostro de Dios, dejando tu camino espiritual en nada. Minará tu relación con Dios y tu relación con los demás. No puedes dejar que el miedo te debilite porque te pondrá en una espiral de muerte que muchas veces no podrás recuperar.

Sólo a través de una relación con Jesús y el Espíritu Santo puedes superar este miedo y vencer la debilidad que trae. A medida que te empapes de la palabra, ganarás fuerza para combatir este virus llamado miedo. A medida que continúes buscando Su rostro, podrás fortalecer tu Espíritu y tu decisión de no rendirte, sino de seguir adelante y luchar.

El miedo matará tu AMOR, por Dios, tu familia y amigos, y tus sueños y metas. Si permites que el miedo destruya tu amor por las cosas de Dios, te vuelves frío e insensible a las cosas del Espíritu. Si tu pasión por las cosas de Dios muere, experimentarás una sequedad en tu vida que no puede ser llenada por nadie ni por nada.

El miedo también destruirá la pasión y el amor por tus sueños y metas. Desafortunadamente, aquí es donde muchas personas se dan por vencidas. Se frustran y tienden a culpar a los demás por su falta de acción, un mecanismo para ocultar las emociones genuinas de que su AMOR por perseguir sus sueños y metas está abandonado.

Cuando el amor muere, entra la frustración y comienza el juego de la culpa. Sin embargo, no puedes permitir que el miedo mate tu pasión; no puedes permitir que el miedo entorpezca tu amor a causa de algunos contratiempos que puedas encontrar en la vida. Vendrán momentos difíciles, ocurrirán pérdidas, pero no son razón suficiente para permitir que tu amor por Dios se marchite en la nada.

No puedes permitir que las frustraciones maten tu impulso; tu carrera no es un sprint sino un maratón, y tu amor no sólo por Dios sino por las cosas de Dios y por tus metas y sueños personales a morir. Todo se pone en peligro cuando permites que el miedo mate tu amor, y todo se derrumbará cuando permitas que el miedo destruya tu amor.

El miedo también atacará tu mente, controlando tu forma de hablar, actuar y reaccionar. Si tu mente está controlada por el miedo, no tomarás decisiones correctas; obstaculizará tu capacidad de generar nuevas ideas y dejará muertas tus acciones.

Si tu mente está afectada por el miedo, verás los resultados manifestados en tu discurso, y la evidencia del miedo se verá en tus acciones. El miedo en tu mente destruirá la capacidad de pensar con claridad, poniendo en peligro las decisiones críticas; tu ansiedad se traducirá en decisiones que alterarán el curso de tu camino. El miedo en la mente es peligroso porque tu mente es un campo de batalla de un millón y uno de pensamientos que se cruzan en ella cada día.

Salmos 27:3 "Aunque un ejército acampe contra mí, mi corazón no temerá; aunque se levante una guerra contra mí, estaré confiado".

El corazón envía señales de que tiene miedo, y su capacidad de funcionamiento se pone en duda. Hoy en día, puede que no tengamos un ejército acampado a nuestro alrededor físicamente hablando, pero el enemigo libra una guerra contra ti para afectar tu mente y tu corazón.

La guerra es feroz y desordenada; te hará perder el sueño, el hambre y otras cosas. Es una guerra de la que no estás exento, pero es una guerra que debes enfrentar de frente. Una batalla que DEBES ganar, y enfatizo DEBES porque si empiezas a caminar hacia tu sueño y empiezas a construir tu futuro, no puedes permitirte el lujo de abandonar o rendirte.

La biblia dice en 2 Corintios 10:4," Porque las armas de nuestra guerra no son carnales, sino poderosas en Dios para derribar fortalezas,"

Lo mejor sería que reconocieras que tu guerra no es carnal, tu lucha no es física, sino que tu batalla y tu guerra tienen implicaciones espirituales de proporciones épicas. Pero él te dio armas lo suficientemente fuertes como para permitirte luchar y ganar.

Él dijo que tus armas son PODEROSAS EN DIOS-esto es clave porque son poderosas no por ti o porque estén en tus manos, sino que son poderosas en DIOS y sólo en Dios.

Santiago 4:7 dice: "Someteos, pues, a Dios. Resistid al diablo, y huirá de vosotros".

La sumisión a Dios es tu primera línea de defensa. Te permite someter tus sueños y metas a Dios; te permitirá matar tu orgullo y te permitirá continuar la búsqueda de tus sueños y metas.

La sumisión a Dios mantendrá vivo tu amor por Él, y también mantendrá el deseo de caminar hacia adelante y luchar con nuevas fuerzas y determinación para tener éxito. Tu sumisión a Dios te permitirá luchar y resistir las obras del enemigo que ha tramado contra ti.

La palabra también dice, RESISTE al enemigo; aquí es donde debes activar tu Fe, y la palabra debe estar activa y viva en tu mente, corazón y boca.

Ser capaz de hablar la palabra de Dios en tu situación, y verás el poder que tiene para cambiar el ambiente y alterar el curso de tu caminar. Si la palabra está viva en ti, podrás rechazar los ataques a tu mente y a tu corazón. La palabra de Dios te permite tener la columna vertebral espiritual para resistir al enemigo y sus ataques.

Cuando sometes a Dios tus sueños, metas y visiones, estás, en esencia, incluyendo a Dios en ellos, y si Dios está incluido en ellos, entonces el fracaso nunca es una opción, sino que lograrás enormes éxitos y victorias. El problema de muchos es que hacen planes sin incluir a Dios; intentan hacer cosas GRANDES sin tener a Dios en esas conversaciones o proyectos.

La biblia dice que no te apoyes en tu entendimiento; en otras palabras, no trates de hacer las cosas sin Dios, porque seguramente fracasará. Ahora puedes decir, mucha gente tiene éxito sin tener a Dios en sus planes; son paganos, y Dios está lejos de sus conversaciones, y sin embargo siguen prosperando; ¿cómo es esto posible?

Siempre hay un precio que pagar; no importa la decisión que tomes, o el camino que elijas recorrer, pagarás una cuota por esa decisión. Para perder peso, debes pagar el precio, algunos de los cuales son el sacrificio, la disciplina y el autocontrol. Sacrificio e invertir el tiempo en el gimnasio, disciplina para mantener el rumbo de tu entrenamiento y dieta, y autocontrol para resistir la tentación de no comer lo que no deberías comer.

El precio que pagas para ser usado por Dios es invertir tiempo en oración, humildad, paciencia y mucho más. Por todo lo que elegimos, debemos pagar ese precio. Nada viene gratis, nada que importe, al menos.

Isaías 35:4 "Di a los que tienen un corazón inquieto: '¡Esfuérzate, no temas! He aquí que vuestro Dios vendrá con la venganza, con la recompensa de Dios. Él vendrá y te salvará".

No puedes vivir en un estado de miedo toda tu vida; ¡debes ser capaz de ser fuerte y no temer! Se puede decir que es más fácil decirlo que hacerlo, pero en realidad, cuando sometas tus metas, sueños y visiones al Señor, entonces es cuando tu corazón estará realmente libre de temor.

Lo más emocionante de este versículo es que Isaías dice que tu Dios vendrá con venganza, con la recompensa de Dios. Él vendrá y te salvará.

No sólo viene Dios con venganza, sino también con recompensa. ¡Con una venganza para tus enemigos pero al mismo tiempo con una recompensa para ti! Cuando tu corazón tome la palabra, la crea y la aplique, entonces tu corazón descansará y se liberará del miedo que lo atenaza.

Cuando te liberes del miedo en el corazón, activarás tu Fe en una dimensión mayor. Una vez que tu corazón esté libre, entonces podrás liberar tu Espíritu para ser usado por Dios en una mayor capacidad, llegando más cerca de tu destino, y un espíritu de excelencia se apodera de ti.

EL PODER DE TENER UN ESPÍRITU DE EXCELENCIA

Cualquiera puede realizar cualquier tarea que se le asigne. Cualquiera puede hacer cosas si se le da el entrenamiento y la orientación adecuados, pero lo que separa a esas personas de alcanzar su destino es el espíritu de excelencia que poseen.

Es lo que separa lo mediocre de lo genial, lo mediocre de lo impresionante, y lo cojo del factor sorpresa. Para alcanzar tu destino, debes tener un espíritu de excelencia, o mejor dicho, comprometerte con un espíritu de excelencia al hacer las cosas que Dios te ha llamado a hacer.

En Mateo 25, la biblia nos cuenta una historia bastante poderosa; dice en el verso 14: "Otra vez será como un hombre que se va de viaje, que llamó a sus siervos y les confió sus riquezas.

El versículo 15 dice: Y a uno le dio cinco talentos, a otro dos y a otro uno, a cada uno según su capacidad; y enseguida se puso en camino.

Deténgase aquí por un momento.

¡Le dio a cada uno SEGÚN SU CAPACIDAD!

Dios nunca te dará una carga que no puedas llevar,

1ª Corintios 10:13 No os ha sobrevenido ninguna tentación que no sea la común de los hombres; pero fiel es Dios, que no os dejará ser tentados más de lo que podéis, sino que junto con la tentación os dará también la salida, para que podáis soportarla.

Él siempre te dará algo que puedas manejar; puede parecer que no puedes y que serás aplastado por la carga, pero Dios te hizo lo suficientemente fuerte para llevarla y manejarla y perseverar sin importar lo que pueda venir en tu camino.

Tu destino es tan grande como quieras que sea y tan pequeño como quieras que sea. Dios estará contigo sin importar el camino que elijas recorrer; la elección es absolutamente toda tuya. Dios tiene un gran destino para todos, pero no todos aceptan ese destino.

Tu destino depende de ciertos factores como tu Fe, tu deseo de lograrlo, tu determinación de seguir adelante sin importar las circunstancias, tu empuje y por último, tu deseo de lograr la excelencia.

La biblia dice que a cada uno le dio unos talentos, pero lo que hizo la diferencia no fue el talento sino lo que cada persona decidió hacer.

Mateo 25:16-18 dice Entonces el que había recibido los cinco talentos fue y negoció con ellos, y ganó otros cinco talentos. Asimismo, el que había recibido dos, ganó también otros dos. Pero el que había recibido uno fue y cavó en la tierra y escondió el dinero de su señor.

Y ahí está el problema; tomó lo que su señor le dio, no prestó atención a los demás y lo enterró. No tuvo visión, ni deseo, ni impulso, ni nada, excepto el hecho de que enterró lo que su señor le dio.

¿Cuántas veces la gente, tú, entierras lo que Dios te ha dado? Por miedo, o por falta de creencia, entierran ese don que Dios les ha dado y entierran su destino junto con él.

Los otros dos tenían una visión; los otros dos habían agarrado lo que se les había dado y produjeron más. Un espíritu de excelencia siempre te impulsará a hacer mucho más por el reino; nunca te permitirá no hacer nada con lo que Dios te dio.

Ellos tomaron lo que se les dio y lograron la grandeza con lo que se les dio. El otro no hizo nada, pero pensó que estaba haciendo algo. No puedes cometer el error de tomar lo que Dios te ha dado y no hacer nada con ello.

La biblia dice en Mateo 7:16, ¡por sus frutos los conoceréis!

Lo que hagas con lo que Dios te da determinará el resultado de tu vida. Lo que hagas con los dones y talentos que él te ha confiado determinará tu felicidad y el índice de éxito en la consecución de tus objetivos y sueños.

Enterró los talentos que su amo le había dado; en otras palabras, fue perezoso, se dio por vencido, no quiso molestarse con ello. ¿Cuántas veces somos como este hombre? Nos damos por vencidos porque oímos a la gente decir que no podíamos hacerlo, renunciamos porque culpamos a la educación de nuestra infancia, y eso no quiere decir que no sean valoraciones justas de nuestra vida, pero por muy justas que parezcan, nunca deberían ser suficientes para hacer que renuncies o dejes de perseguir tus sueños.

Cuando era apenas un niño, recuerdo que mis padres hablaban de dar a Dios lo mejor de lo que éramos y de maximizar los dones y talentos que nos dio a cada uno de nosotros. Yo era joven y aún no había descubierto el verdadero significado de lo que decía mi padre. Estaba más interesado en jugar y hacer lo que los niños hacen mejor.

Dar a Dios lo mejor de sí mismo no significa darle la perfección, porque eso en sí mismo es imposible, pero dar a Dios lo mejor de sí mismo significa, en primer lugar, darle tu corazón. Luego, después de haberlo hecho, dar el 110% de esfuerzo en todo lo que él pone ante ti

Por aquel entonces no sabía tocar el piano, pero quería convertirme en el líder de la alabanza en la iglesia. Mi padre era un gran teclista y había grabado algunas cintas por aquel entonces, pero con su horario y sus responsabilidades en la iglesia, verle llegar a casa e irse directamente a la cama hacía que mi corazón se entristeciera por él, sabiendo la presión a la que estaba sometido. No me atreví a pedirle que me enseñara a tocar cuando supe lo cansado que estaba

Sé que si se lo hubiera pedido, estoy segura de que se habría tomado 5 minutos para enseñarme algo cada noche. Así que decidí encargarme de aprender a tocar el teclado. Me ponía al lado del teclista de aquella época y le miraba tocar, y después de cada servicio, mientras todos estaban en comunión, te encontrabas a un chico joven en el santuario intentando recordar lo que yo veía y tratando de reproducirlo.

Mi hermano y yo volvíamos a casa, y en nuestro tiempo libre, poníamos una cinta, CDs que no existían entonces, y seguíamos en un teclado que mi padre nos había comprado. Cada día avanzaba, cada día estaba lleno de errores, y seguíamos en ello, ¡pero nunca nos rendíamos!

Cuanto más nos equivocábamos, más queríamos intentar resolverlo y tratar de perfeccionar lo que la canción intentaba enseñarnos. Pero nunca nos dimos por vencidos, no nos rendimos, no paramos ni abandonamos; eso es lo que significa tener un espíritu de excelencia: ¡querer ser mejor que ayer!

¿Nos conformamos con la dejadez y la pereza? ¿Nos alegramos de habernos rendido? Es fácil hacerlo, pero ¿estamos mejor? Mi padre tenía una regla, que dice: "sé el primero en la iglesia, y sé el último en salir".

Nunca podrás alcanzar tu destino con una actitud perezosa y una mentalidad de abandono. Dios se merece lo mejor de ti, lo mejor de tu tiempo, esfuerzo, voluntad, impulso, pasión y habilidad. Así que dale a Dios lo mejor de ti y observa lo mejor que tiene para ti siempre en acción.

Caminar por la Fe no se supone que sea fácil, pero se supone que te hace entender que si haces tu parte en confiar en Él, entonces Dios nunca te decepcionará. La linterna de tu teléfono no te da mucha más luz que dos o tres pies delante de ti, sin embargo confías en que la luz que ves, aunque sólo brilla lo suficiente para que puedas caminar, te ayudará a navegar por el camino que estás recorriendo.

La fe funciona de la misma manera; la fe solo te permite ver un par de pasos adelante y nada más, el propósito de la fe no es hacerlo fácil como dije antes, el objetivo de la fe es crear en ti una dependencia de Dios, que no sepas lo que hay adelante. Sin embargo, confías en Él lo suficiente como para seguir caminando.

Repito que no puedes enterrar lo que Dios te ha dado, sino que debes abrazarlo con todo lo que tienes. No es una competencia con nadie más, sino con uno mismo. Entonces, ¿cómo puedes hacer mejor y ser mejor de lo que eras ayer? La fe en acción.

Un espíritu de excelencia nace cuando te das cuenta de que puedes y debes hacerlo mejor para Dios. Un espíritu de excelencia se alcanza cuando sabes que los talentos y dones que Dios te ha dado no pueden ser enterrados sino activados. Un espíritu de excelencia nace cuando decides que lo que has hecho por Dios y por el reino puede ser mejor.

Un mejor esposo, padre, hermano, tío, predicador, hijo, hija, mejor que ayer, mejor que tu antigua versión de ti.

Mateo 25:19 dice: "Después de mucho tiempo, vino el señor de aquellos siervos y ajustó cuentas con ellos. "Nunca puedes olvidar que el Señor siempre requerirá un informe de las cuentas de tu vida y de lo que hiciste con lo que te dio mientras estabas aquí en la tierra.

El versículo 20 dice: "El que había recibido cinco talentos vino y trajo otros cinco talentos, diciendo: "Señor, me entregaste cinco talentos; mira, he ganado otros cinco talentos además de ellos". ¡Fue recompensado con el doble al que invirtió y activó ese Espíritu de excelencia!

Siempre hay una recompensa por tu esfuerzo y trabajo en el reino-¡siempre! Nunca es en vano, sino que siempre tendrá una recompensa.

El versículo 21 dice: "Su señor le dijo: 'Bien hecho, siervo bueno y fiel; fuiste fiel en lo poco, te pondré a gobernar en lo mucho. Entra en el gozo de tu señor".

Siervo bueno y fiel esas palabras son confiables y poderosas, Bueno no por quien era, sino bueno por su ética de trabajo, disciplina e inteligencia. No sólo recibió una recompensa, sino que se le puso una etiqueta que no se le podía quitar de por vida. ¡Pasó de ser un siervo a ser un GOBERNADOR de muchas cosas!

Todo porque eligió hacer algo, tuvo ese espíritu de excelencia que le hizo actuar para mejorar el reino y a su amo. Alcanzó su destino simplemente tomando la iniciativa y superando a todos los demás, y de repente dejó de ser un siervo para convertirse en un gobernante.

Mateo 25:22-23 dice: "También el que había recibido dos talentos se acercó y dijo: Señor, me entregaste dos talentos; he aquí que he ganado otros dos talentos además de ellos. Su señor le dijo: 'Bien hecho, siervo bueno y fiel; has sido fiel en lo poco, te pondré al frente de lo mucho. Entra en la alegría de tu señor".

Este siervo también era inteligente y había duplicado lo que se le había dado, y por eso fue recompensado, y su vida cambió en ese mismo momento. Ahora, este siervo no se quejó porque sólo recibió dos talentos, y los primeros cinco, no, él maximizó lo que se le dio.

Deja de mirar alrededor quién tiene más que tú, quién es mejor que tú, quién tiene más talentos y habilidades que tú; lo que importa es lo que haces con lo que Dios te ha dado en ese momento. Así que él no se quejó porque el otro tenía más que él, él bloqueó todo eso y corrió su carrera, se mantuvo en su carril e hizo lo mejor con lo que Dios le había dado, y al final, resultó ser un ganador.

Miremos hacia adelante; los versículos 24-25 dicen: "Entonces el que había recibido el único talento se acercó y dijo: 'Señor, yo sabía que eres un hombre duro, que cosechas donde no has sembrado, y recoges donde no has esparcido la semilla. Y me asusté y fui a esconder tu talento en la tierra. Mira, ahí tienes lo que es tuyo'.

Su respuesta parecía estar llena de conocimiento y razón, pero era superficial y hueca por dentro en realidad. Así que, primero, descubres que estaba incapacitado por el miedo, lo que le hacía inútil. Luego, descubres que hizo lo que nadie hizo y trató de justificarlo con su razonamiento.

Fue y lo enterró; luego tuvo que desenterrarlo y devolvérselo a su amo; esto requirió trabajo. Se necesitó tiempo, energía, voluntad y empuje para que alguien tomara su talento y lo enterrara. Pero, ¿imagina si hubiera utilizado esos mismos principios en la dirección correcta? ¿Imagina cuáles habrían sido los resultados que habría obtenido?

¿Con qué frecuencia utilizamos la energía que Dios nos ha dado, el talento, la habilidad, la pasión y mucho más, en la dirección correcta? ¿O estamos usando todas esas cosas y empeorando nuestras vidas?

El versículo 26 de Mateo 25 dice: "Pero su señor respondió y le dijo: 'Siervo malo y perezoso, sabías que cosecho donde no he sembrado, y recojo donde no he esparcido la semilla'".

Dos palabras me saltan a la vista en este texto: son malvado y perezoso. Según el diccionario, malvado es malo o moralmente incorrecto. ¿Malvado por enterrar el talento? un poco duro, ¿dirías tú? Todo lo contrario, el que no hace nada por nada es malvado y moralmente incorrecto.

Hay que hacer algo; hay que actuar, y no se puede permanecer callado o perezoso; hay que intentarlo y no renunciar-perezoso significa sin voluntad de trabajar o usar energía-.

No hay nada más horrible que una persona perezosa en la vida. No sé tú, pero estar cerca de una persona perezosa es tan frustrante y exasperante que me hierve por dentro. Una persona perezosa puede infectar rápidamente a otros, y arruinará a otros muy rápidamente si no se trata con prontitud.

Mira lo que la escritura dice a continuación; el verso 30 de Mateo 25 dice, "Y echad al siervo inútil en las tinieblas de afuera. Allí será el llanto y el crujir de dientes".

¡Qué final para este siervo; no sólo le quitaron lo que tenía y se lo dieron al que tenía diez talentos, sino que lo echaron a las tinieblas exteriores! Un triste final para un hombre que había comenzado en la misma página que los demás.

Todos comenzamos en el mismo nivel en esta vida, pero nuestras elecciones rápidamente comienzan a crear una división y separación entre tú y los demás, y es ahí donde ves que algunos tienen éxito y otros no. Todos nos enfrentamos a la adversidad en la vida; todos lo hacemos, pero lo que hacemos ante la adversidad es lo que importa.

Por favor, no me malinterpreten, sí, ciertas cosas suceden que están más allá de nuestro control, ciertas cosas vienen a destrozarnos y a golpearnos hasta hacernos papilla, pero una cosa es segura que la biblia dice en 1 Juan 4:4 "Vosotros sois de Dios, hijitos, y los habéis vencido; porque mayor es el que está en vosotros que el que está en el mundo".

Cuando te des cuenta de la magnitud del Dios al que servimos y de su poder, entonces en ese momento, empezarás a cambiar tus palabras y a cambiar tus acciones. Por supuesto, como dije antes, los desafíos vendrán, pero esa es la oportunidad para que te agarres de la verdad en la palabra de Dios y la apliques a tu vida.

No dejes que nada te derrote, y si alguien te vence, ¡que seas tú quien te derrote! Derrota a tu viejo yo, lleno de excusas y quejas. Derrota a tu viejo yo lleno de miedo e inseguridades, vence a tu viejo yo acercándote a Dios y decidiendo que un revés no significa que hayas fracasado, sino que lo usas como un peldaño para llegar más alto.

Un espíritu de excelencia no se conforma con lo ordinario; no se conforma con el promedio ni se conforma con lo mínimo. Por el contrario, significa dar a Dios el mejor "producto" o sacrificio posible. No significa competir con el impulso o la pasión de otra persona, sino correr tu carrera y mantenerte en tu carril.

El error que puedes cometer rápidamente es comparar tu carrera y sacrificio con los de otros; no puedes permitir que el enemigo te atraiga a esa arena. Es una arena en la que perderás permanentemente la lucha. Así que debes permanecer enfocado en tu llamado, y si otros te pasan, que así sea, y si otros lo hacen mejor que tú, que así sea, pero debes enfocarte en ti mismo, y TÚ debes ser capaz de darle a Dios lo mejor de TI.

Tu éxito no depende de los demás y de lo que puedan pensar de ti; no, depende un poco de que actives tu Fe, de que confíes en Dios, de que corras tu carrera, de que subas tu montaña, de que derrotes a tus gigantes y de que termines la tarea que tienes entre manos.

El Monte Everest es la montaña más grande de la tierra, con una altura de 29.032 pies. Las personas que escalan esa montaña son consideradas únicas, y al hacerlo, son realmente fantásticas por hacerlo. Pero permítanme que les hable de una pequeña colina cerca de donde vivo que, en verano, me desafía cada vez a subirla corriendo lo más rápido posible tres veces. Esa pequeña colina es mi monte Everest; esa pequeña colina presenta un desafío cada año; esa pequeña colina debe ser conquistada cada vez que decido correr hacia arriba.

Digo esto porque cada uno debe enfrentarse a su pequeño monte Everest, ahora bien, mi monte Everest puede ser diferente al tuyo, y el hecho de que mi colina sea más prominente o viceversa no la hace menos significativa.

Debes decidirte a desafiarte a ti mismo con un espíritu de determinación, con un corazón de excelencia y resolución, que no se te negará ni se te disuadirá; no renunciarás ni te rendirás. Sin embargo, primero debes estar a la altura de las circunstancias, subir esa colina y, cuando lo hagas, subir la montaña y llegar a la cima: celébralo y no mires la cima de los demás ni sus celebraciones.

Celebre sus logros, celebre sus logros, y nunca compare su victoria con las victorias de otros. Pablo lo dijo muy bien en 2ª Timoteo 4:7-8 "He peleado la buena batalla, he terminado la carrera, he guardado la Fe. Por último, me está reservada la corona de la justicia, que el Señor, el juez justo, me dará en aquel día, y no sólo a mí, sino también a todos los que han amado su aparición.

Con espíritu de excelencia, decide de una vez por todas que te vas a levantar, que vas a ser mejor y, sobre todo, que vas a dar a Dios lo mejor de lo que eres.

CAPÍTULO 3

TU DESTINO AHORA PREPARACIÓN Y DISCIPLINA

Para que cualquier cosa sea grande, debe ser preparada correctamente; uno debe prepararse para lograr esa meta para alcanzar la grandeza. Por lo tanto, la preparación y la disciplina son fundamentales para la excelencia de tu futuro. Por muy devoto que seas, sin preparación y disciplina la ejecución de dichas metas y sueños nunca se hará realidad.

Jeremías 29:11 Yo sé los pensamientos que tengo para ustedes, dice el Señor, pensamientos de paz y no de mal, para darles un futuro y una esperanza.

Para cada pensamiento, debe haber un plan que debe seguir, porque si no hay un plan que siga, ese pensamiento morirá y no se realizará. Así que cada sueño necesita un plan de acción; cada proyecto requiere disciplina para ejecutarlo. Habrá gigantes y adversidades que vendrán a desafiar tus sueños y metas. Vendrán a matar tu Fe y a asegurar que tu visión nunca vea la luz del día.

Tus enemigos tratarán de desprestigiarte a ti y a tu Fe; se te presentarán muchas oportunidades para abandonar y rendirte. Te animarán a dejar de construir hacia tu sueño, te instarán a dejar de correr hacia la línea de meta, pero cuando sus gritos para que te detengas sean más fuertes, es cuando debes empujar más fuerte, correr rápido y sobre todo, ¡no te rindas!

Más vale que des gracias a Dios porque tus enemigos han hecho más por ti que cualquiera de tus amigos. Si lo ves desde la perspectiva de la Fe, sabrás que te harán presionar; si tu enemigo supiera lo que está haciendo por ti cuando te lo hace, te habría dejado en paz.

Nunca se habrían metido contigo; por eso la Biblia dice que ores por tus enemigos. Mateo 5:44 dice: "Pero yo os digo: Amad a vuestros enemigos, bendecid a los que os maldicen, haced bien a los que os odian, y orad por los que os ultrajan y os persiguen... Por ejemplo, la Nueva Versión Internacional dice: "Pero yo os digo que améis a vuestros enemigos y oréis por los que os persiguen".

Mis enemigos me hacen caer de bruces; me hacen decir: Dios, te necesito ahora más que nunca. Me obligan a ayunar, a rezar, a creer y a seguir caminando. Puedes dejar que tus enemigos te derriben y te mantengan al margen, o puedes permitir que tus enemigos te empujen más cerca de Dios y más cerca de tus sueños y visiones.

Hay una cosa fascinante en los funerales: cuando sacan el féretro, normalmente hay seis personas sacando el ataúd. Sin embargo, en la vida, cuando trabajas para alcanzar tus sueños y metas, a menudo te encuentras solo. ¿Dónde están esas seis personas cuando está más oscuro antes de que llegue la luz? ¿Dónde están esas seis personas cuando te sientes derrotado?

En esos momentos, necesitas apoyarte en el Dios eterno que nunca deja de estar ahí cuando nadie más lo está. Así lo dijo en su palabra en Hebreos 13:5, "...Porque Él ha dicho: "Nunca te dejaré, ni te abandonaré".

Tienes que ser un hacedor de problemas a la pereza; tienes que ser un hacedor de problemas al conformismo; tienes que ser un hacedor de problemas a tu duda, dar más dolores de cabeza al enemigo que el enemigo te da dolores de cabeza a ti. Veamos esta historia;

Hechos 17:6 dice, Pero como no los encontraron, arrastraron a Jasón y a algunos otros creyentes ante los funcionarios de la ciudad, gritando: "Estos hombres que han causado problemas en todo el mundo han venido ahora aquí,

Creo firmemente que ser un creador de problemas, espiritual y proféticamente, es darle la vuelta al guión y agitarlo; hay que levantarse y declarar una guerra a la incredulidad y a la duda. Pero, para obtener la victoria, debe haber un precio que pagar. Tal vez el dolor que sientes es el precio que debes pagar para dar a luz a tu milagro.

Tal vez el dolor que sientes es el precio que debes pagar para dar a luz a lo que Dios quiere hacer A TRAVÉS de ti, siempre hay un precio que pagar, y en tu angustia, Dios te engrandecerá.

Cuando te das cuenta de que Dios lo hace todo, Dios lo hace a propósito con propósito y para propósito. Y te quedas pensando ¿por qué es que nadie ha pensado en esto? Tal vez sea un puñado de propósitos sólo para ti.

Hay una razón por la que Dios hace lo que hace, y hay una razón por la que Dios permite que las cosas sucedan y tengan lugar; la Biblia dice en

Isaías 55: 8-9, "Porque mis pensamientos no son vuestros pensamientos, ni vuestros caminos son mis caminos, dice el Señor. Porque como los cielos son más altos que la tierra, así mis caminos son más altos que vuestros caminos, y mis pensamientos más que vuestros pensamientos.

Puede que nunca entendamos, y nunca entenderemos, los caminos de Dios y sus pensamientos, nunca podremos entender su razonamiento, nunca podremos entender cómo piensa Dios. Sin embargo, en el mundo de la Fe, el entendimiento no es necesario, la comprensión no es necesaria, la verdadera Fe no es cuando lo entiendes todo; no sabes nada y aún así eliges caminar hacia adelante.

La verdadera Fe es cuando estás rodeado de dudas e incredulidad y aún así eliges creer en la palabra de Dios. Los sentimientos siguen el enfoque; si me concentro en la paz y me concentro en la cura y el proceso, me siento confiado.

Cuando estoy confiado, me siento en paz y alegre, pero si estoy enfocado en el problema, me siento ansioso, y me siento temeroso. Si me centro en lo que está mal, me siento nervioso. Si me centro en lo que he perdido en lugar de en lo que me queda, mis sueños están en peligro.

Cuando me doy cuenta de que si Dios crea un milagro en tu vida, a menudo no será con lo que has perdido; en cambio, usará lo que te queda.

Jesús tomó las sobras de pescado y pan y alimentó a los cinco mil, permíteme recordarte que Dios puede tomar lo que te queda y convertirlo en un milagro sobrenatural.

Puedes estar roto porque nadie creyó o cree en ti y en tus sueños, pero Dios tomará lo que te queda y te bendecirá con ello. El te bendecirá con lo que el mundo piensa y cree que es insignificante; el usará eso para "mostrar" su poder y gloria a través de tus actos de Fe.

Dios nunca hará lo que tú tienes que hacer; tu preparación es crítica, tu disciplina es crucial, y tu Fe debe ser implacable.

La verdadera pregunta que debes hacerte es: ¿ves lo que te queda? ¿Lo valoras? ¿Crees que Dios puede utilizarlo para cambiar las cosas? Por supuesto, la respuesta a todas estas preguntas debe ser un sí rotundo.

2 Reyes 4 nos habla de una mujer sorprendente y de sus actos de confianza y fe en la palabra que salió de la boca del profeta.

Su marido había muerto, y ella tenía una deuda pendiente, tanto que venían a llevarse a sus dos hijos como siervos para pagar la deuda. Cuando creía que todo había terminado, cuando pensaba que ya no había nada que hacer, entonces Dios se presentó a través del profeta.

Lo único que le quedaba era una jarra de aceite; Eliseo le dijo: "¿Qué puedo hacer por ti? Dime, ¿qué tienes en casa?". Y ella respondió: "Tu sierva no tiene nada en casa, salvo una vasija de aceite". 2 Reyes 4:3

De una vasija de aceite iba a salir un gran milagro; de algo tan pequeño e insignificante iba a salir un avance para ella y su familia. Así que no le preguntó qué había perdido, aunque sabía que lo había perdido todo, sino que le preguntó qué tenía en su casa.

La fe siempre mirará lo que te queda y nunca lo que has perdido. La fe nunca verá la copa medio vacía, sino que la verá medio llena. Para obtener la fuerza para dar el siguiente paso, necesitará mucha paciencia y disciplina para que las cosas empiecen a suceder en su vida.

El profeta procede entonces a pedirle que haga algo muy inusual; le pide que reúna muchas vasijas y llene las jarras vacías con el aceite que le queda. Esa orden puede haber parecido sin ninguna lógica a la mente natural, pero no se necesitaba una explicación para el pueblo de la Fe; sólo se requería Fe. La verdadera Fe no requiere comprensión; no requiere una razón, pero sí requiere paciencia y disciplina no convencionales.

En medio de un momento de crisis, fue llamada a trabajar por su milagro. En medio de sus pruebas, se le ordenó que tomara a sus dos hijos y se pusiera a trabajar. El hombre de Dios podría haber orado fácilmente, y el milagro podría haber tenido lugar allí mismo, pero en lugar de eso, se le ordenó que se pusiera a trabajar.

¿Por qué no rezó? Porque la oración sin acción es nula. Un milagro sin trabajo realizado creará en usted una mentalidad de niño mimado. Fíjate que la mujer no se quejó ni cuestionó lo que se le ordenaba; no levantó las manos y se rindió; se arremangó con sus dos hijos y se puso a trabajar.

Sus sueños, sus visiones y sus objetivos siempre le harán trabajar por ellos. Ella y sus hijos estaban preparados para trabajar, y eso requería disciplina. Se comprometieron con el plan; estaban decididos a salir del lío en el que se encontraban. Debes estar preparado y disciplinado para ir más allá, sin importar lo que Dios te pida.

A menudo he dicho en la iglesia que si Dios dijera: "Te daré un millón de dólares, y todo lo que tienes que hacer es correr alrededor de la cuadra diez veces, ¿cuántos de ustedes permanecerían en sus asientos? Casi puedo garantizar que muy pocas personas permanecerían sentadas en sus asientos.

Los que se quedaran serían los que se negaran a hacer lo que se les pide y se quejarían diciendo, ¿por qué correr? ¿Por qué Dios no me da el millón sin dar la vuelta a la manzana?

Como dije antes, los verdaderos milagros nunca se harán por ti mientras estés en un estado mental perezoso. Si genuinamente quieres una bendición, entonces debes estar dispuesto a levantarte, vestirte y hacer lo que se te pide. Si la mujer decide quedarse en su estado mental negativo, habría perdido a sus hijos y nunca habría visto los milagros ante sus propios ojos.

Si se hubiera quejado o hubiera pedido una explicación, su milagro habría muerto, y la historia habría terminado de forma diferente. Sin embargo, ella eligió no cuestionar la instrucción, sino que mostró su preparación y determinación para hacer lo que fuera necesario para realizar el trabajo. Si ella decide abandonar, también lo habría hecho su milagro.

Si decides abandonar la persecución de tus sueños y objetivos sólo porque no te gustan las instrucciones que te han dado, no estás de acuerdo con el método o crees que lo que se te pide no es razonable. Entonces, puedes despedirte de tus sueños y metas porque en el momento en que decidas adoptar esa actitud, nunca alcanzarás tu destino.

Ayudaría si estuvieras preparado y disciplinado para estar mental, emocional y espiritualmente listo para recibir la palabra o instrucción, y luego encontrarlo en ti mismo para levantarte y proceder en el camino para lograr la grandeza.

Debes, y enfatizo, debes estar listo para hacer lo que Dios te ha llamado a hacer en un momento dado. Si te sientas y te quejas, entonces no te quejes cuando las cosas mueran, estás llamado a la grandeza, y por lo tanto debes, a toda costa, seguir adelante y nunca detenerte. Con preparación y disciplina, desbloquearás grandes cosas para ti y activarás tu Fe. Cuando eso ocurra, empezarás a ver cómo se producen milagros sobrenaturales, no sólo bendiciones sino dones sobrenaturales.

GANANDO IMPULSO

Cuando se lanza una honda, primero hay que tirar hacia atrás para soltar la piedra; cuanto más se tire hacia atrás, más lejos viajará la piedra.

En nuestra búsqueda por alcanzar nuestros sueños y metas, a menudo pasamos por el proceso de ser jalados hacia atrás. Esa sensación no siempre parece agradable y aceptada, pero es necesaria. Cuando te tiran hacia atrás, parece que te impiden ir más allá.

Das un paso adelante y tres hacia atrás; es una sensación deprimente, y a menos que estés dispuesto a depositar tus metas y sueños en las manos de Dios, nunca entenderás este proceso. Finalmente, te arqueas hacia atrás para coger impulso mientras lanzas el brazo hacia delante para conseguir la máxima distancia, incluso para lanzar una piedra con la mano desnuda.

No puedes desanimarte.

La honda es el proceso que Dios utilizará a menudo para impulsarte hacia adelante a una velocidad máxima. Aunque no entendamos lo que está sucediendo cuando nos tiran hacia atrás, puede parecer que vamos hacia atrás y no hacia adelante; debemos saber que ganaremos impulso a través de este proceso, lanzándonos hacia nuestro destino.

Aquí en Canadá, sabemos un par de cosas sobre quedarse atascado en la nieve, y conocemos el dolor de cabeza que supone quedarse atascado. Haces girar los neumáticos pisando el acelerador, pero no vas a ninguna parte. Haces girar los neumáticos a derecha e izquierda, y nada es aún más complicado si eres tú mismo.

Pero benditos seamos los canadienses, que tarde o temprano alguien pasa y se ofrece a echarte una mano. Así que he estado en los dos lados de este escenario, y ambos son geniales porque, por un lado, consigues ayudar a alguien en apuros, y por otro, te están apoyando en tu momento de dolor.

Ahora bien, esto tiene que ser exacto; primero empiezas a intentar salir con la pala; después, empiezas el proceso de balancear el coche hacia delante y hacia atrás para darte algo de tracción. Cuando empiezas a balancear el coche hacia adelante y hacia atrás, estás creando un impulso para salir del lío en el que te encuentras.

Te mueves hacia adelante y hacia atrás hasta que finalmente te liberas y tienes tracción para seguir adelante. Pero, de nuevo, el retroceso fue necesario para que tuvieras la oportunidad de avanzar.

Nunca te desanimes por la idea de que debes ir "hacia atrás" o por la idea de que estás siendo arrastrado hacia atrás. Dios manifiesta su más extraordinario poder en una idea que puede no tener sentido para ti en ese momento.

La historia de Daniel es interesante; todo iba muy bien hasta que fue condenado al foso de los leones. No es hasta el versículo 25 del capítulo 6 de Daniel que encontramos el poder de redención.

La Biblia dice en Daniel 6:25: "Entonces el rey Darío escribió a todas las naciones y pueblos de todas las lenguas de toda la tierra: "¡Prosperen en gran manera! "Doy un decreto para que en todas las partes de mi reino se tema y reverencie al Dios de Daniel. "Porque él es el Dios vivo, y perdura para siempre; su reino no será destruido, su dominio no tendrá fin. Él rescata, y salva; realiza signos y prodigios.

Fue enviado a la muerte, pero Dios tenía un plan diferente; puede que te encuentres en un momento de crisis, retrocediendo en lugar de avanzar. Debes confiar en Dios y en su plan perfecto y omnisciente para tu vida. A menudo, que te hagan retroceder es lo mejor que te puede pasar, porque Dios ve lo que tú no puedes, y su retroceso es para impulsarte hacia adelante y darte el impulso que buscas.

Cuando no entendemos que Dios tiene el control, nos frustramos y nos enfadamos ante la idea de ir hacia atrás. No podemos controlar lo que nos sucede, pero sí podemos controlar cómo reaccionamos ante esas cosas. El impulso a menudo va hacia atrás, pero sólo para impulsarlo hacia adelante.

Daniel se enfrentó a una muerte inminente al ser enviado al foso de los leones; su futuro era cierto, la muerte estaba asegurada, pero se olvidaron de que Daniel tenía un Dios al que rezaba constantemente. Parecía que tenía que retroceder, y así lo parecía en aspectos concretos, pero Dios estaba a punto de aparecer poderosamente.

Lo mejor sería que nunca olvidaras que el Dios de la Biblia es un Dios vivo, y que aún no ha perdido ninguna batalla. Por lo tanto, ganar impulso sólo puede atribuirse a Dios, pues es él quien te permite sobresalir, crecer y expandirte.

La Biblia dice en 1ª Corintios 3:6: "Yo planté, Apolos regó, pero Dios dio el crecimiento."

¡La clave aquí es que Dios da el incremento! En este punto, no podemos olvidar que Dios es el que da el crecimiento y el impulso. La Biblia también dice en Apocalipsis 3:8: "Yo conozco tus obras. Mira, he puesto ante ti una puerta abierta, y nadie puede cerrarla; porque tienes un poco de fuerza, has guardado mi palabra y no has negado mi nombre".

Cuando Dios te da impulso, te acelerará a lugares que pensabas que eran sólo un sueño. Cosas que deberían tomar meses y años para lograrse, se logran en días y horas. El impulso en Dios aumenta el favor en tu vida; hace que las bendiciones se pongan delante de ti, provoca un cambio en la búsqueda de tus sueños y metas.

Salmos 23:5 dice: "Preparas una mesa delante de mí en presencia de mis enemigos; unges mi cabeza con aceite; mi copa está llena".

Este es un verso poderoso para considerar; Uno, Tú preparas una mesa delante de mí en presencia de mis enemigos. Esto me lleva de nuevo a la gracia y el favor que Dios pone en tu vida, las cosas que no deberían suceder-suceden, y tus enemigos hacen que estés en paz, y sólo pueden ser testigos de lo que Dios está haciendo por ti y a través de ti.

Significa que cuando tus enemigos quieren luchar contra ti, Dios dice NO-y comienza a bendecirte en presencia de aquellos que pueden no gustarte o estar a tu favor.

En segundo lugar, dice: Unges mi cabeza con aceite. El aceite que aleja a los mosquitos, el aceite que te convierte en un repelente para aquellas cosas que podrían venir a hacerte daño. Te unge con aceite precioso, dándote un aroma dulce que atrae a la gente y a la bendición a tu vida. No me malinterpretes; no estoy diciendo que el enemigo no vendrá y te atacará, pero lo que estoy diciendo es que irán contra ti pero no prevalecerán contra ti.

La Biblia dice Salmos 91:7 "Mil pueden caer a tu lado y diez mil a tu derecha, Pero no vendrá contra ti".

Eso es lo que hace el aceite; te da una cobertura alrededor tuyo en la cual tus enemigos no pueden penetrar. Ese aceite sólo viene a través de tu búsqueda de Dios; cuanto más lo busques, más aceite te ungirá.

En tercer y último lugar, dice: Mi copa está llena. Aquí habla de la abundancia y de lo que a mí me gusta llamar impulso. Aquí en Canadá, tenemos un gran lugar que me gusta visitar: Las cataratas del Niagra.

Las cataratas del Niagra, en Ontario, son una ciudad canadiense en la que se encuentra la famosa cascada del mismo nombre, unida a Estados Unidos por el puente del arco iris. Se dice que las cataratas del Niagra tienen el mayor caudal del mundo. Unos veintiocho millones de litros o unos 700.000 galones de agua bajan por las cataratas del Niagra cada segundo.

Eso es mucha agua fluyendo, ¡y la Biblia dice que tu copa se llena! De repente, te llega tanta bendición que no puedes explicarla con una explicación humana, sólo dar la gloria a Dios.

Tu copa se desborda, lo que significa que tienes tanto impulso, y estás en un rollo tal que te expandes en formas que pensabas que nunca lo harías. Empiezas a dar pasos de gigante, saltos y saltos, hasta el punto de no poder explicar lo que está ocurriendo en ese momento, sólo para decir que Dios está detrás de lo que está ocurriendo.

Tu primer lugar de ganancia es sobre tus quillas en la oración; aquí es donde todo comienza, sobre tus rodillas. La oración te hace tener no sólo una relación con Dios, sino que te permite volar alto y ganar mucha distancia en la búsqueda de la visión y las metas que puedas tener.

La oración hace que corras más rápido, que vueles más alto, que subas más y que nunca te rindas en la búsqueda de lo que estás tratando de lograr.

LA RECTA FINAL

Me encanta ver las carreras de relevos en línea porque analizo constantemente por qué pusieron a ese corredor en esa posición de carrera. Sin embargo, la experiencia más estimulante es ese tramo final que lleva a la línea de meta. Cada corredor es cuidadosamente elegido y colocado estratégicamente para dar ventaja al equipo durante la carrera.

En 2015, en los Juegos Olímpicos de Pekín, los jamaicanos ganaron la carrera final de relevos 4x100 metros. Ver a Usain Bolt despegar en los últimos 100 metros fue tan emocionante que hay que verlo una y otra vez. Cada posición importa; cada segundo cuenta, los relevos deben ser perfectos para que el equipo tenga éxito.

En tu viaje hacia la línea de meta, debes recordar que cada asociación que tienes importa; cada vez que inviertes tiempo en alguien o en algo importa, y esa inversión producirá negativa o positivamente en tu vida.

Ves la línea de meta, el final está cerca, pero la parte más desafiante acaba de empezar; conseguir cruzar la línea de meta es fundamental, y normalmente, las batallas más complejas se dejan para el final.

A menudo he hablado del poder de la asociación, y cuando ves la línea de meta, esto se vuelve aún más importante que nunca. Soy un firme creyente de que hay que ser amable con todo el mundo, independientemente de cómo sean contigo. Sé que puede parecer más fácil decirlo que hacerlo, pero es la verdad: sé amable con todo el mundo.

Sé amable con la gente a todos los niveles porque una relación o asociación puede cambiar de la noche a la mañana. Esa relación o asociación a menudo puede marcar la diferencia entre cruzar la línea de la victoria o no cruzar esa línea en absoluto.

El éxito siempre está relacionado con el movimiento; debes ponerte en marcha; estos son los verdaderos principios de la grandeza; trabajar, tener una gran actitud, amor y amabilidad.

Tienes que ser el individuo que más trabaje en la sala; no puede haber nadie que te supere. El impulso que debes tener debe ser copiado por todos los demás; debes ser el primero en llegar y el último en salir. Tu ética de trabajo debe ser de primera categoría; una ética de trabajo de segunda categoría nunca alcanzará la grandeza.

La gracia te da confianza y postura; es un ejecutor silencioso que rodea poderosamente tu vida. La gracia es lo que otros ven en ti, pero tú mismo no lo ves. La gracia abre puertas que el dinero muchas veces no puede; te pone frente a personas que no podrían en otras circunstancias.

La gracia cubre tus errores, hace que tus defectos no se noten, te da un brillo cuando hablas y hace que tus enemigos estén en paz contigo.

En cambio, el orgullo es lo contrario a que tengas gracia; es un excelente divisor, que te cierra las puertas allá donde vayas. El orgullo es ofensivo y resulta desagradable. Si Dios mismo se resiste a los orgullosos y no puede soportar a una persona orgullosa, esto también ocurre de forma natural.

El orgullo acaba con la buena voluntad que los demás puedan sentir hacia ti; mata la disposición a ayudar a alguien, ofende a los demás, hiere, corta y, a menudo, quema puentes que nunca podrán ser reparados. Pero, por otro lado, el orgullo puede venir por los logros y o progresos que hagas, y es aquí donde debes tener cuidado de no destruir todo lo que has estado trabajando duro porque, en un momento, todo puede arruinarse.

Proverbios 11:12 "Cuando viene la soberbia, entonces viene la desgracia, pero con los humildes está la sabiduría."

1 Pedro 5:5: Igualmente, vosotros que sois más jóvenes, estad sujetos a los mayores. Revestíos todos de humildad unos con otros, porque "Dios se opone a los soberbios, pero da gracia a los humildes".

La humildad se caracteriza a menudo como una gratitud genuina y una falta de arrogancia, una visión modesta de uno mismo. Sin embargo, la definición bíblica de humildad va más allá. La humildad es un énfasis crítico y continuo de la piedad en la Biblia, ya que estamos llamados a ser humildes seguidores de Cristo y a confiar en la sabiduría y la salvación de Dios. Por lo tanto, seamos humildes ante nuestro creador por el don de la vida que se nos ha dado.

La humildad bíblica se basa en Dios. El Padre desciende para ayudar a los pobres y afligidos; el Hijo encarnado manifiesta humildad desde su nacimiento hasta su crucifixión. El uso conjunto de "manso" y "humilde de corazón" en Mateo 11:29 subraya la humildad de Cristo ante la humanidad, a la que vino a servir, y su sumisión ante Dios. La humildad y la mansedumbre suelen estar interrelacionadas, ya que ambas son rasgos justos para hacer la voluntad de Dios.

"Confía en el Señor con todo tu corazón y no te apoyes en tu entendimiento"; Proverbios 3:5

La importancia de la humildad está directamente relacionada con las consecuencias mortales del orgullo. El orgullo nos separa de Dios al no reconocer y apreciar la soberanía eterna de nuestro Señor. Por lo tanto, la importancia de la humildad se ve en la profunda gratitud que tenemos al reconocer debidamente la divinidad y el amor de Dios por nosotros. La importancia de la humildad también se encuentra en el reconocimiento de nuestra naturaleza defectuosa como seres humanos en la tierra y nuestra susceptibilidad al pecado si no estamos atentos a la tentación.

"Sed sobrios y velad. Vuestro adversario, el diablo, ronda como un león rugiente, buscando a quien devorar". ~ 1 Pedro 5:8

Durante la recta final, debes tener cuidado de no permitir que el orgullo nuble tu juicio y no dejar que los logros o los elogios que puedas recibir arruinen todo lo que has conseguido hasta ahora.

Mantenerse humilde significa reconocer que Dios fue quien le dio el poder para llegar hasta este punto y darse cuenta de que sin Él, nada sería posible, y gracias a Él, todas las cosas son posibles.

Juan 15:5 dice: "Yo soy la vid, vosotros los sarmientos. El que permanece en mí, y yo en él, da mucho fruto; porque sin mí nada podéis hacer".

2ª Timoteo 4:7-8 dice: "He peleado la buena batalla, he terminado la carrera, he guardado la Fe. Finalmente, me está reservada la corona de la justicia, que el Señor, el Juez justo, me dará en aquel día, y no sólo a mí, sino también a todos los que han amado su aparición."

La carrera no termina hasta que la haces, hasta que debes seguir trabajando duro, mantener la cabeza baja, reconocer a Dios en todos tus caminos y presionar, presionar, porque estás demasiado cerca para que todo se venga abajo.

Será muy tentador desviarse, por supuesto, debido a tus logros, perder el enfoque sin esfuerzo debido a los elogios que recibes, y todo esto sucede justo cuando estás cerca de alcanzar tus metas.

Hay una batalla para llegar a donde vas, pero nunca olvides que habrá una batalla para permanecer donde vas. La lucha no termina porque lo hayas conseguido; debes reconocer que lo has hecho pero que la guerra acaba de empezar. Durante ese tramo final, cuando veas el final a la vista no es el final; es el comienzo de algo nuevo. Está a punto de comenzar un nuevo capítulo en tu vida, y es aquí donde no debes bajar el ritmo ni dormirte en los laureles; es aquí donde te preparas, encuentras esa nueva fuerza y te esfuerzas aún más.

Todo lo que has hecho bien te ha llevado a este punto de tu vida, y ahora no es el momento de ceder. Recuerdo el invierno de 1997, cuando atravesé las puertas del 212 de la calle Murray por primera vez y le dije a mi padre: "Este es el lugar, papá". "

Lo habíamos conseguido, pensé; era el momento cumbre de la iglesia; estábamos a punto de construir nuestro primer edificio. Estaba vacío, pero ya podía ver a la gente, sucia, pero todo lo que podía ver era una belleza; esto era una obra maestra esperando a suceder.

Mientras recorríamos el edificio, me sentía como un niño en una tienda de caramelos, emocionado por lo que estaba a punto de suceder, emocionado por el comienzo de este nuevo capítulo. Recuerdo que le dije a mi madre lo emocionante que era esto, lo genial que sería; mi madre se limitó a sonreír y a aceptar mantener su alegría en el interior mientras el agente inmobiliario nos daba la gran visita al lugar.

Lo habíamos conseguido, pensé, lo que mi Padre había predicado durante tantos años, por fin salía a la luz; lo que se había hablado y soñado por fin veía la luz del día. Ahora sólo había que poner los puntos sobre las íes, y el sueño se había cumplido. Pero, ¿lo estaba?

Mi mente había saltado de lo sucio a lo bello y se había saltado todo lo que había entre medias. Había ido de lo vacío a lo lleno y había obviado todo lo necesario para llegar allí. Pensé que mi resultado se manifestaría instantáneamente en un chasquido de dedos, y vaya si me equivoqué.

A menudo nos quedamos atrapados en las imágenes del producto acabado y olvidamos que hay un proceso para llegar a él, y no siempre es bonito.

El edificio estaba al revés y del revés, pero mi presente no vio nada de eso; todo lo que vi fue el producto acabado y pulido. Así que lo mejor sería entusiasmarse con el producto terminado, pero nunca deprimirse al contemplar el proceso para llegar a él.

La compra del edificio era sólo el comienzo, pero para mí era el final, sin darme cuenta de que el camino hacia la grandeza en la consecución de tus objetivos y sueños nunca termina; está en constante crecimiento y expansión.

Estamos a punto de celebrar 25 años de ministerio en el 212 de la calle Murray, aquí mismo, en la capital del país, y puedo decir sinceramente que no hemos llegado a la meta final, ni mucho menos. Hemos pasado por múltiples renovaciones, amplias reparaciones y modificaciones, y aún queda por hacer.

Se han gastado miles de dólares en mejorar y adaptarse a los tiempos a lo largo de los años, y aún no hemos terminado. Las cosas que una vez fueron estupendas se han quedado obsoletas, pero no nos achantamos al pensar en la cantidad de dinero que se ha ido por la puerta; nos damos cuenta de que era el precio a pagar en este camino que llamamos ministerio.

No puedes mirar hacia atrás y reprenderte por las decisiones que debiste tomar o el camino que debiste cruzar; no importa qué decisión tomaste o qué ruta decidiste seguir, eso te ha traído a este punto aquí y ahora. No podemos cambiar el pasado, pero sí podemos influir en nuestro futuro.

Si nos detenemos por un momento y nos damos cuenta de que deberíamos estar agradecidos por no estar muertos o peor en el infierno, entonces deberíamos estar agradecidos por tener la oportunidad de cambiar nuestro futuro ahora mientras estamos en el presente. Mirar hacia atrás con arrepentimiento no hace bien a nadie; ¿qué podrías haber sido? Y tantas otras preguntas son un sinsentido y una completa pérdida de tiempo y energía.

En ese momento en el que crees que lo has conseguido y has llegado a la meta, da un paso atrás, respira y date cuenta de que has llegado al final de un hito, pero que otro está a punto de empezar.

El tramo final suele ser el más difícil porque está lleno de emoción y de ilusión. Emoción porque has creído de verdad que lo has conseguido, pero ilusión porque el camino sigue su curso. Entonces, ¿por qué se llama tramo final?

Cada hito tiene un "tramo final" cada vez que llegas al final del paso de crecimiento en tu vida; entras en esa zona en la que muchos fracasan. Entonces, finalmente, llegas a ese punto en el que piensas y crees que lo has conseguido, y de repente levantas las manos al aire y lo celebras, pero sólo para darte cuenta de que el siguiente paso está a punto de empezar.

Muchos se desaniman porque, al igual que yo, se lanzan al resultado final cuando no vemos que llegar a nuestra meta es algo que cambia y evoluciona constantemente, y nunca terminamos. Repito que no puedes desanimarte ante el hecho de que lo que creías que era el "todo" es sólo el principio para que tus sueños y objetivos se cumplan.

Cuando un avión viaja del punto A al punto B, debe pasar por unos "marcadores" específicos en su ruta hacia su destino. Estos marcadores permiten a los pilotos saber que están en el camino correcto hacia su destino. El piloto no celebra el marcador; lo celebra hasta que ha llegado a su destino.

Cada marcador debe ser celebrado en la vida porque representan nuestro crecimiento en madurez, conocimiento, confianza, obediencia y relación con Dios. Observamos que cada día aprendemos y crecemos a través de las experiencias por las que podemos pasar. Cada adversidad y prueba que enfrentamos son una oportunidad si dejamos que nos mejoren y nos conviertan en una mejor persona mientras nos esforzamos por alcanzar la meta.

Una vez que aceptes el hecho de que nuestra verdadera meta es el cielo y que las metas terrenales son necesarias pero son secundarias a nuestra meta eterna, entonces estaremos en paz cuando alcancemos esos hitos que parecían el final pero que, en realidad, son sólo el lugar de nacimiento de tu siguiente nivel.

¡El nacimiento del NUEVO TÚ!

AQUÍ ES DONDE COMIENZA EL NUEVO TÚ

2ª Corintios 5:17 "Por lo tanto, si alguien está en Cristo, es una nueva creación; las cosas viejas han pasado; he aquí que todo es nuevo".

Siempre hay un nivel mayor, y cada nivel mayor requiere un tú mayor. Has llegado hasta aquí para no volver atrás, pero has alcanzado y cruzado el punto de no retorno.

Múltiples señales te indican lo que puedes y no puedes llevar a través del control de seguridad cuando viajas y estás a punto de pasar por el control de seguridad. No importa a dónde vayas, ni el motivo por el que vayas, todo el mundo debe pasar por este control de seguridad. Si llevas algo que no debes llevar, se te negará la entrada.

Cuanto más alta sea tu búsqueda de la grandeza, requerirá cambios específicos en tu vida que no irán bien con el lugar al que Dios quiere llevarte. Ciertas cosas que pueden haber funcionado para usted en el pasado pueden no funcionar con usted en el futuro. Los métodos, planes y estrategias que pueden haberte ayudado anteriormente no significan que funcionarán en esta nueva temporada o nivel en el que estás a punto de embarcarte.

Uno de los mayores errores que puedes cometer es vivir una nueva temporada con una vieja mentalidad. La palabra dice, "todas las cosas son hechas nuevas", no algunas, sino todas las cosas son hechas nuevas.

Cada persona perseguirá sus propias metas y sueños, y no uno es mejor que el otro, sino que no debes mirar cuál es la visión de tus amigos o familiares y comparar la tuya con la de ellos; debes alcanzar tus sueños y metas.

Alcanza ese sueño, ora por ese sueño, ayuna y siembra por él, porque al hacerlo, activarás tu Fe, y Dios responderá. No te detengas hasta que alcances la meta, y cuando lo hagas, encuentra en ti la capacidad de superarte y pasar a la siguiente estación.

Ya que hay un nuevo tú, habrá nuevos retos, nuevos gigantes que enfrentar, nuevas adversidades vendrán a tu camino, pero recuerda que la Biblia dice, en 1 Juan 4:4, "Vosotros sois de Dios, hijitos, y los habéis vencido; porque mayor es el que está en vosotros que el que está en el mundo".

Dios siempre será más grande que esas cosas, incluyendo las personas que se levantarán contra ti. Debes creer que eres digno de esa bendición que estás persiguiendo. No puedes permitir que nadie te diga que eres indigno de tus metas y sueños debido a tu pasado.

Tu pasado no te descalifica todas las cosas buenas, pero a través de la sangre de Jesús, somos una nueva creación, el viejo tú es lavado y de nuevo, todas las cosas son hechas frescas, incluyéndote a ti.

A menudo la gente deja de perseguir sus sueños y metas porque los demás les dicen que son locos o descabellados. Esas son frases indirectas que te dicen que no eres digno. Esa negatividad es tan venenosa que paraliza a la persona haciéndole creer que no merece un sueño o una meta tan descabellada.

Tus sueños, objetivos, aspiraciones y visiones deben ser enormes. Sin embargo, lo mejor sería recordar que los sueños, objetivos, aspiraciones e ideas más pequeños deben completarse antes para llegar al producto final. Conseguir estas cosas al final te permitirá llegar a ese producto final.

Cuando se construye un coche, siempre se empieza con un renderizado del coche, se hacen modificaciones, se sacan diseños en 3D y, tras varias versiones, el fabricante decide el producto final.

Tras la aprobación de los renders, se procede a la construcción del coche; primero se fabrica el armazón del vehículo, seguido de todos los demás componentes y, tras varias semanas, el coche sale y llega al concesionario listo para que sus nuevos propietarios tomen posesión de él.

Había un proceso para crear el coche; ahora, el diseñador no se desanima porque el vehículo no aparezca al instante ni se frustra porque tenga que hacer revisiones; no, sabía que había un proceso. Cuando entiendes el proceso, la frustración no tiene cabida en tu vida.

Repito, cada nuevo nivel requiere un nuevo tú, una nueva forma de pensar, hablar, comprometerse y adaptarse. Dicen que no se pueden enseñar trucos nuevos a un perro viejo, ¡oh, pero sí se puede!

Cuando tienes un sueño, a menudo te susurra; Dios no grita, te susurra. Cuanto más cerca estés de Dios, más suave será su voz. Dios debe ser tu fuente de inspiración; cuando se convierta en tu fuente de inspiración, empezarás a recibir sabiduría y comprensión en todas las cosas que hagas y quieras hacer.

Nunca te rindas; sin compromiso, nunca empezarás nada; sin constancia, nunca terminarás; no es fácil; si lo fuera, la historia sería diferente. Así que en lugar de eso, debes seguir trabajando en el nuevo tú, caer siete veces pero levantarte ocho, golpearte a ti mismo para reconocer que el viejo tú no puede llevarte más allá de puntos específicos de tu vida.

1ª Corintios 13:11 dice: "Cuando era niño, hablaba como niño, entendía como niño, pensaba como niño; pero cuando me hice hombre, dejé las cosas de niño".

Debes crecer cada día, buscar a Dios, crecer en madurez, conocimiento, obediencia, sumisión y respeto. Crecer en el aprecio por los demás, crecer en tu amor por la palabra de Dios, crecer en el deseo de estar cerca de Dios y escuchar su voz.

Uno de mis factores de motivación más significativos para continuar este viaje es la duda, y la incredulidad que otros pueden tener en mí o en mis sueños. Su duda sobre mí me motiva a esforzarme más, a servir mejor, a alcanzar lo más alto y a superar a todos los presentes.

El nuevo tú tendrá que dejar muchas cosas atrás, adaptarse a nuevos entornos y, sobre todo, seguir persiguiendo la grandeza para la que Dios te ha llamado. Por supuesto, el viejo tú se aferrará y luchará por no dejarlo ir, pero es imperativo que renuncies a tu viejo nuevo y aceptes el nuevo tú al que Dios te ha llamado.

El nuevo tú debe aceptar que surgirán desafíos más significativos, y por lo tanto tu vocabulario debe cambiar, las palabras que salgan de tu boca deben estar alineadas con la palabra de Dios. Por lo tanto, es crucial para el nuevo tú entrar en la palabra de Dios, memorizarla, estudiarla, declararla y vivir de acuerdo a ella.

La Biblia dice en 2 Corintios 5:7, "Porque por fe andamos, no por vista".

Tu viejo yo quiere caminar basado en lo que ve y escucha, basado en una experiencia que le ayude a seguir caminando. El viejo tú necesita evidencia para creer, necesita cosas que se sienten para caminar. El nuevo tú no necesita nada de lo natural; no requiere de lo que se oye, se siente y se ve para caminar; nuestra confianza está en el Señor Dios, y esa es la energía que necesitamos para caminar.

El nuevo tú no necesita que la motivación o el estímulo vengan de otra persona; eso lo encuentras en el Señor. Así que 1 Samuel 30:6 dice, "...pero David se animó en el Señor su Dios.

Encuentra el ánimo y la motivación en saber que todo es posible con Dios, y que nada es posible sin Dios. Porque si no aceptas este hecho, ¿cuándo verás la Gloria de Dios manifestada en tu vida?

Ahora es el momento para que el nuevo tú surja de las cenizas y entierre tu viejo tú. Dejar ir aquellas cosas que te han servido sólo para bloquearte, liberarte de la culpa, la vergüenza y tu pasado, y aceptar que hoy Dios te ha llamado para algo más grande.

Cada día, mes, año, hora y segundo que pasa viviendo en el viejo tú, lleno de decepciones y fracasos, de culpa y vergüenza, es un momento que nunca volverá a nosotros. Por supuesto, nunca vuelve a nosotros cuando pasa el tiempo, pero la semilla que plantamos en ese momento dará frutos en nuestro mañana. Sean buenos o malos, esas semillas te ayudarán a crecer o te mantendrán en los pozos de la desesperación.

Porque este es el momento, este es el momento en el que debes decidir levantarte y hacerte cargo ante todo de ti mismo. Conviértete en una nueva versión de ti mismo, redefine quién eres, desafíate a ser mejor; este es ese momento. La Biblia dice, en Eclesiastés 3:1, "Hay un tiempo para todo y una temporada para cada actividad bajo el cielo".

Pues esta es la temporada en la que Dios quiere hacer grandes cosas contigo, a través de ti y para ti.

SI NO ES AHORA, ¿CUÁNDO?

¿Cuándo es el momento adecuado para hacer algo? ¿Debemos esperar hasta que no tengamos problemas? ¿O hasta que tengamos todo el dinero necesario? ¿Cuándo es el momento adecuado para actuar?

Si esperamos a que todo se alinee, podríamos estar aquí algún tiempo. Si Pedro hubiera esperado a que las aguas se calmaran, es posible que entonces nunca hubiera caminado sobre las aguas; si Daniel hubiera esperado a que no hubiera un decreto, nunca habría visto las maravillas de Dios en el foso de los leones.

Si David hubiera esperado a hacerse más grande y fuerte, Goliat no habría sido derrotado. Si estos hombres, entre otros, hubieran esperado a actuar, tendríamos una historia diferente para leer en la Biblia.

Si esperamos a que las cosas sean perfectas para actuar, nunca funcionaremos porque nada será perfecto. La Biblia dice, Proverbios 3:5-6, "Hay un tiempo para todo, y una temporada para cada actividad bajo los cielos".

Pedro tuvo que confiar en Dios, y caminó sobre el agua; Daniel tuvo que ser fiel en su oración, y Dios envió la liberación, David tuvo que creer en sí mismo, y su Dios y Goliat bajaron.

No puedes sentarte a esperar que las cosas se resuelvan solas, a veces lo hacen, pero debes arremangarte y ponerte a trabajar cuando no lo hacen. Esperar que Dios lo haga todo es una completa pérdida de tiempo y energía. Dios nunca hará lo que tú debes hacer, él hace lo que tú no puedes hacer, pero espera que tú hagas lo que te ha dado la capacidad de hacer.

No hay un momento perfecto para hacer nada; no hay un escenario correcto para empezar, tú debes decidirlo y depende de ti decirte a ti mismo, ¡este es mi momento! La fe no espera el momento adecuado; la fe crea el momento para actuar. La fe no espera a que las estrellas se alineen; la fe es audaz y activa, la fe provoca el movimiento.

Las excusas te dicen que debes esperar el tiempo correcto, y sí, como dije antes, hay un tiempo y una temporada para todo bajo el sol, pero debes actuar cuando se trata de tu Fe.

La Biblia dice, Santiago 2:14, "¿De qué sirve, hermanos míos, que alguien diga que tiene fe y no tenga obras? ¿Puede la fe salvarle?

El versículo 18 dice: "Pero alguien dirá: "Tú tienes fe, y yo tengo obras". Muéstrame tu fe sin tus obras, y yo te mostraré mi fe por mis obras

Este es un verso poderoso, especialmente al final, cuando dice, "¡Te mostraré mi fe por mis obras!"

Tus obras resultan directamente de tu Fe y viceversa; tu falta de obras resulta directamente de tu falta de confianza. Así que decir que estás esperando el momento "adecuado" es simplemente enmascarar el hecho de que tienes razones por las que no quieres empezar.

Pueden ser razones justificables o puntos de vista válidos, pero la realidad es que si nunca te decides a empezar, nunca lo harás. ¿Cuándo será un buen momento? Por muy buen momento que parezca, siempre habrá cosas que no sean perfectas, y si te centras en las cosas que no están bien, servirán para bloquearte incluso antes de empezar.

Las excusas a menudo se enmascaran como cosas legítimas, y por favor, entiéndeme, puede que lo sean. Sin embargo, estoy tratando de transmitir que si siempre dejas que esas cosas te detengan, ¿cuándo conseguirás hacer las cosas?

Ester era una mujer audaz, confiada en su vocación, de mente sana, pero su momento no era el mejor. No podía acercarse al rey sin ser llamada; hacerlo significaría una muerte segura. Estaba entre la espada y la pared; el enemigo la rodeaba, las restricciones estaban fuera de su control, pero sabía lo que tenía que hacer.

Sabiendo cuál era la ley y el castigo por acercarse al rey sin avisar, decidió hacer lo impensable. Con una frase, selló su destino y lo dejó en manos de Dios cuando dijo en Ester 4:16: "Ve, reúne a todos los judíos que se encuentran en Susa, y ayunad por mí; y no comáis ni bebáis durante tres días, ni de noche ni de día. Así también ayunaremos yo y mis doncellas. Y así entraré al rey, lo cual no es conforme a la ley; y si perezco, perezco".

Ella no podía esperar el momento adecuado o ser llamada por el rey; necesitaba activar su Fe y actuar de acuerdo a su Fe y a lo que había que hacer. Hay momentos en los que hay que esperar a que ocurran ciertas cosas para poder trabajar, pero también hay momentos en los que hay que actuar antes de que llegue el momento adecuado.

Ambos puntos de vista son esenciales, pero si te quedas atascado en esperar siempre el tiempo, el momento o la circunstancia adecuados para actuar, entonces puede que el momento nunca llegue a ti. Durante tu búsqueda para lograr lo que Dios te ha llamado a hacer, te encontrarás con momentos que requerirán que esperes a que se abra una ventana; esos momentos necesitan paciencia, consejo y guía.

Paciencia para ver que la ventana se abre lo suficiente como para que aproveches tu oportunidad, recibir consejo sobre si debes actuar o no, y orientación de aquellos que han pasado por ello para que no se repitan errores similares.

Luego están esos momentos en los que se requiere fe en la acción. Nuevamente, Pedro para caminar sobre las aguas no tomó un voto de los otros discípulos; no revisó para ver cómo se sentían sobre él caminando sobre el agua. Pedro tampoco esperó hasta que no hubiera tormenta y los mares estuvieran en calma. Pedro reaccionó con fe, asumió el momento y caminó sobre las aguas.

Habrá días para que des un paso atrás y analices la situación, pero luego habrá días en los que deberás actuar y ver las maravillas que Dios tiene para ti.

Ester dijo, ¡bien, si perezco, perezco! Sin embargo, ella estaba dispuesta a arriesgar su propia vida para ver que ocurriera un milagro.

Daniel 3:16-18 dice: Sadrac, Mesac y Abednego respondieron y dijeron al rey: Oh Nabucodonosor, no tenemos cuidado de responderte en este asunto. Si es así, nuestro Dios, a quien servimos, puede librarnos del horno de fuego ardiente, y nos librará de tu mano, oh rey. Pero si no es así, que sepas, oh rey, que no serviremos a tus dioses, ni adoraremos la imagen de oro que has levantado.

Y si no, que sepas, oh rey, que no serviremos a tus dioses ni adoraremos la imagen de oro que has levantado. Como dicen, trazaron una línea en la arena, y se mantuvieron firmes.

Frente a un horno de fuego, frente a la muerte, se mantuvieron firmes y declararon audazmente su fe en Dios. Esa audaz declaración les hizo actuar "desafiantemente" ante el rey, pero era la única salida.

Ante la perspectiva de la muerte, eligieron defender con valentía aquello en lo que creían en lugar de ceder para salvar su propia vida. ¿Qué estás dispuesto a hacer ahora? ¿Estás dispuesto a ceder o a resistir?

Tú, y sólo tú, puedes tomar esa decisión; debes ser dueño de la decisión y mantenerte firme en ella, sin importar lo que te ocurra. Debes apartar el miedo de tu mente, de tu corazón y de tus palabras. Debes ser capaz de levantarte y decir,

"¿Qué diremos entonces a estas cosas? Si Dios está a nuestro favor, ¿quién podrá estar en contra de nosotros? Romanos 8:31

Ese "quién" puede simbolizar una persona o una cosa, ese "quién" debe ser derrotado en tu vida, aunque ese "quién" seas tú mismo.

Estamos en una temporada que es tan impredecible, tantas variables están sucediendo a nuestro alrededor, y las cosas están cambiando a cada minuto. Así que la palabra de Dios dice, en 2 Timoteo 1:7, "Porque no nos ha dado Dios un espíritu de temor, sino de poder y de amor y de una mente sana".

El miedo no puede tener un lugar en tus pensamientos y o palabras. El miedo no puede tener un lugar para vivir en tu mente; el miedo no puede tener un lugar en cómo vives; debes ser libre de todo lo libre.

La única manera de liberarte del miedo es rodeándote y sumergiéndote en la presencia de Dios. Entonces, estarás libre de ese miedo cuando lo hagas, y podrás tomar decisiones claras y directas sobre tu futuro.

Cometerás errores en tu toma de decisiones, te equivocarás, tomarás el camino equivocado, y a veces tomarás decisiones horribles de las que luego te arrepentirás. Pero recuerde, "Pero en cuanto a usted, usted quiso hacer el mal contra mí; pero Dios quiso hacer el bien para que se produjera como en este día, para salvar a mucha gente con vida. Génesis 50:20

A veces te equivocarás, pero Dios, en su infinita sabiduría, en su gran gracia, te dará la vuelta a las cosas de la manera que Él sólo sabe hacerlo.

Pedro pudo haber pensado fácilmente cuando se estaba ahogando, "este fue un movimiento equivocado de mi parte" ¿cuántas veces has dicho esas palabras? Te puedo decir que yo he dicho esas palabras muchas veces durante mi vida. Sin embargo, a lo largo de todos mis errores, he llegado a la conclusión de que la misericordia de Dios es tan inmensa y muy especial que nos da gracia y compasión incluso cuando deberíamos recibir un juicio.

Momentos en que somos culpables, nos da un perdón, que este el gran amor de Dios. Puede que nunca seamos capaces de entenderlo o comprenderlo, pero la realidad es que si confiamos en el Señor con todo nuestro corazón, entonces podemos tener la garantía de que su misericordia nunca nos fallará.

Puede que tengas razón, pero Dios es absoluto, tú puedes tener una perspectiva, Dios lo ve todo, nosotros podemos tener una idea, Dios tiene el camino; porque sin Dios, no podemos hacer nada.

Es mi sincera oración que tu vida sea edificada y desafiada a hacer lo impensable a través de este libro. Rezo para que te levantes hoy y persigas el sueño, la meta o la visión que Dios ha puesto en tu corazón y que lo veas realizado.

Porque esta es la temporada, que es el momento que Dios ha estado esperando, el momento en que decides levantarte, desempolvarte y ser lo que Dios te ha llamado a ser.

Tus problemas son tan grandes como tú les des crédito, y Dios puede ser tan grande como tu fe se lo permita. Entonces, puedes levantarte hoy y lograr lo que te propongas.

Sé el Daniel que fue implacable en la oración, sé la intrépida Débora, sé el David que derribó a un gigante y salvó a una nación, sé la Ester y levántate ante la incertidumbre, sé el Pedro que caminó sobre las aguas.

La Biblia está llena de héroes de la fe y nada menos que nuestro Señor y Salvador Jesucristo.

De nuevo, el mundo está lleno de héroes, pero ahora es el momento de que se escriba un nuevo capítulo y surja un nuevo héroe, ¡y ese héroe tienes que ser tú!

Sé el héroe para tu familia, el héroe para tus amigos, sé el héroe para ti mismo. Reconoce que Dios está de tu lado, y que nunca te dejará ni te abandonará.

Este es tu momento y tu tiempo, agárralo, conquista el momento, levántate, levántate y grita desde la cima de la montaña;

¡HE SIDO DESTINADO A LA GRANDEZA!

DESTINÉ À LA GRANDEUR ET C'EST AINSI QUE TOUT COMMENCE....

C'est là que tout commence, une auto-déclaration de qui vous êtes, car tant que nous n'aborderons pas l'ancien vous, le NOUVEAU VOUS ne pourra jamais apparaître. Vous devez donc être honnête pour aborder l'ancien vous, ouvert à l'idée d'aborder vos défauts, car lorsque vous le faites, vous vous libérez des chaînes et la liberté est vécue pour commencer le processus vers votre destinée.

Des faiblesses? Ai-je des défauts? C'est la première question qui met tout en perspective. Avez-vous des défauts? La réponse à cette question est: je n'ai que des faiblesses. Je ne suis pas naturellement sûr de moi, rapide ou souple; je ne suis certainement pas l'homme le plus intelligent du monde; je deviens émotif pour des choses pour lesquelles je ne devrais pas l'être.

Je mange les mauvais aliments, je ne dors pas assez, je procrastine et je perds mon temps. Je me soucie trop des choses sans importance et pas assez des choses essentielles.

Mon ego est trop grand, et mon esprit trop petit pour essayer ne serait-ce que de commencer à comprendre les plans illimités que Dieu a pour ma vie. Mes pensées sont donc piégées, souvent à l'intérieur d'elles-mêmes.

Cela dit, j'ai un dicton qui dit à peu près ceci: la force d'une personne est souvent sa plus grande faiblesse. Pourtant, leurs défauts peuvent devenir des forces.

Vous ne pouvez pas accepter la façon dont le monde vous étiquette ou vous définit. Vous ne pouvez pas accepter leurs conclusions sur la façon dont vous allez finir, surtout s'ils déclarent que vous êtes voué à l'échec et condamné à n'aller nulle part.

Les prévisions du monde sur vous et vos objectifs sont sombres et peu encourageantes. Souvent, nous passons tellement de temps à lire ces prévisions et à les entendre qu'elles deviennent soudainement ce que vous croyez et ce que vous êtes. Il s'empare de votre esprit et de vos émotions et se manifeste dans votre vocabulaire, vous façonnant en quelque chose d'extérieur au plan et au moule de Dieu pour votre vie.

Nous sommes tellement pris par l'opinion que chacun a de nous que nous oublions le chemin que nous devrions suivre. Le combat est honnête, précis chaque jour, du moment où vous ouvrez les yeux au moment où vous les fermez, et il semble que le combat soit terminé alors, mais il continue dans vos rêves et vos pensées.

Je me bats tous les jours, je lutte, je me débats, je gratte, et je m'attaque à ces faiblesses parce que la bataille est réelle! Votre plus grand ennemi, c'est VOUS; votre plus grand défi, c'est VOUS. La lutte pour changer vos faiblesses est réelle; la lutte pour empêcher vos faiblesses de se développer est réelle, et soit elle vous vainc, soit vous la vainquez.

Il y a des jours où je gagne, et d'autres où je ne gagne pas, mais chaque jour je me relève et j'avance, les poings serrés, l'œil sur le prix, avec tout ce que j'ai pour surmonter ces faiblesses. Alors je me relève et je cours vers le combat, vers la lutte, vers la peur qui me regarde en face, car la seule façon de réussir est de ne JAMAIS FAIRE FACE, mais de toujours se lever et se battre.

Vos lacunes et vos insécurités crieront toujours à tue-tête pour essayer de vous faire dévier de votre chemin, mais si vous pouvez vous réveiller chaque matin et décider que vous serez meilleur aujourd'hui qu'hier, alors mon cher ami, vous avez commencé à gagner ce combat. Beaucoup de gens décideront que vous êtes une menace pour eux, que vos objectifs sont une menace pour eux, et c'est là que vous décidez de céder ou d'insister.

Vous n'êtes pas façonné par ce que disent les autres; vous êtes façonné chaque jour par ce que vous vous dites à vous-même. La Bible dit: "Je puis tout par le Christ qui me fortifie" Phil 4:13. Ce mot est une déclaration qui devrait être prononcée dans votre vie chaque jour et chaque minute de votre vie. Il commence par dire "Je peux"! Pensez-y un instant.....I CAN! et il continue en disant, FAITES TOUTES LES CHOSES! Cela signifie que vous pouvez faire toutes les choses! Si ce mot ou cette phrase ne vous excite pas et ne vous motive pas, je ne pense pas que quoi que ce soit puisse le faire.

Mais voici la clé, il dit par le Christ qui me fortifie! Donc, vous pouvez faire toutes choses, mais vous ne pouvez pas faire toutes choses sans Christ. Jean 15:5 dit: "Je suis la vigne, vous êtes les sarments. Celui qui demeure en moi, et moi en lui, porte beaucoup de fruit; car sans moi vous ne pouvez rien faire.

Encore une fois, il nous dit que nous pouvons porter beaucoup de fruits SI nous demeurons en lui, et ce SI est important! Nos faiblesses nous font souvent sortir du chemin qui nous permet de porter du fruit. Nos faiblesses assèchent notre Foi et notre vie de Prière si on les laisse faire. Et il termine la phrase en disant une expression définitive, et c'est CAR SANS MOI VOUS NE POUVEZ RIEN FAIRE! Non seulement c'est une déclaration audacieuse, mais c'est une déclaration qui ne laisse aucune place à la négociation; laissez-moi vous expliquer...

Nous voulons souvent négocier avec Dieu ou jouer la carte de la victime avec Lui. Mais, malheureusement, cela ne fonctionne pas! Il nous a donné la clé du succès, la clé de la grandeur et cette clé, c'est LUI!

En LUI se trouve le pouvoir de surmonter une grande partie de ce que nous essayons de surmonter et d'échouer par nous-mêmes. Je peux vous dire tout ce que j'ai fait, mais la seule chose que je ne peux pas faire est de moudre pour vous! Nous lisons les clés, entendons le message, et pensons que juste parce que nous le lisons ou l'écoutons, tout d'un coup, il va se manifester en quelque chose d'extraordinaire dans notre vie. C'est alors que nous commençons à échouer, cet état d'esprit s'empare fréquemment de nous, et si nous ne nous battons pas, nous serons vaincus avant même de commencer.

J'adore regarder les émissions sur la nature, principalement celles où les prédateurs chassent leurs proies. J'aime analyser leurs pensées, leurs mouvements, tant du côté du prédateur que de la cible. Par exemple, regardez la gazelle et le lion pendant un moment. Quelle est la différence entre la gazelle et le lion, à part l'évidence? La gazelle court toujours dans la peur; elle sait que ses jours sont comptés tant que le lion est là. Elle court dans la peur, sachant qu'au moment où elle se relâche, elle meurt.

Leur peur est leur moteur, et beaucoup de gens ne sont souvent pas conduits par Dieu, ni par leurs objectifs et leurs visions; leur peur les conduit. La peur vous poussera toujours vers votre mort. Vous avez souvent entendu l'expression: "Quel est votre pourquoi? "Le lion ne demande pas pourquoi; il fait ce qu'il fait de mieux: il chasse! Le problème avec cette question, c'est qu'on la trouve souvent sans aucune substance. Votre "Pourquoi" n'est pas essentiel si votre "Pourquoi" ne l'inclut pas LUI. Dieu doit être au centre de tout ce que nous faisons et de ce que nous sommes.

Chaque opportunité doit être saisie comme si c'était la dernière opportunité que vous aurez jamais. Mais, en réalité, c'est peut-être le cas, car nous ne savons pas quand la Mort viendra frapper à notre porte et nous rappellera à la maison. Donc, la vraie question devrait être: qu'est-ce qui vous motive? Qu'est-ce qui vous excite? Qu'est-ce qui vous donne envie de vous lever chaque matin? Chaque jour, vous devez vous remettre en question, en apprenant toujours, en grandissant toujours, car le jour où vous vous satisferez est le jour où vous ne vivrez plus; vous existerez mais ne vivrez pas.

Le jour où tu arrêtes de grandir, le jour où tu arrêtes d'apprendre, le jour où tu arrêtes de te reprocher, c'est le jour où tu meurs intérieurement, et c'est le jour où la personne qui essayait de te dépasser le fait.

Je suis ici pour vous dire que vous ne pouvez pas pleurer parce que vous avez abandonné, pleurez parce que vous allez continuer, ne pleurez pas pour abandonner! Tu as déjà mal, tu as déjà des bleus, tu as fait tout ce chemin et maintenant tu veux t'arrêter? Vous êtes déjà blessé, autant en tirer une récompense.

Une femme sur le point d'accoucher ne s'arrête pas simplement parce que les contractions sont trop rapprochées ou que la douleur est insupportable? NON! Elle va de l'avant parce qu'elle est sur le point de donner naissance à quelqu'un d'incroyable. Vous devriez faire de même, il n'y a pas de place pour l'abandon, il n'y a pas de place pour l'arrêt, il n'y a pas de place pour le ralentissement lorsque les contractions de la vie vous frappent l'une après l'autre, vous n'abandonnez pas-vous poussez en avant et vers l'avant.

LE COMBAT EST RÉEL!

Oui, il l'est, et on dit que vous devez vous battre, mais je vous le dis plus souvent qu'à mon tour, vous ne vous battrez pas du tout; vous gagnerez. Mais vous devez intégrer cette attitude dans votre vie quotidienne. Faites ce que les autres ne font pas, faites ce qui vous retourne l'estomac, car c'est souvent ce qui rapporte le plus. En termes de gymnastique, faites la répétition supplémentaire, courez les 5 minutes supplémentaires, essayez un exercice que vous n'aimez pas parce que ce qui vous fait sortir de votre zone de confort vous amènera plus haut et plus près de vos objectifs.

Les choses qui nous effraient, celles qui nous intimident et celles qui semblent impossibles sont les choses que vous devez et devez faire parce que ce qui se cache derrière ces mirages d'impossibilités sont des récompenses qui dépassent de loin nos attentes.

J'avais une vingtaine d'années, je regardais mon premier-né, juste un bébé qui dormait, puis je me suis regardée dans le miroir et j'ai réalisé que je devais changer ma vie, sinon, il était possible que mon fils ne vive jamais longtemps. J'avais 25 ans et j'étais dans la pire forme de ma vie, physiquement parlant. J'étais en surpoids et je me sentais comme un morse, sans vouloir offenser le morse. À ce moment-là, j'ai décidé que ça suffisait, que j'allais agir sur ma santé pour changer la trajectoire de ma vie, et que j'allais le faire pour mon fils.

Beaucoup de gens font une erreur parce qu'ils veulent plaire à tout le monde et rendre les autres heureux tout en vivant misérablement. Mais, malheureusement, vous devez le faire pour vous et votre premier! Psaume 139:14 Je te rendrai grâce parce que j'ai été créé de façon si étonnante et miraculeuse. Tes œuvres sont miraculeuses, et mon âme en est pleinement consciente.

Éphésiens 5:29 Car personne n'a jamais haï son propre corps, mais il le nourrit et en prend tendrement soin, comme le Seigneur le fait pour l'Église.

Il est essentiel que vous vous fixiez un objectif et que vous soyez heureux et motivé. Ce n'est pas être égoïste; non, en agissant ainsi, vous étendez la joie que vous apportez à quelqu'un d'autre. Hypothétiquement parlant, je me suis regardé dans le miroir et j'ai décidé que j'étais bien comme je suis et que je devais être accepté tel que je suis. Quelle erreur cela aurait été.

Mon manque d'action aurait causé une grande souffrance à moi-même et à ma famille. Des complications de santé auraient annulé toute activité future que j'aurais pu partager avec mon fils; j'aurais également apporté du stress à ma femme, tout cela parce que j'avais décidé de ne rien faire.

LE PRIX À PAYER POUR NE RIEN FAIRE

Le prix à payer est élevé et douloureux, mais un prix doit être payé. Vous voyez donc que, quel que soit le chemin que vous décidez de prendre, vous en paierez le prix! Il est garanti que le prix que vous paierez pour ne rien faire sera toujours plus élevé et plus coûteux que le prix à payer pour faire quelque chose afin de changer votre vie. Alors faites les bons choix, renforcez-vous mentalement, physiquement et spirituellement.

Si vous ne faites rien, votre faiblesse fera tout pour devenir dominante dans votre vie. Quand vous ne faites rien, la peur grandit; les problèmes deviennent plus importants qu'ils ne le sont; quand vous ne faites rien, le chaos éclate; quand vous ne faites rien, le mal prévaut. Vous voyez, le coût de l'inaction est exceptionnellement élevé et douloureux. Il vous fait reculer de plusieurs jours, voire de plusieurs années. Ne rien faire vous envoie sur une route remplie de dépression, de tristesse, de frustrations et de déceptions. Lorsque vous ne faites rien, vous tuez l'essence même de ce que Dieu a mis en vous.

Proverbes 19:8 Acquérir la sagesse, c'est s'aimer soi-même; les gens qui aiment l'intelligence prospéreront. Acquérir signifie agir, il faut faire quelque chose au lieu de ne rien faire. Acquérir quelque chose, c'est investir dans la connaissance de ce que vous allez réaliser, c'est-à-dire agir et ne pas rester immobile.

Chaque jour est un combat, combat contre la peur, combat contre la faiblesse, contre le temps, contre la décadence, contre le désir de ne rien faire; chaque jour est un combat que vous seul devez mener pour réaliser ce que Dieu a placé en vous.

Lorsque vous êtes confronté à un défi ou à une situation que vous savez ne pas pouvoir gagner, rappelez-vous que vous avez tout à perdre si vous ne faites rien. Le coût de l'inaction ne sera pas seulement ressenti par vous, mais aussi par tous ceux qui vous entourent, même ceux qui vous connaissent de loin.

Levez-vous, allez de l'avant, sortez dans un flamboiement de gloire, en vous battant avec tout ce que vous avez, chaque once d'énergie, chaque battement de votre sueur et chaque goutte de sang jusqu'à votre dernier souffle et alors, et alors seulement, vous aurez franchi la première étape qui consiste à surmonter l'inaction!

LES EXCUSES-QUAND ON EN A, ON NE PERD JAMAIS

C'est une arme puissante que l'ennemi utilise. Les excuses semblent parfaitement légitimes dans leur raisonnement; elles semblent justifiées et justes, mais elles sont un poison qui pénètre dans votre esprit et votre cœur et commence lentement et effectivement à ronger votre vision, vos objectifs et votre désir de réussir. Lorsque vous leur permettez de rejoindre votre vocabulaire, ils dominent votre état d'esprit. À ce stade, à ce moment-là, vos rêves et vos visions, vos objectifs et vos ambitions commencent à partir en vrille dans une spirale mortelle que très peu ont pu surmonter et renverser.

Les excuses sont la licence que vous vous donnez pour ne rien faire et finalement échouer. Les excuses vous donnent la liberté de blâmer tout et tout le monde pour votre incapacité ou votre manque de capacité à ne rien faire. Elles vous permettent de ne pas dire ce que vous ressentez ou ce que vous voulez faire ou ne pas faire. Elles sont si convaincantes qu'elles deviennent une "loi" pour vous une fois que vous les acceptez et que vous les respectez. Ce sont des limites que vous fixez à votre esprit, des limites à vos objectifs et à vos visions, des limites à votre cœur qui l'empêchent de grandir dans la foi.

Vous ne pouvez pas grandir lorsque des excuses vous entourent. Vous ne pouvez pas exceller lorsque des excuses vivent dans votre esprit et votre cœur. Vous ne pouvez pas atteindre la grandeur lorsque les excuses sont devenues une forme d'expression et un mode de vie.

La vie n'est pas facile; personne n'a dit qu'elle le serait, Jésus lui-même a dit dans Jean 16:33 Je vous ai dit ces choses, afin qu'en moi vous ayez la paix. Vous aurez des tribulations dans le monde; mais prenez courage, j'ai vaincu le monde. J'aurais aimé qu'il dise problèmes, questions, ou dilemmes, mais il a noté tribulations!

Avoir des problèmes est une chose, mais avoir des tribulations est d'un autre niveau. La pression et le stress que les épreuves peuvent apporter à quelqu'un peuvent être écrasants, et à ce moment-là, les excuses sont le moyen parfait d'échapper à la peur et à la douleur que l'on peut ressentir. Les personnes raisonnables ne peuvent pas gérer au niveau que quelqu'un de grand est. Le problème est que nous voulons être le PDG mais ne pas avoir les problèmes ou le stress du PDG. Nous voulons la grandeur, mais pas le processus de douleur pour y parvenir. Nous voulons avoir du succès, mais nous le voulons sur un plateau d'argent, mais la réalité est que rien de grand ne sort jamais d'excuses. Rien de ce qui vaut la peine n'est le fruit d'excuses-rien!

Nous disons que nous le voulons, nous en rêvons et nous y pensons, mais nous nous rendons compte qu'au moment où nous décidons de nous y mettre, nos excuses prennent vie, et soit vous les écrasez, soit elles vous écrasent.

La vie n'est pas juste, mais les excuses ne sont pas acceptables sur la grande scène pour atteindre la grandeur. Il n'y a pas de place pour que les excuses aient un siège à la table de vos rêves. Si vous leur accordez une chaise, alors vous leur donnez une voix, vous donnez une voix à vos excuses, alors vous vous donnez une raison "légitime" d'échouer. Une raison "légitime" d'échouer. Personne ne vous en voudra car votre raisonnement ou vos excuses semblent justifiables et doivent être acceptés par tous.

Pourtant, la partie suivante de ce verset est passionnante; il est dit: "Soyez de bonne humeur". Attendez un instant, être de bonne humeur? au milieu des tribulations, être de bonne humeur? Comment cela peut-il avoir un sens? En général, les tribulations ne sont pas des moments de grande joie ou d'humeur joyeuse. Quand je pense aux tribulations, je pense souvent à la douleur et au chagrin, mais dans ce verset, Jésus dit de prendre courage! De plus, il poursuit en disant: "Car j'ai vaincu le monde."

Lisez cela attentivement; Jésus a vaincu le monde; il n'a jamais dit vous. Nous devons comprendre la chose suivante: la victoire ne commence pas avec vous; le succès commence avec Jésus et seulement Jésus. Si nous sommes en LUI et qu'IL est en nous, alors cette victoire que Jésus a revendiquée est aussi une victoire que nous pouvons revendiquer et dont nous pouvons nous réjouir. Il a vaincu le monde et toutes ses tribulations, ses épreuves et ses peurs. Puisque nous sommes en LUI et qu'IL est en nous, cette revendication de la victoire est également donnée à ceux qui sont en lui.

Plus vous attendez pour mettre vos excuses de côté, plus vos rêves deviennent une réalité. Chaque minute, chaque heure, et chaque jour que vous attendez est une minute, une heure et un jour qui prolonge les rêves et les objectifs de devenir une réalité vivante dans votre présent. Vous ne pouvez pas tarder à mettre ces peurs au repos; vous ne pouvez pas tarder à mettre ces excuses au lit; vous devez vous lever avec le désir de surmonter ces peurs et ces excuses, le désir d'être une meilleure version de vous-même chaque jour.

L'opportunité est devant nous chaque jour, et elle exige que vous donniez 120% de vous-même, mais vous ne fournissez que 70% d'effort et 50% d'effort, et nous voulons ce que ceux qui paient de leur sueur, de leurs larmes et de leur sang ont, et cela n'arrivera pas, ce n'est pas gratuit!

Il faut à la fois de l'émotion et de la logique pour atteindre votre potentiel maximum; vous ne pouvez pas atteindre le sommet seulement avec l'un ou l'autre; vous avez besoin des deux.

LE POUVOIR DE L'ÉMOTION

L'émotion peut vous propulser vers la grandeur et vous faire tomber à des niveaux si bas que vous ne pouvez même pas l'imaginer. Vous devez donner tout ce que vous avez pour dépasser vos limites, car l'émotion et la logique atteignent toutes deux leurs limites, et lorsque l'une d'entre elles est atteinte, vous devez compter sur l'autre. Quand il n'est pas logique de continuer, vous devez utiliser l'émotion pour passer à l'étape suivante.

Il serait préférable que vous appreniez à utiliser votre colère et vos peurs pour vous pousser à aller plus loin et à dire: JE NE M'ARRÊTERAI PAS! Il est facile d'abandonner, facile d'abandonner et de se cacher derrière une excuse; tout cela est facile, mais la facilité ne vous mènera jamais là où Dieu veut que vous arriviez. Tant de gens croient que Dieu les mènera à leur destinée, et c'est là qu'ils font une erreur en supposant cela. Dieu a un plan de grandeur pour votre vie; il l'a dit clairement dans Jérémie 29:11 "Car je connais les pensées que je forme pour vous, dit le Seigneur, des pensées de paix et non de malheur, pour vous donner un avenir et une espérance."

Paul déclare également dans le 2ème Timothée 4:7, "J'ai combattu le bon combat, j'ai achevé la course, j'ai gardé la foi."

Jérémie explique clairement que les plans de Dieu pour vous sont GRANDS! Ils sont énormes, remplis d'opportunités et remplis de paix, d'espoir et d'avenir. Pourtant, Paul dit: "J'ai combattu le bon combat! "Il n'a pas dit que quelqu'un l'a fait pour lui ou que c'était facile, il l'a dit, j'ai combattu le bon combat!

Les plans de Dieu sont grands, ce qui signifie que le combat sera grand, promet un avenir et de l'espoir, mais Paul dit qu'il y a une course à faire et à terminer, et enfin, il dit, j'ai gardé la Foi! Ces deux choses vont de pair. Je répète, et vous l'avez entendu, que personne n'a dit que ce serait facile ou une promenade dans le parc, et s'ils l'ont fait, soit ils vous ont menti, soit ils ne savent pas de quoi ils parlent.

Lorsque vos émotions vous crient qu'elles en ont assez, et que vous pensez que vous allez craquer, passez outre cette émotion avec trois ingrédients clés: la logique, la prière et l'action!

La logique pour réaliser que le retour en arrière n'est pas une option, la prière pour stimuler votre foi, sachant qu'avec Dieu tout est possible, et l'action, car ce n'est pas une vraie prière si elle ne stimule pas votre foi en action. La Bible dit dans Hébreux 11:6, Et sans la foi, il est impossible de plaire à Dieu, car quiconque s'approche de lui doit croire qu'il existe et qu'il récompense ceux qui le cherchent sincèrement.

Vous devez combattre les émotions qui paralysent vos actions, avec des sentiments qui donnent un sens à votre combat. Le mieux serait que tu trouves la force et la ténacité de te regarder dans le miroir, et avec tout ce que tu as, de te dire: JE NE PEUX PAS M'ARRÊTER!

Votre place n'est pas au fond du trou, et il est temps pour vous de le réaliser et de vous relever, de vous battre et de commencer à marcher vers là où Dieu veut que vous soyez. Deut 28: 13 dit, Et l'Eternel fera de toi la TÊTE, et non la queue, et tu seras SEULEMENT EN HAUT, et tu ne seras pas en bas, si tu écoutes les commandements de l'Eternel ton Dieu que je te commande aujourd'hui, pour les observer et les mettre en pratique.

Ce sont des mots puissants qui doivent être prononcés dans ta vie quotidienne chaque fois que ces émotions commencent à murmurer dans ton cœur, ton esprit et ton âme d'abandonner. Il est temps que vous vous sentiez mal à l'aise d'être au fond du trou, et vous vous demandez peut-être si c'est même possible? Mais, malheureusement, c'est une réalité pour beaucoup de gens de nos jours. Les émotions de peur et de doute vous maintiennent au plus bas, alimentant la sympathie et l'empathie des autres à votre égard. Bien que tout cela soit "bon", cela devient comme un auto-virus qui vous empêche de vous relever et de devenir tout ce que vous devez être dans la vie.

Même s'il peut être agréable d'avoir la sympathie et l'empathie des autres, cela ne vous donne pas la force de vous relever, et beaucoup s'en servent pour rester là parce qu'il n'y a pas de pression en étant au fond. Il n'y a pas de pression pour réussir quand les autres vous donnent de la sympathie; il n'y a pas de raison de grandir quand les autres travaillent pour que vous vous sentiez mieux ou vous donnent l'illusion de devenir meilleur. Il n'y a aucune pression sur vous pour vous améliorer parce que vos émotions vous ont paralysé, et vous vous nourrissez de la sympathie des autres. Finalement, la mort survient sur le plan mental, spirituel et physique.

La Bible raconte que le fils prodigue était dans une fosse à cochons (Luc 15) et qu'il mangeait leur nourriture, et que lorsqu'il est revenu à lui, il a décidé de retourner chez son père. Analysez cela un instant: il est passé de la richesse à la nourriture des porcs; pensez à l'impact émotionnel que cela a dû avoir sur la vie de cet homme. Ensuite, pensez aux étapes qu'il a dû franchir pour arriver à ce stade de sa vie. On ne passe pas de la richesse à la nourriture pour porcs du jour au lendemain.

Ses émotions ont dû être tellement décomposées pour l'amener à cet état d'esprit et à ces actions. Il a perdu tout espoir, toute motivation et toute foi; au lieu de retourner immédiatement à la maison de son père, l'orgueil s'est installé et a pris le contrôle de ses émotions, ce qui l'a conduit à la fosse aux cochons. L'orgueil tue le destin; l'orgueil tue les rêves; rien de bon ne vient de l'orgueil. C'est pourquoi la Bible dit dans Jacques 4:6, Mais il donne plus de grâce. Il dit donc: "Dieu résiste aux orgueilleux, Mais il fait grâce aux humbles."

Dieu résiste aux orgueilleux! L'émotion de l'orgueil contredit tout ce que Dieu veut faire dans votre vie. L'orgueil du fils prodigue était si élevé qu'il préférait manger la nourriture des cochons plutôt que de retourner dans la maison de son père. Son orgueil était si élevé qu'il a décidé que la nourriture des porcs était préférable au retour dans la maison de son père, malgré la perte de son argent et de sa fortune. Non seulement il avait perdu sa fortune, mais il avait également perdu tous ses soi-disant "amis", où sont-ils allés?

Finalement, lorsque toute la sympathie est épuisée, et qu'il n'y a plus d'empathie à recevoir, ces mêmes personnes qui vous ont donné ces choses vous tourneront le dos et diront "ça suffit avec cette personne". Cette zone est donc critique et très dangereuse, car une fois que tout le soutien est perdu, beaucoup se retrouvent dans un espace très sombre et, malheureusement, beaucoup sont couchés six pieds sous terre parce qu'ils ont choisi de ne jamais se relever.

Est-il possible de se relever même si l'on est seul, sans rien et en mangeant des cochons? La réponse est un OUI retentissant!

Encore une fois, la Bible dit: Je peux tout faire par le Christ qui me fortifie! Phil 4:13

La Bible dit aussi dans Luc 15:17, "Mais quand il fut revenu à lui, il dit: Combien de mercenaires de mon père ont du pain en suffisance et à volonté, et moi je péris de faim!

LE POUVOIR DE LA LOGIQUE

La Bible dit qu'il est revenu à lui et qu'il a dit: Combien de mercenaires de mon père ont du pain en suffisance et à volonté, et je meurs de faim!

Il arrive un moment à chacun; par la miséricorde et la grâce de Dieu, une "ampoule" s'allume dans notre esprit et l'incite à se réveiller! Mais, d'abord, il a dû reconnaître où il était, il a dû reconnaître son environnement, sa condition, et réaliser ce qu'il avait laissé derrière lui.

Réaliser où nous sommes est une tâche douloureuse; accepter que vous avez fait une erreur est là où vous êtes à cause de ces erreurs. Il est essentiel d'accepter que c'est votre faute et celle de personne d'autre. Porter sa croix est aussi important que de respirer. Vous ne renaîtrez jamais de vos cendres en rejetant la faute de votre état sur quelqu'un d'autre.

Le fils prodigue est revenu à lui, mais vous constatez qu'il n'a blâmé personne pour la situation dans laquelle il se trouvait. Il a assumé la responsabilité de ses actes et n'a pas reproché aux autres sa condition. Il est élémentaire de dire que c'est à cause de ceci ou cela, ou de cette personne, que la vie n'est pas juste, ou tout ce que vous voulez évoquer, mais en fin de compte, vous devez être responsable de là où vous en êtes dans la vie et de personne d'autre.

Les émotions finissent par s'arrêter, et la logique entre en jeu. Elle peut vous pousser à blâmer les autres et à rester là où vous êtes, ce qui ne fera qu'empirer les choses, ou elle peut vous pousser à décider de changer votre situation. La Bible dit dans 1 Pierre 2:9: "Mais vous êtes une race élue, un sacerdoce royal, une nation sainte, un peuple qui lui est propre, afin que vous proclamiez les louanges de celui qui vous a appelés des ténèbres à son admirable lumière";

Vous ne pouvez pas abandonner maintenant; c'est le dixième round, il vous en reste encore deux, et lorsque vous atteignez un certain niveau de succès et de grandeur, cela n'a pas grand-chose à voir avec la compétence et tout à voir avec l'endurance.

La Bible dit dans Matthieu 24:13 que celui qui persévérera jusqu'à la fin sera sauvé. Endurer signifie que vous devez avoir de l'endurance, pas de l'habileté. Vous pouvez avoir toute la puissance et tous les muscles, mais si votre adversaire peut vous dépasser un round de plus, alors vous perdez et il gagne!

Votre ennemi n'a pas besoin d'être le plus fort ou le plus rapide; il doit durer plus longtemps que vous dans la course. La Bible dit dans 1 Corinthiens 9:24-27: "Ne savez-vous pas que, dans une course, tous les coureurs courent, mais qu'un seul reçoit le prix? Courez donc pour l'obtenir. Tout athlète fait preuve de maîtrise de soi en toutes choses. Ils le font pour recevoir une couronne périssable, mais nous une impérissable. Ainsi, je ne cours pas sans but, je ne fais pas de la boxe comme si je battais l'air. Mais je discipline mon corps et le garde sous contrôle, de peur qu'après avoir prêché aux autres, je ne sois disqualifié.

Ce verset est très puissant; permettez-moi de le décomposer pour vous. Premièrement, il commence par reconnaître qu'il s'agit d'une course et que vous n'êtes pas seul à essayer d'obtenir le prix. Il s'agit d'un réseau d'éléments complexes, qui se déplacent tous simultanément, car même si nous courons tous cette course et qu'un seul recevra le "prix", c'est symbolique car nous avons tous des objectifs, des visions et des plans différents. Même si certains courent peut-être après le même prix que le vôtre.

Tout athlète fait preuve de maîtrise de soi en toutes choses; il voit chaque personne comme un athlète, une excellente visualisation. La maîtrise de soi est si nécessaire car elle vous sépare des autres. La discipline est essentielle car pour atteindre la fin, atteindre le but et recevoir le prix; vous devrez faire des choses qui peuvent vous sembler inconfortables. Pour atteindre l'avenir, vous devrez payer le prix, faire des sacrifices et faire preuve de logique. La préparation est nécessaire pour réussir; sans elle, nous sommes voués à l'échec.

Ils le font pour recevoir une couronne périssable, mais nous une impérissable. Je ne cours donc pas sans but. C'est ici que nous devons réaliser que notre but éternel est beaucoup plus important que notre but physique. Nous nous concentrons tellement sur la logique naturelle et les objectifs réalistes que nous oublions que nous sommes dans ce monde, mais que nous ne sommes pas de ce monde. Nos yeux doivent être fixés sur les objectifs réels, mais nous ne pouvons jamais perdre la perspective de notre objectif éternel.

Par conséquent, nous ne courons pas sans but; en d'autres termes, notre course doit être menée avec un but et une perspective. La résistance vous donne l'endurance nécessaire pour avancer sans relâche, avec le désir d'atteindre la fin et de l'atteindre dans la victoire. Il n'y a pas de victoire dans l'abandon; il n'y a pas de joie dans le renoncement; il n'y a pas de satisfaction à vivre une vie sans but-nous ne courons pas sans but!

Je ne fais pas de la boxe comme si je battais l'air. Mais je discipline mon corps et le garde sous contrôle. Il met un point d'honneur ici à nous dire que nos actions doivent être ciblées et avoir un but. Chaque pas que nous faisons doit être discipliné et garder nos émotions sous contrôle. Je ne le fais pas, dit-il; c'est une déclaration audacieuse que vous devez faire chaque jour. Je n'abandonne pas; je n'abandonne pas, je ne cherche pas d'excuses, je ne cède pas à mes émotions négatives, je ne blâme pas les autres pour mes erreurs, je ne deviens pas paresseux, je ne fais pas marche arrière-ce sont les mots que vous devez vivre chaque jour.

Je discipline mon corps et le garde sous contrôle, ce qui signifie que la grandeur exige discipline et maîtrise de soi. Il est trop facile de céder à toutes ces choses négatives, trop facile de se cacher derrière un mur d'excuses, mais aucun grand athlète ne trouve d'excuses pour ne pas continuer.

Si vous me connaissez depuis assez longtemps, vous verrez que j'adore le hockey; je ne suis pas né au Canada, mais en arrivant ici à l'âge de 5 ans, le Canada est mon chez-moi. Je suis un vrai Canadien qui aime le hockey et le chocolat chaud.

En 2017, les Penguins de Pittsburgh ont remporté leur deuxième Coupe Stanley consécutive. Un grand accomplissement. Le hockey est un sport rapide, intense et amusant à regarder. Je me souviens avoir regardé le match, et alors que le chronomètre approchait de la dernière seconde, l'excitation sur le banc des Penguins était électrique. Le buzzer a retenti et les joueurs ont sauté sur la glace pour se féliciter mutuellement. Les étreintes sont profondes, le sourire sur leurs visages est contagieux, et la foule est en feu!

Mais personne ne se doutait qu'un de leurs joueurs avait joué et gagné dans des circonstances que personne ne connaissait. Commençons par le défenseur des Penguins, Ian Cole. Le joueur de 28 ans a joué un peu plus de 18 minutes par match pour son équipe, et il l'a fait avec une main et des côtes cassées depuis le début de la série des Capitals (deuxième tour). Oui, vous avez bien lu, une main et des côtes cassées! Alors comment quelqu'un peut-il jouer dans de telles circonstances?

Si je me cogne l'orteil sur le bord du lit, je suis fini; je suis hors jeu! Encore moins jouer un match de haute intensité avec une main ou une côte cassée, d'ailleurs. Il a joué en dépit de sa douleur, il a joué en dépit de son agonie, il a joué en dépit de l'adversité-il a continué à jouer. Il aurait été facile et justifiable pour lui d'arrêter de jouer, et personne ne lui aurait reproché de s'arrêter. Mais ce qui l'a poussé à continuer, c'est le désir de gagner!

Lorsque votre désir de gagner l'emporte sur votre douleur, vous gagnez; lorsque votre passion d'exceller l'emporte sur votre lutte, vous gagnez à chaque fois. Je ne peux pas imaginer la douleur de jouer dans ces conditions, mais tout ce que nous pouvons dire, c'est qu'il a gagné! Par conséquent, votre histoire doit raconter comment vous avez connu la victoire à travers votre douleur, votre lutte et votre désordre.

Les gens aiment raconter votre histoire, mais ils ne parleront le plus souvent que de votre douleur, de vos peurs, de vos luttes et de votre désordre, et rarement de vos réalisations. Personne ne savait qu'il jouait dans ces conditions jusqu'à ce que ces choses soient révélées après la fin de la série. Alors ne montrez pas votre douleur, ne diffusez pas votre combat, ne montrez pas votre faiblesse, car cela ne vous apportera jamais rien de bon.

Ses coéquipiers savaient, ses entraîneurs savaient, sa famille savait, mais personne d'autre ne le savait. Il doit en être de même dans votre vie; seules certaines personnes doivent connaître vos faiblesses, vos peurs, vos luttes et vos douleurs, et parmi ces personnes spécifiques, il n'y en aura que quelques-unes qui se tiendront à vos côtés pour vous aider à vous relever. Cet homme devait avoir les meilleurs médecins pour le conseiller et lui dire quoi faire pour continuer, et non pour lui suggérer comment abandonner.

Il y a suffisamment de gens dans le monde qui feront tout pour vous empêcher d'accomplir quoi que ce soit dans la vie. Il y aura suffisamment de gens autour de vous pour vous apitoyer sur votre sort, mais seuls ceux qui sont liés à vous comprendront votre combat et vous aideront à le gagner.

Regardez cette histoire, Jésus ressuscite la jeune fille morte; la Bible dit dans Marc 5:37-40, "Il ne laissa personne le suivre, si ce n'est Pierre, Jacques et Jean, le frère de Jacques. Lorsqu'ils arrivèrent à la maison du chef de la synagogue, Jésus vit une agitation, des gens qui pleuraient et se lamentaient bruyamment. Il entra et leur dit: "Pourquoi cette agitation et ces gémissements? L'enfant n'est pas mort, mais il dort." Mais ils se moquèrent de lui.

Après les avoir tous mis dehors, il prit le père et la mère de l'enfant, ainsi que les disciples qui étaient avec lui, et il entra là où était l'enfant.

Jésus avait un cercle restreint, mais il avait aussi un cercle intérieur, montré ici dans ce verset. Il n'a laissé personne le suivre, sauf Pierre, Jacques et Jean, le frère de Jacques. Vous devez être capable de réduire votre cercle intérieur aux personnes qui vous sont proches, afin que, dans les moments difficiles, elles vous soutiennent. Sur les 12 disciples, seuls Pierre, Jacques et Jean ont été autorisés à suivre Jésus là où se produisait le miracle. Qu'est-il arrivé aux autres? Où sont-ils allés? La Bible ne dit pas où ils sont allés, mais mentionne seulement ceux qui ont suivi Jésus plus loin.

Il n'est pas toujours bon d'avoir beaucoup de monde autour de soi; dans ce cas, beaucoup de gens prenaient de la place et ne mettaient pas l'endroit en valeur. Jésus s'était montré, et personne ne semblait se soucier du fait qu'il avait la réputation de faire des miracles; la Bible dit qu'ils se moquaient de lui! Combien de soi-disant amis entendent vos rêves, votre vision et vos objectifs, et au lieu de vous aider à les réaliser, ils se moquent.

Jésus était dérangé par le fait qu'il y avait tant d'agitation et de gémissements; il était contrarié par leur manque de foi et de croyance. Mais ensuite, ces mêmes personnes qui créaient le vacarme et les gémissements se sont soudainement mises à rire de Jésus!

Protégez votre cercle, vos rêves, vos visions et vos objectifs, protégez ce que Dieu a placé en vous. Protégez vos plans, car ils ne doivent pas être partagés avec tout le monde, car tout le monde ne voudra pas être là pour vous voir réussir.

Protégez vos paroles, car elles ont du pouvoir et du poids, car c'est par elles que les choses se créent ou se défont. Vous devrez vous battre et vous battre et vous battre, et beaucoup perdent le combat non pas parce qu'ils ne sont pas assez forts, mais simplement parce qu'ils ne peuvent pas battre l'ancienne version de vous. Vous êtes battus par la version négative de vous, la version de vous qui ne veut pas renaître de ses cendres, qui parle naturellement et non par la Foi.

Vous perdez contre l'ancien vous qui n'avait ni espoir ni rêve parce que vous ne vous battez pas assez longtemps pour voir le NOUVEAU VOUS surgir. Mais je peux vous dire qu'il y a une lumière au bout du tunnel, elle peut être petite, mais si vous vous engagez à prendre une bonne décision après l'autre, vous en tirerez des dividendes dont vous n'avez jamais rêvé.

Les choses vont s'améliorer, peut-être pas du jour au lendemain, peut-être pas dans le style micro-ondes; ce ne sera pas instantané autant que nous le voudrions; il faut du temps! Mais le processus construit le caractère, vous donne une peau épaisse; avoir du caractère est tout dans la vie; avoir la parole de Dieu dans votre vie est la chose la plus significative que vous pouvez avoir pour obtenir le meilleur que Dieu a pour vous.

LE POUVOIR DE VOS PAROLES

Votre attitude va déterminer votre altitude! Vos mots créent le monde dans lequel vous vivez. La chose la plus difficile que j'ai dû apprendre au fil des ans a été de croire au pouvoir de mes mots.

Quelles que soient vos circonstances ou les situations qui se présentent à vous, vos paroles ont de l'importance ici sur terre et au ciel. Le monde vous rendra capable et essaiera de vous définir par ses mots, et c'est là que vous acceptez leurs termes prononcés sur vous, ou que vous commencez à parler dans votre propre vie et à créer un nouveau vous.

Nous nous fions tellement aux paroles des autres; si ce sont des paroles encourageantes, elles nous élèvent, et si ce sont des paroles négatives, elles nous font tomber. Nos mots sont des pierres. Nous ne sommes que des lanceurs de pierres à chaque mot que nous prononçons. Mais, d'un autre côté, si nos mots contiennent de la beauté, les gens les chérissent. Si nos paroles contiennent de la douleur, les gens les jettent, mais pas avant d'avoir soigné la blessure qu'elles ont causée.

Proverbes 15:4 "Les paroles douces apportent la vie et la santé; une langue trompeuse écrase l'esprit." Les mots que vous prononcez ou que vous permettez qu'ils soient prononcés sur vous constituent le monde dans lequel vous marchez. Vous constaterez que deux personnes seront dans deux atmosphères différentes alors qu'elles se trouvent dans la même pièce, simplement parce qu'elles ont permis aux mots de changer leur perspective ou leur humeur. Les mots doux apportent la vie et la santé, donc vos mots peuvent élever quelqu'un, lui donner de l'espoir, et apporter la santé à son corps, son esprit et son âme.

Mais d'un autre côté, dit-il, une langue trompeuse écrase l'esprit; elle ne le fait pas descendre, elle l'écrase. C'est dire le pouvoir que détiennent nos paroles.

Proverbes 16:24 "Les paroles aimables sont comme le miel, douces pour l'âme et saines pour le corps." Oui, il est possible de changer votre avenir et votre présent par vos mots. Les mots que vous prononcez sur vous-même sont plus importants que les autres mots que quiconque peut prononcer sur vous, même si ce sont de bonnes paroles. Ils viennent en second lieu par rapport aux termes que vous devriez prononcer sur votre vie.

Combien de fois les gens se privent-ils de la grandeur ou du succès? Combien de fois nous nous privons de ce que Dieu a préparé pour nous, simplement parce que nous n'y croyons pas et que les mots que nous avons prononcés dans nos vies ont créé une fosse de désespoir et de doute dont beaucoup ne sortent jamais?

Le mieux serait que vous le fassiez; chaque jour, changez votre vocabulaire qui vous édifiera et vous construira. Vous ne pouvez pas attendre que les autres parlent dans votre vie. Alors quand vous vous voyez dans le miroir chaque matin, profitez-en pour parler à votre nouveau vous, et ne laissez pas l'ancien vous revenir, n'arrêtez pas de parler dans votre vie de foi, d'espoir et de puissance, n'arrêtez pas car si vous arrêtez, vous permettez à l'ancien vous de revenir vivant. Il reviendra avec une vengeance.

Vous devez être le plus incroyable agent commercial pour vous-même. Demandez-vous chaque jour, qu'est-ce que je vais me vendre aujourd'hui? Achèteriez-vous des tomates pourries au marché? La réponse serait sans aucun doute non! Mais combien de fois vous vendez-vous à vous-même et acceptez-vous ces expressions pourries que vous avez laissé s'insinuer dans votre esprit et votre cœur ou que vous avez entendu quelqu'un vous dire?

Combien de fois vous êtes-vous servi un plat de mots pourris qui ne vous rapprochent pas de vos rêves mais vous ramènent aux cendres de l'endroit d'où vous essayez de sortir.

Car quelle que soit la gravité de la situation, vos paroles ont le pouvoir de changer et d'affecter la tempête. Marc 4:39 Il se réveilla, menaça le vent et dit à la mer: "Paix! Sois tranquille!" Et le vent cessa, et il y eut un grand calme.

2 Corinthiens 12:9 Mais il m'a dit: "Ma grâce te suffit, car ma puissance s'accomplit dans la faiblesse." C'est pourquoi je me vanterai d'autant plus volontiers de mes faiblesses, afin que la puissance du Christ repose sur moi.

Nourrissez votre esprit de la parole de Dieu, Nourrissez votre esprit de la parole de Dieu, Nourrissez votre âme de la parole de Dieu, Romains 10:17 Car la foi vient de ce qu'on entend, et ce qu'on entend vient de la parole de Dieu. Plus vous vous nourrissez de la parole de Dieu, plus vous verrez vos paroles changer.

Quand tu changes tes mots, tu changes la trajectoire de ce que l'ennemi voudrait à ce que Dieu a toujours voulu qu'il soit. Alors nourris ta Foi, regarde tes doutes et tes peurs s'affamer, nourris ta Foi en creusant dans les écritures, et nourris ta Foi jusqu'à ce que tu commences à voir un changement dans tes paroles.

Ce que vous nourrissez dans votre esprit est ce que votre bouche va dire. Si vous ne regardez que les nouvelles, les nouvelles seront la seule chose dont vous parlerez, et tout à coup, vous permettrez aux mots que vous entendez aux nouvelles de commencer à influencer vos commentaires.

J'ai entendu mon père dire un jour que si aujourd'hui était le dernier jour de votre vie, serait-ce la dernière chose que vous vous diriez à propos de vous-même? Cela m'a poussé à m'arrêter, à me regarder dans le miroir chaque jour et à m'obliger à changer mon vocabulaire et ce que je dis de moi.

Nous n'y pensons généralement pas; nous croyons que les mots ne sont que des mots, mais ils ont un pouvoir incroyable en réalité. Par exemple, Dieu lui-même a donné l'existence à toutes choses; d'un seul mot, la lumière est apparue; d'un seul mot, les choses sont passées du néant au tout.

Proverbes 18:4 "Les paroles d'une personne peuvent être une eau vivifiante; les paroles de la vraie sagesse sont aussi rafraîchissantes qu'un ruisseau bouillonnant."

La première étape pour changer votre présent et avoir un impact sur votre avenir est de croire que vos mots comptent. Il n'y a pas de plan B, car le plan B vous détourne du plan A. Le plan A consiste à modifier vos propos et à croire que ce que vous dites fait une différence pour ceux qui l'entendent et, surtout pour vous, pour votre rêve, vos objectifs et votre avenir.

Les mots d'une personne peuvent être de l'eau qui donne la vie; c'est dire à quel point nos mots peuvent être puissants, peuvent être de l'eau qui change la vie! Vous ne pouvez pas prendre vos mots pour acquis; vous ne pouvez pas prendre vos mots comme s'ils n'avaient aucune signification; nos mots ont de l'importance. Ils peuvent produire la vie ou prendre la vie en une seule phrase.

Proverbes 18:21 "La mort et la vie sont au pouvoir de la langue, et ceux qui l'aiment en mangeront les fruits."

Votre langue a un pouvoir que nous ne pouvons pas commencer à comprendre. J'ai donc dû faire quelques recherches sur la langue et j'ai découvert que la langue est un groupe de muscles qui travaillent sans le soutien de votre squelette. (Aucun autre muscle du corps humain ne peut faire cela!) Cela la rend incroyablement flexible, ce qui te permet de former des sons, de siffler, de déplacer la nourriture dans ta bouche, d'avaler, et tu peux même l'utiliser pour te nettoyer les dents après avoir mangé.

Non seulement tu peux tirer ta langue, la rétracter à l'arrière de ta bouche et la déplacer d'un côté à l'autre, mais tu peux aussi changer complètement sa forme! Chaque fois que vous roulez votre langue, que vous la rentrez, que vous la recourbez ou que vous la formez en pointe, vous changez sa forme.

L'empreinte de la langue de chaque personne est aussi unique que ses empreintes digitales. Imaginez un avenir où nous utiliserions les empreintes digitales, les scans de la rétine (yeux) et les scans de la langue pour confirmer nos identités. Imaginez un peu!

Une langue gonflée est appelée macroglossie et peut indiquer d'autres problèmes de santé sous-jacents. Par exemple, si vous avez des indentations sur le côté de votre langue à cause de vos dents, votre langue est probablement gonflée. Ce gonflement peut être causé par une hypothyroïdie, une infection, des allergies, des maladies inflammatoires et de nombreuses autres affections.

Combien de fois avons-nous un vocabulaire gonflé ou des mots gonflés qui provoquent des douleurs dans notre vie quotidienne? Les mots gonflés font mal à la personne qui les prononce, mais aussi à ceux qui les entendent. Les mots gonflés peuvent endommager des relations, détruire des amitiés et causer des blessures durables qui prennent souvent des années à guérir et à surmonter.

Les paroles enflées ne peuvent être guéries que par la prière et la lecture de la parole; la Bible dit dans Ephésiens 4:29 qu'aucune parole corrompue ne sorte de votre bouche, mais ce qui est bon pour l'édification nécessaire, afin qu'elle communique la grâce à ceux qui l'entendent.

Les mots sont si puissants qu'ils peuvent non seulement créer ou détruire votre monde, mais aussi avoir un effet sur ceux qui les entendent. Car nous ne pouvons pas commencer à imaginer les dommages qu'une phrase peut avoir dans le monde spirituel, et si nous le faisions, nous changerions et nous nous abstiendrions des mots que nous prononçons.

Colossiens 3:8 "Mais maintenant, vous devez vous débarrasser de tout cela, de la colère, de l'emportement, de la malice, du blasphème, du langage vulgaire qui sort de votre bouche."

J'ai toujours pensé que la colère, le courroux et la malice étaient des actions, mais selon Colossiens, ils ont été formés à partir des mots que nous avons prononcés dans l'existence. Nous créons l'environnement dans lequel nous vivons, nous créons l'atmosphère dans laquelle nous marchons et nous créons un monde qui a un impact sur chaque personne que nous rencontrons.

Ne laissez pas le bruit des paroles des autres étouffer la voix de Dieu dans votre vie. Il y aura beaucoup de voix autour de vous, toutes vous parlant simultanément, mais vous devez vous rappeler que lorsque vous vous immergez dans la parole, vous investissez dans vos paroles.

Lorsque vous investissez du temps dans la parole de Dieu, vous faites un investissement important dans votre présent et votre avenir. Un investissement qui enrichira votre vocabulaire et stimulera votre Foi pour une croissance personnelle plus significative. Car c'est par votre foi que les mots sont prononcés, et c'est par ces mots prononcés que les montagnes sont déplacées, que les géants tombent et que les murs s'écroulent.

Ma femme est portugaise, et elle le parle très bien. Cependant, nous avons trois enfants formidables, nous sommes mariés depuis plus de 15 ans et, à ce jour, je n'ai toujours pas appris la langue-je m'en excuse. Je peux l'entendre parler et retenir certains mots ou certaines phrases, mais je ne peux pas les parler. Combien de fois écoutons-nous la voix de Dieu qui nous parle à travers sa parole, et parce que nous l'entendons sans la pratiquer, nous ne pouvons pas la parler quand l'ennemi vient nous attaquer?

Il est temps de commencer à travailler sur votre rêve, pas demain, aujourd'hui! Les limites n'existent que dans notre esprit, et elles n'existent que pour nous lier et ne pas nous permettre de grandir ou d'aller de l'avant. La peur se répand dans notre vocabulaire, faisant taire notre voix de la Foi, et nous nous attachons à la peur, et nous la disons, et une fois que nous la disons, nous la croyons, et une fois que nous la pensons, cette pensée s'empare de notre vie.

Proverbes 12:18 "Il y en a un dont les paroles irréfléchies sont comme des coups d'épée, mais la langue du sage apporte la guérison."

Vous rencontrerez beaucoup de déceptions, d'échecs et de défaites en changeant votre vocabulaire. Cependant, en passant par là, vous découvrirez de nombreuses choses sur vous-même que vous ne connaissez pas pour le moment. Il y a de la grandeur en vous, et vos mots ont du pouvoir. Lorsque vous réaliserez l'ampleur du pouvoir de vos propos, vous commencerez alors rapidement et sans hésitation à changer ces mots.

Vous réaliserez que vous êtes plus important que vos circonstances et que les mots que vous prononcez affectent directement ces circonstances. À ce moment-là, vous commencerez à comprendre que vous êtes assez puissant pour dire à cette montagne de s'écarter du chemin et de se jeter dans la mer.

Vous réaliserez que le ciel prête une grande attention à ce que vous dites, non seulement lorsque les choses vont bien, mais surtout lorsqu'elles vont au plus mal.

Prenez une décision aujourd'hui; décidez aujourd'hui que vous allez changer la trajectoire de votre vie en changeant votre façon de parler! Choisissez qu'aujourd'hui vous allez changer votre avenir en changeant les mots qui sortent de votre bouche. Nous n'avons pas à parler de l'obscurité et de la peur dans notre présent; non, nous pouvons au milieu de ces temps sombres et au milieu de cette peur, nous pouvons choisir de nous lever et de parler de la lumière, de parler du courage, de parler de la parole de Dieu et regarder comment le ciel et Dieu répondent à vos commentaires de Foi.

En prenant cette décision, vous serez confronté à l'ancien vous, parlant de l'ancienne manière, et vous ne pouvez pas fuir votre ancien moi; vous devez vous engager et gagner cette bataille. Contre toute attente, vous devez croire que vos mots comptent et qu'il n'est pas question de revenir à votre ancien moi. Vous avez emprunté cette voie; vous savez ce que cela fait et à quoi cela ressemble; il n'y a rien là-bas pour vous, seulement la défaite. Ainsi, lorsque nous ne savons pas quoi dire, parlons alors de la parole de Dieu; lorsque nous ne savons pas comment le dire, disons-le selon la parole de Dieu. Car le ciel et la terre passeront, mais sa parole restera.

Vous devez rester cohérents car sans cohérence, nous ne finirons jamais cette course, si c'était facile, alors nos résultats seraient tous grands, mais parce que la grandeur n'est pas facile, seuls quelques-uns l'atteignent. Mais chaque jour est une bataille pour être grand, non pas pour être comparé à quelqu'un d'autre, mais pour vous mettre au défi de devenir la meilleure version de vous-même possible.

N'oubliez pas que votre concurrent dans la vie n'est personne d'autre que vous! Vos mots vous donnent l'avantage dans cette bataille ou peuvent être votre désavantage. Soit vous gagnez la bataille avec vos mots, soit vous la perdez à cause de votre choix de mots. Nous avons tous un choix à faire dans cette bataille. Vos mots sont les armes de votre choix, et vous seul pouvez les sélectionner.

Les grands mots sont comme des épées qui sont aiguisées avant chaque combat; vous aiguisez votre épée par la lecture de la parole de Dieu. Plus vous creusez dans SA Parole, plus vos mots deviennent aiguisés. Maintenant, tu ne parles plus à partir de ton imagination, mais non Dieu lui-même appuie tes paroles car non, tu cites sa parole, et il répond toujours à ce que tu répètes sa parole.

Colossiens 4:6 "Que votre parole soit toujours aimable, assaisonnée de sel, afin que vous sachiez comment il faut répondre à chacun."

Matthieu 12:37 "Car c'est par vos paroles que vous serez justifiés, et c'est par vos paroles que vous serez condamnés."

Vos mots doivent être en avant et non en arrière. Les temps difficiles viendront, mais vous devez rester ferme sur SA parole; les temps difficiles viennent pour défier notre résolution, tester nos mots, tester nos émotions qui contribuent à nos mots, mais vous devez rester ferme dans votre détermination à changer votre vocabulaire!

Dieu nous a donné sa parole pour vaincre quand nous ne pouvons pas nous tenir sur nos forces.

CHOISISSEZ VOTRE AVENIR

Votre avenir est ce que vous en faites, il n'est pas ce que les autres disent qu'il est, ni ce que les autres veulent qu'il soit, mais plutôt ce que vous voulez qu'il soit, il sera. Peu importe les questions ou les problèmes qui peuvent survenir, votre avenir est entre vos mains. Vous avez le pouvoir de le changer, de l'affecter et de le créer par le pouvoir de vos mots.

Proverbe 3:5-6 dit: "Fais confiance au Seigneur de tout ton cœur et ne t'appuie pas sur ta propre intelligence. Dans toutes tes voies, reconnais-le, et il rendra droits tes sentiers."

Peu importe à quel point nos chemins peuvent sembler tortueux, dès que vous reconnaissez le Seigneur par vos paroles, il rendra les chemins droits. Ce n'est pas un secret que le Seigneur veille sur vous et prend soin de vous, bien qu'il puisse sembler loin, et parfois on peut avoir l'impression qu'il n'est pas là-il l'est!

Il dit Crois au Seigneur de tout ton cœur, non pas en marchant parce que tu le comprends, mais plutôt en marchant parce que tu le crois. La confiance est également entendue et ressentie à travers les mots que vous prononcez. Vous êtes l'artiste; vos mots sont le pinceau que vous utilisez pour créer votre chef-d'œuvre. Pourtant, il voit et sait tout; par conséquent, il corrigera nos erreurs et les fera tourner à notre avantage. Faire confiance, c'est faire confiance, aveuglément, hardiment, en sachant qu'il veille sur nous.

Notre incapacité à parler de vie et à parler de bénédiction nous empêche de les recevoir; notre manque de recherche de la parole limite notre vocabulaire, nos déclarations sont liées à notre incrédulité où il n'y a pas de vie du tout.

Plus la parole entre en vous, plus vous devenez la parole, plus vous devenez la parole, plus vous devenez capable de choisir votre avenir. Si les mots sont prononcés mais ne sont pas crus, ils ne sont que du bruit. Les paroles qui ne sont pas suivies d'effet deviennent un bruit de crécelle et ne portent aucun fruit.

Si vous voulez une nouvelle voiture, vous ne pouvez pas simplement prier pour l'avoir, vous devez aller la demander, mais avant de la demander, vous devez aller voir la voiture; avant de voir le véhicule, vous devez être intéressé par un véhicule, et avant d'être intéressé par un véhicule, vous devez ouvrir la bouche et dire, je veux une nouvelle voiture.

Tout commence par ce qui sort de nos bouches. Vous ne pouvez pas arrêter de rêver; vous ne pouvez pas arrêter de croire; il est nécessaire que vous vous aligniez avec des gens qui parlent le même langage que vous, le langage de la foi. Alignez-vous avec des gens qui ont faim comme vous, des gens qui n'accepteront pas de refus, des gens qui sont acharnés dans leur quête de grandeur, des gens qui non seulement vous pousseront plus loin, mais vous propulseront à votre prochain niveau.

Si vous vous alignez sur des personnes qui ne créent pas leur avenir dans la bénédiction et l'espoir, alors votre avenir sera perdu et entre les mains de quelqu'un d'autre. Par conséquent, vous devez prendre en main votre avenir, prendre en main vos paroles, les soumettre à la parole de Dieu et observer comment le Seigneur honorera sa parole et fera de vos rêves une réalité.

Vous pouvez échouer tôt, voire échouer souvent, mais allez de l'avant. Je trouve toujours un peu frustrant que les gens associent une connotation négative à l'échec. L'échec peut être utilisé pour rester en bas de l'échelle ou pour progresser dans la vie et atteindre les objectifs que vous vous êtes fixés.

Soyez à l'aise avec l'échec car si vous prenez du recul et analysez la situation, vous verrez les leçons de l'échec. L'échec est terrible si vous le laissez être une chose terrible, mais il peut être votre plus excellent professeur si vous le laissez vous guider. Il fera de vous un maître, vous donnera les connaissances nécessaires pour votre avenir et vous permettra d'aider les autres, alors oui, l'échec peut être une mauvaise chose si vous le laissez être, ou il peut être la meilleure chose qui vous soit jamais arrivée.

Les personnes qui réussissent échouent plus que vous ne le pensez; elles tombent tellement que leurs histoires comportent plus d'échecs que de succès. Alors comment cela peut-il avoir un sens? Les personnes qui réussissent savent qu'elles se relèveront avec un vaste éventail de connaissances pour les aider dans leur parcours si et quand elles tombent. Tandis que d'autres se contenteront de l'échec et resteront en mode échec, sans en tirer la leçon qui leur permettrait de réessayer et d'atteindre le succès qu'ils recherchaient.

Tout, et je dis bien tout, commence par les mots qui sortent de votre bouche; tout! Avec une seule phrase, vous avez le pouvoir de faire la journée ou la semaine de quelqu'un, et pourtant en une seule phrase, vous pouvez détruire la journée et la semaine de quelqu'un. Mais, d'un autre côté, vous pouvez apporter de la joie dans la vie de quelqu'un, et par de simples mots, vous pouvez amener le moral de quelqu'un à de nouveaux bas niveaux.

Changez votre présent et créez un nouvel avenir pour vous et les vôtres dès aujourd'hui; que rien ne vous arrête ou ne vous fasse dérailler; que les paroles qui sortent de votre bouche changent la vie et portent du fruit. Car lorsque nous changeons nos paroles, nous changeons notre être même, et lorsque celui-ci est changé, Dieu fera en excès et en abondance au-delà de tout ce que nous pourrions jamais demander ou rêver, il en est capable.

Changez vos mots, changez votre monde!

CHAPITRE 2

LEÇONS APPRISES
L'ORGUEIL LE PLUS GRAND VIRUS

Nous trouvons dans la Bible une histoire extraordinaire sur le roi Ézéchias; il avait vingt-cinq ans lorsqu'il a commencé à régner sur Israël. Dans 2e Chroniques 29, nous trouvons que la parole de Dieu dit au verset 2: "Il fit ce qui était juste aux yeux de l'Éternel, comme avait fait David, son père."

Un jeune homme a ouvert les portes du temple et les a réparées, a reconstruit l'autel du temple, a ramené les holocaustes et a rétabli les lévites et les grands prêtres.

Tout allait si bien en Israël qu'au chapitre 30, verset 27, la Bible dit: "Les prêtres et les lévites se levèrent pour bénir le peuple, et Dieu les exauça, car leur prière parvint jusqu'au ciel, sa sainte demeure ".

Pensez-y un instant: leurs prières sont parvenues jusqu'au ciel, sa sainte demeure! C'est puissant, et le chapitre 31 raconte que les Israélites qui se trouvaient là se rendirent dans les villes de Juda, brisèrent les pierres sacrées et coupèrent les mâts d'ashère. Ils ont détruit les hauts lieux et les autels dans tout Juda et Benjamin, Ephraïm et Manassé. Puis, après les avoir tous détruits, les Israélites retournèrent dans leurs villes et sur leurs terres.

Un puissant mouvement de Dieu a eu lieu; une sorte de réveil a frappé le pays. Le verset 20 des 2èmes Chroniques dit: "Voici ce qu'Ézéchias fit dans tout Juda, faisant ce qui est bon, juste et fidèle devant l'Éternel, son Dieu. 21 Dans tout ce qu'il entreprit pour le service du temple de Dieu et l'obéissance à la loi et aux commandements, il chercha son Dieu et travailla de tout son cœur. Et c'est ainsi qu'il prospéra.

La prospérité régnait dans le pays; le peuple fixait sa vie et se consacrait au Seigneur. Tout allait bien jusqu'au chapitre 32. Nous découvrons alors que Sennacherib, roi d'Assyrie, envahit Juda et assiège les villes fortifiées, pensant les conquérir pour lui-même.

Au verset 20, la Bible dit: "Le roi Ézéchias et le prophète Ésaïe, fils d'Amoz, crièrent au ciel en priant à ce sujet.

21 Et le Seigneur envoya un ange qui anéantit tous les combattants, les commandants et les officiers dans le camp du roi assyrien. Et celui-ci se retira dans son pays, en disgrâce. Et quand il entra dans le temple de son Dieu, certains de ses fils, sa chair et son sang, le tuèrent par l'épée.

22 Ainsi le Seigneur sauva Ézéchias et le peuple de Jérusalem de la main de Sennacherib, roi d'Assyrie, et de la main de tous les autres. Il prit soin d'eux de tous côtés.

23 Beaucoup apportèrent à Jérusalem des offrandes pour le Seigneur et des cadeaux de valeur pour Ézéchias, roi de Juda. Dès lors, il fut très apprécié de toutes les nations.

Jusqu'à présent, le roi Ézéchias a conduit Israël à la victoire, a tout bien fait aux yeux du Seigneur son Dieu, et soudain, la maladie s'abat sur lui jusqu'à la mort. Mais, dans sa maladie, il a fait ce qu'il faisait de mieux, c'est-à-dire chercher la face du Seigneur son Dieu, il a prié, et Dieu a entendu sa prière et lui a envoyé un signe.

Un signe? il demandait la guérison, et Dieu lui a envoyé un signe? Arrêtez-vous un instant: combien de fois Dieu répond-il à nos prières par une réponse que nous n'attendons pas ou que nous n'avons pas demandée? Cependant, le signe était unique, et la réponse à sa prière était la bonté!

De la bonté pour une personne malade et mourante? Mais le vrai problème n'était pas la maladie; le problème n'était pas la réponse à sa prière; le vrai problème était que l'orgueil s'était installé dans son cœur!

La Bible dit au verset 24 de 2e Chroniques 32: "En ce temps-là, Ézéchias tomba malade et fut sur le point de mourir. Il pria l'Eternel, qui l'exauça et lui donna un signe miraculeux.

25 Mais le cœur d'Ézéchias était orgueilleux, et il ne répondit pas à la bonté qui lui était témoignée; c'est pourquoi la colère du Seigneur s'abattit sur lui, sur Juda et sur Jérusalem.

Vous voyez, l'orgueil est un virus qui entre dans la vie d'une personne non pas pour la blesser mais pour la tuer. C'est un virus qui est si agressif qu'il ronge les fibres de votre âme. Il ne vous permet pas de profiter du présent; vous vous plaignez de votre passé et détruisez votre avenir.

L'orgueil s'installe, tue les relations, brise les partenariats et finit par aspirer la vie même de cette personne. Il tue les rêves et les visions, et tous les progrès que vous avez faits jusque-là sont détruits en une seconde; c'est dire à quel point l'orgueil est puissant et destructeur.

La Bible est claire quant à sa position sur l'orgueil,

Proverbes 11:2 "Quand vient l'orgueil, alors vient la disgrâce, mais avec l'humilité vient la sagesse."

Proverbes 16:5 "L'Éternel a en horreur tous les orgueilleux du cœur. Soyez donc certains de ceci: Ils ne resteront pas impunis."

Proverbes 16:18 "L'orgueil précède la ruine, un esprit hautain précède la chute."

Rien de bon ne peut jamais sortir de l'orgueil-rien! Le roi Ézéchias était malade à mort, et dans sa maladie, il est devenu fier dans son cœur et a attiré la colère de Dieu sur lui et les Israélites.

L'orgueil est un tueur de rêves, un destructeur de destinée; si vous l'avez et décidez de ne pas vous en débarrasser, il s'avérera être une puissante pierre d'achoppement sur votre chemin vers la grandeur. L'orgueil a le pouvoir de vous faire reculer de plusieurs mois, voire d'années et de décennies, car il ferme la porte à de grandes choses pour votre vie.

Vous regardez la rouille sur une voiture; elle ne commence jamais assez gros pour que vous la remarquiez. Au lieu de cela, elle commence petit et innocent, comme si rien ne se passait. Pendant ce temps, elle ronge la peinture et la voiture elle-même et, si l'on n'y prend garde, elle envahira tout le véhicule. Peu importe où elle commence sur la voiture, ce n'est qu'une question de temps avant qu'elle ne se propage et que ce qui était autrefois une belle voiture ne soit plus qu'un tas de rouille dont personne ne veut.

L'orgueil fait mal; il tue, vous sépare des autres, vous maintient sur une île pour vous seul, sans personne pour vous aider. Il vous isole tellement que même si les gens veulent vous aider, ils choisissent de ne pas le faire à cause de votre orgueil. C'est une puanteur imaginaire qui vient sur vous, que les autres sentent et voient, mais malheureusement, il devient difficile pour vous de la voir.

S'il n'est pas traité, l'orgueil est comme une tornade, il arrive et détruit tout et n'importe quoi sur son passage, laissant une traînée de destruction et de désespoir. Selon la Bible, le roi Ézéchias s'est vu montrer de la gentillesse, mais il s'est enflé d'orgueil dans son cœur, au point d'offenser Dieu, qui a décidé de répondre à cet orgueil par la colère et le jugement.

Vos rêves sont bloqués par l'orgueil, et la grandeur ne sera jamais atteinte parce que vous avez choisi l'orgueil dans votre cœur plutôt que l'humilité. Une personne orgueilleuse est arrogante et dédaigneuse. Les personnes orgueilleuses n'ont généralement pas beaucoup d'amis, car elles se croient supérieures à tous les autres.

Le péché biblique de l'orgueil fait référence à une attitude élevée ou exaltée, à l'opposé de la vertu de l'humilité, qui est la position appropriée que les gens devraient avoir avec Dieu.

Un cœur orgueilleux est rempli d'égoïsme et perd de vue le véritable objectif d'un leader: transformer la vie des autres. Mais, malheureusement, il est souvent difficile de s'en rendre compte avant qu'il ne soit trop tard. Nous allons donc de l'avant, poussés par notre cœur orgueilleux, jusqu'à ce que nous soyons transformés en pierre spirituelle.

L'orgueil est souvent motivé par une mauvaise estime de soi et la honte. Nous nous sentons si mal dans notre peau que nous compensons en nous sentant supérieurs. Nous recherchons les défauts des autres afin de dissimuler les nôtres. Nous prenons plaisir à critiquer les autres pour nous défendre contre la reconnaissance de nos défauts.

Proverbes 8:13 "La crainte de l'Éternel, c'est de haïr le mal. Je hais l'orgueil, l'arrogance, la voie mauvaise et la bouche fuyante.

Maintenant, qu'est-ce que cela signifie de s'humilier devant Dieu? Pour moi, cela signifie venir devant Jésus avec crainte et révérence, sans tenir compte de ce que les gens peuvent penser de vous. C'est être prêt à dire: "J'avais tort". ... C'est se décentrer de soi-même pour se concentrer sur ce qui compte-Dieu! Enfin, venez à la croix avec une conscience claire.

L'orgueil nous pousse à évaluer notre vie à l'aune de nos réalisations plutôt qu'à celle de l'identité que Dieu nous a donnée. L'orgueil (ou, comme on dit, "l'ego") nous sépare du dessein de Dieu de vivre dans une relation avec les autres. Nous sommes poussés à l'isolement par notre confiance en nous-mêmes, croyant au mensonge selon lequel la vie est meilleure seule.

Sur votre chemin vers la grandeur, vous aurez de nombreuses "occasions" d'accepter la fierté en raison de vos réalisations, mais faites le choix judicieux de rejeter cette opportunité, restez humble, soyez et soyez gentil, appréciez ce que vous avez et soyez reconnaissant pour les choses que vous n'avez pas. Appréciez et aimez ceux qui sont dans votre vie, chérissez la parole de Dieu comme pierre angulaire et fondement de votre progrès et regardez Dieu tourner les choses en votre faveur.

1 Pierre 5:5 De même, les plus jeunes, soyez soumis aux anciens. Revêtez-vous tous d'humilité les uns envers les autres, car "Dieu s'oppose aux orgueilleux, mais il fait grâce aux humbles".

C'est puissant, la grâce aux humbles! J'ai appris qu'être humble ouvre des portes que l'argent ne peut pas ouvrir. Être humble ouvre des opportunités qui autrement ne seraient pas ouvertes. Alors restez humble lorsque vous réalisez des choses, et ne prêtez jamais l'oreille à l'orgueil-jamais!

NE PROCRASTINEZ PAS

La procrastination est "l'acte de retarder volontairement l'accomplissement de quelque chose qui devrait être fait". Chez certaines personnes, c'est une façon habituelle d'accomplir une tâche. Bien que le mot lui-même ne se trouve pas dans la Bible, nous pouvons y trouver quelques principes pour nous guider.

Parfois, la procrastination résulte de la paresse, et la Bible a beaucoup à dire à ce sujet. La Bible loue le travail acharné et l'industrie (Proverbes 12:24; 13:4) et met en garde contre la paresse et le laisser-aller (Proverbes 15:19; 18:9).

L'un des remèdes à la procrastination est une plus grande diligence, quelle que soit la tâche. Nous devrions être suprêmement motivés pour être diligents dans notre travail puisque nous servons en fin de compte le Seigneur. "Tout ce que vous faites, travaillez-y de tout votre cœur, comme travaillant pour le Seigneur, et non pour des hommes" (Colossiens 3:23).

Si nous mettons notre cœur dans notre travail, comme ce verset nous dit de le faire, nous trouverons probablement difficile de trop procrastiner.

La procrastination, c'est le fait de remettre sans cesse à plus tard une chose que l'on devrait faire maintenant. Il existe de nombreuses raisons pour lesquelles les gens procrastinent: La peur, l'anxiété, le refus d'affronter le changement... Peut-être même la peur du succès.

La vérité est que lorsque nous remettons à plus tard, nous déclenchons une réaction en chaîne d'événements qui peuvent avoir un impact négatif sur les autres-et pas seulement sur nous. Et Dieu nous appelle à faire du bien aux autres. Mais, au contraire, lorsque nous remettons à plus tard, nous faisons le contraire du bien!

Quand les gens pensent à la procrastination, ils pensent à la paresse. Ils peuvent même se demander "que dit la Bible sur la paresse?". Mais la vérité est que ce sont deux choses très différentes.

La paresse signifie que vous n'êtes pas disposé à travailler ou à utiliser votre énergie (Dictionary.com).

En revanche, la procrastination ne signifie pas que vous n'êtes pas disposé à travailler, mais que vous remettez quelque chose à plus tard.

Les rêves peuvent être mis en veilleuse non pas parce que vous n'y croyez pas, mais parce que vous tardez à travailler sur votre vision. Bien sûr, consacrer du temps à la planification de votre rêve et à l'exécution de l'objectif est important, mais il ne faut pas que la procrastination prenne le dessus.

La procrastination tuera le même élan que vous pourriez avoir pour réaliser vos rêves et vos objectifs; elle vous paralysera et vous mettra à l'arrêt. Si nous continuons à dire "je le ferai demain" et que, le lendemain, nous n'avons toujours pas commencé, nous mettons essentiellement nos rêves dans un cercueil et les enterrons six pieds sous terre.

La procrastination peut devenir très confortable et tout à fait raisonnable.

Car, dans l'ombre de la procrastination, il y a des excuses qui se cachent dans l'obscurité, vous faisant croire que le faire demain serait une meilleure décision, alors qu'en réalité, le faire demain vous prive de l'opportunité de vous surpasser aujourd'hui!

Les gens procrastinent souvent à cause de leurs échecs passés, et ils pensent à ce qu'ils ont ressenti lorsqu'ils ont échoué et à la douleur que cela a causé, alors pour éviter la douleur et les peurs, ils procrastinent en se donnant une autre chance!

VAINCRE LA CULPABILITÉ DE L'ÉCHEC

Il y a deux mots essentiels dans ce titre-Culpabilité et Échec, qui seront tous deux abordés ici. L'échec est toujours associé à des émotions de défaite et à une mauvaise expérience. Il n'est jamais vraiment associé à quelque chose de bon. Nous échouons tout le temps; nous échouons même lorsque nous ne voulons pas échouer. Nous échouons volontairement, et nous échouons sans le vouloir.

Nos échecs ne doivent pas nécessairement être associés à une connotation négative; l'échec peut aussi être une bonne chose qui vous arrive. Vous pouvez soit voir votre échec comme une chose terrible qui vous est arrivée, et ne vous méprenez pas, certains événements qui surviennent dans notre vie sont des événements bouleversants.

Certains événements détruisent nos émotions et nous mettent à genoux, brisant toute pensée que tout ira bien. Des événements qui contiennent des épreuves, qui testent la fibre même de notre être. Des moments de notre vie qui nous font nous réveiller au milieu de la nuit avec des sueurs froides, effrayés par ce que nous avons vécu ou devons encore vivre.

L'échec ajoute au stress et à la douleur, la culpabilité étant si importante que nous devenons paralysés par la culpabilité de l'échec qui nous fait croire que l'espoir a disparu depuis longtemps. La culpabilité nous fait penser que nous ne pouvons pas faire un pas de plus, et que nous sommes sûrs de mourir dans le gouffre de cette culpabilité et de cette honte.

Nous remettons en question notre foi, nous doutons de la parole, nous déversons notre colère et nos frustrations sur ceux qui ne la méritent pas, nous dépassons les bornes et nos paroles offensent ceux qui nous sont proches, et surtout, nous pensons souvent que c'est la faute de Dieu pour ce qui est arrivé.

L'ennemi utilise la culpabilité de l'échec pour souligner que Dieu ne s'est pas montré comme il l'avait promis. Pourtant, Dieu a une façon passionnante d'arranger les choses. Il a dit dans sa parole Esaïe 55:8-9: "Car mes pensées ne sont pas vos pensées, Et vos voies ne sont pas mes voies, dit le Seigneur. "Car, comme les cieux sont plus élevés que la terre, Mes voies sont plus élevées que vos voies, Et Mes pensées plus que vos pensées.

Ses voies sont mystérieuses, et rien ne le surprend ou ne le prend au dépourvu. Il sait tout et voit tout, entend tout et a toujours une réponse à ces choses que nous n'avons pas. Votre échec n'a donc pas pris Dieu au dépourvu; il ne l'a pas surpris, il ne dormait pas quand cela vous est arrivé, et avant que cela ne vous arrive, il avait la réponse.

Si l'échec était si grand, pourquoi s'est-il produit? Voilà la vraie question et une question parfaite. Nous n'avons pas la réponse à certaines des questions les plus complexes parfois, pourtant, il y a certaines choses dont je peux être assuré, et c'est que mon échec n'est pas absolu peu importe comment il est ou comment il devient mauvais si Dieu devant vous alors qui peut être contre vous! Romains 8:31 dit: Que dirons-nous donc de ces choses? Si Dieu est pour nous, qui peut être contre nous?

Ce "Qui" peut être traduit non seulement par une personne, mais aussi par une "chose". "Car il dit Que dirons-nous donc à ces CHOSES? LES CHOSES! Les choses arrivent, et les personnes nous arrivent; les deux sont tout aussi mortelles et blessantes. Paul l'a donc bien dit aux Romains, et à ce stade, les choses sont déjà arrivées, quelque chose a eu lieu, traumatisant et tout. Cependant, il n'offre pas de sympathie à ce stade, non pas parce qu'il était antipathique mais parce qu'il voulait qu'ils ne restent pas dans cette émotion de culpabilité et d'échec.

Des choses vont nous arriver, nous affecter et nous ébranler, mais il insiste sur le fait que si Dieu est pour nous, qui peut être contre nous? Il est passé des choses à un qui; il s'est adressé aux deux en même temps. Si nous choisissons de rester dans cette émotion de culpabilité et d'échec, nous passerons à côté de la véritable leçon que Dieu voulait nous enseigner.

Regardez Job; la Bible dit dans Job 1:1 Il y avait au pays d'Uz un homme dont le nom était Job; cet homme était parfait et droit, il craignait Dieu et se détournait du mal. Vous lisez la vie de cet homme du verset 2 au verset 5; vous vous rendez compte que cet homme est riche, puissant, qu'il exerce une influence sur le pays, qu'il est pratiquement fixé pour la vie. Pourtant, en un jour, tout son monde s'est écroulé devant lui. En un jour, il est passé de tout à rien! Pourtant, la Bible dit que cet homme était parfait et droit. Comment faites-vous pour recevoir une accolade telle que "parfait" et "droit"?

Pourtant, même en ayant ces deux accolades attachées à son nom, la destruction est arrivée dans sa vie en un seul jour. A-t-il mérité cela? Quel péché a-t-il commis pour que tout cela lui arrive? Peut-être vous êtes-vous déjà posé ces mêmes questions: pourquoi cela est-il arrivé? ou qu'ai-je fait pour mériter cela? Je me suis posé les mêmes questions. Mais, si souvent, ces questions restent sans réponse, on a l'impression qu'il y a un silence, et que Dieu vous a oublié, alors que c'est tout le contraire, Dieu est aux commandes.

Au verset 8, quelque chose d'excitant se produit: "Et l'Éternel dit à Satan: As-tu considéré mon serviteur Job, qu'il n'y a personne comme lui sur la terre, un homme parfait et droit, qui craint Dieu et qui évite le mal?"

Dieu a proposé Job pour l'épreuve; Dieu a proposé Job comme sa "vedette", "Dieu savait qu'il pouvait proposer Job, et Dieu était sûr qu'il passerait l'épreuve. Attendez un moment.....

Se pourrait-il que ce soit la façon dont Dieu vous met en valeur et vous prépare à une bénédiction plus incroyable? Se pourrait-il que ce soit la manière de Dieu de vous promouvoir? Se pourrait-il que ce soit le moyen que Dieu utilise pour apporter une faveur et une bénédiction surnaturelles dans votre vie? Serait-ce la situation qui va changer les choses? Mais, d'un autre côté, Dieu pourrait-il faire de ce désordre un message? Et une épreuve en un témoignage?

La réponse à toutes ces questions est un OUI retentissant!

Avancez jusqu'à la fin de la vie de Job, et la Bible dit dans Job 42:12, L'Éternel bénit la fin de Job plus que son commencement... elle dit aussi dans Job 1:22, "Dans tout cela, Job n'a pas péché et n'a pas accusé Dieu de mal."

Sa femme l'a quitté, ses amis l'ont quitté, il a perdu tout son bétail, ses enfants sont morts, la destruction est arrivée, on lui a dit que c'était sa faute pour tout ce qui était arrivé, on l'a blâmé pour tout, et à travers tout cela, il n'a pas péché ni accusé Dieu, en un mot tout ce que je peux dire est WOW!

Aujourd'hui, nous laissons un orteil de bébé sur le coin du lit, et nous déclarons que c'est la fin du monde tel que nous le connaissons. C'est encore plus profond lorsqu'au milieu de son "échec", il dit dans Job 1:21, "Nu, je suis sorti du ventre de ma mère, et nu, j'y retournerai. L'Éternel a donné, et l'Éternel a repris; que le nom de l'Éternel soit béni."

Béni soit le nom du Seigneur-il dit cela au milieu de sa douleur et de sa souffrance, il bénit le Seigneur à travers la culpabilité de son échec, il fait ce que personne ne pensait faire, il bénit le nom du Seigneur. C'est une leçon à apprendre, que, même si les épreuves et les tribulations arrivent, même si la douleur et la souffrance sont complexes, que la nuit de chagrin est longue, et que la tempête fait rage, vous avez le POUVOIR de vous lever et de bénir le nom du Seigneur. Vous avez le POUVOIR de vous lever et de reconnaître, avec chaque fibre de votre être, que vous êtes dans les meilleures mains possibles et que le Seigneur ne vous quittera ni ne vous abandonnera jamais, mais qu'il sera avec vous tous les jours de votre vie!

Votre échec n'est pas la fin, mais reconnaissez-le comme un nouveau départ-une occasion d'apprendre et de grandir. Votre échec est rempli de douleur et de larmes. Cependant, vous avez le pouvoir de transformer cette expérience négative en une expérience positive, sachant que Dieu a permis que toutes les choses négatives vous arrivent afin que vous puissiez avoir l'expérience de partager une histoire dont le témoignage est si puissant que tous ceux qui l'entendront sauront que c'était Dieu qui était avec vous.

Vous n'avez pas échoué, l'échec n'est pas votre roi, et vous n'avez pas à être lié par la culpabilité de cet échec; vous êtes le fils ou la fille du Dieu suprême, et en tant que tel, votre dernier sera plus significatif à la fin qu'au début! Ce n'est pas fini, tu n'as pas fini, la course n'est pas terminée, tu n'as pas été assommé, relève-toi, dépoussière-toi, tu es libéré de la culpabilité au nom de Jésus.

Si Job a eu le pouvoir de se lever et de dire ce qu'il a dit et n'a pas péché, alors vous avez la capacité de faire la même chose; Dieu donne et Dieu reprend, mais BLESSÉ SOIT LE NOM DU SEIGNEUR!

Il y a trois étapes fondamentales pour surmonter la culpabilité de l'échec; permettez-moi de les partager avec vous.

La première étape pour être libéré de cette culpabilité est de mettre tous vos fardeaux sur lui; la parole dit 1 Pierre 5:7 "Jetez tous vos soucis sur lui, car il prend soin de vous". "Vous ne serez jamais libre si vous essayez de porter ce poids sur vos épaules chaque jour. Une ancre est conçue pour vous maintenir en place, et si le navire prend l'eau, elle le tirera vers le bas. Ne laissez donc pas la culpabilité être votre ancre qui vous tire vers le bas ou vous empêche d'avancer vers votre objectif et votre destinée.

Le second est Proverbes 3:5 "Fais confiance à l'Éternel de tout ton cœur, Et ne t'appuie pas sur ta propre intelligence"; Tu dois croire que Dieu va changer les choses. Vous devez croire, pas seulement penser, mais croire que Dieu est aux commandes et que tout tournera à votre avantage. Croyez que Dieu fera un chemin là où il n'y en a pas. Esaïe 41:10 dit Ne crains pas, car je suis avec toi; ne t'effraie pas, car je suis ton Dieu; je te fortifierai, je te secourrai, je te soutiendrai de ma droite juste.

Enfin, vous ne pouvez pas rester dans cette fosse de chagrin; vous devez vous relever et aller de l'avant. La Bible dit dans Esaïe 43:18: "Ne vous souvenez pas des choses passées, et ne considérez pas les choses du passé." Vous ne pouvez pas rester dans cette condition; c'est arrivé, nous ne pouvons pas revenir en arrière pour changer les choses, mais nous pouvons changer notre demain par nos actions d'aujourd'hui.

2 Corinthiens 5:17 Ainsi, si quelqu'un est en Christ, il est une nouvelle création. Les choses anciennes ont disparu; voici, les choses nouvelles sont venues. Dieu veut vous façonner en quelque chose de plus grand et de meilleur, une nouvelle version de vous, portant toutes les cicatrices de la bataille mais avec une richesse de connaissances.

Jean 5:8 "Jésus lui dit: "Lève-toi, prends ton lit, et marche". Ce sont vos ordres de marche; ce sont les mots pour vous aujourd'hui; alors que vous lisez ceci, peu importe ce que vous traversez ou avez traversé, Dieu vous dit Lève-toi et marche! Si vous suivez ces trois étapes simples mais puissantes, vous verrez la puissance et la main puissante de Dieu sur votre vie.

Votre dernière sera plus significative que vous commencez-vous êtes libre!

LIBÉREZ VOTRE CŒUR DE LA PEUR

Le cerveau est complexe, et le cœur est mystérieux; qui peut le connaître? J'ai donc dû faire une petite recherche et étudier cela, spirituellement et physiquement parlant.

Le cerveau est un organe complexe qui contrôle la pensée, la mémoire, les émotions, le toucher, la motricité, la vision, la respiration, la température, la faim et tous les processus qui régissent notre corps. Le cerveau et la moelle épinière qui en partent constituent le système nerveux central.

Dans votre esprit, une bataille se prépare chaque jour, des décisions doivent être prises, et souvent des décisions qui n'affecteront pas seulement vous mais aussi ceux qui vous entourent. En effet, votre cerveau (esprit) contrôle vos pensées, vos émotions, votre vision et même votre respiration.

L'ennemi se battra pour le contrôle de votre esprit, car c'est là que se gagnent et se perdent les batailles. Le cerveau est très complexe, mais votre cœur l'est encore plus. Le cœur est un organe musculaire de la taille d'un poing, situé juste derrière et légèrement à gauche du sternum. Le cœur pompe le sang dans le réseau d'artères et de veines appelé système cardiovasculaire.

Le cœur comporte quatre cavités:

-L'oreillette droite reçoit le sang des veines et le pompe vers le ventricule droit.

-Le ventricule droit reçoit le sang de l'oreillette droite et le pompe vers les poumons, chargé d'oxygène.

-L'oreillette gauche reçoit le sang oxygéné des poumons et le pompe vers le ventricule gauche.

-Le ventricule gauche (la chambre la plus robuste) pompe le sang riche en oxygène vers le reste du corps. Les contractions vigoureuses du ventricule gauche créent notre tension artérielle.

Proverbes 4:23 dit: "Par-dessus tout, garde ton cœur, car tout ce que tu fais en découle."

Phillippiens 4:7 dit: "Et la paix de Dieu, qui surpasse toute intelligence, gardera vos cœurs et vos esprits en Jésus-Christ.

Votre cœur est précieux, pourtant des personnes peuvent se promener sans cœur, au sens figuré. Un cœur "propre" peut se manifester par des actions significatives de la part d'une personne; il génère de bonnes émotions, vous met dans un endroit sain; de la même manière, un cœur "sombre" peut se traduire par des actions mauvaises et nuisibles.

La bible dit dans Luc 6:45, "Un homme bon, du bon trésor de son cœur, produit du bien; et un homme mauvais, du mauvais trésor de son cœur, produit du mal. Car c'est de l'abondance du cœur que la bouche parle."

La peur s'insinue souvent dans le cœur et peut provoquer une sorte de crise cardiaque spirituelle. La peur cause de la douleur et de l'anxiété, elle peut amener une personne à agir ou à réagir d'une manière particulière alors qu'autrement elle n'agirait ou ne réagirait pas.

Esaïe 41:10 dit: "Ne crains pas, car je suis avec toi; ne t'effraie pas, car je suis ton Dieu; je te fortifierai, je te secourrai, je te soutiendrai de ma droite juste."

Comme vous le savez sans doute, l'expression "ne crains pas" est mentionnée 365 fois dans la bible, une coïncidence? Absolument pas! La peur dans votre cœur vous fera entrer dans un état d'esprit très dangereux. Elle ne vous permettra pas de faire un pas de plus dans la direction de vos objectifs et de votre vision.

La peur dans le cœur vous amènera à manifester des émotions que vous ne révéleriez pas habituellement, souvent couvertes par l'illusion d'être prudent. La peur rouille l'âme et l'esprit de la personne. Si on la laisse perdurer, elle consumera la vie de quelqu'un, et cette personne ne sera plus jamais la même.

Elle fait mourir vos rêves et vos objectifs, les enterrant à jamais dans l'état de simple rêve ou objectif. Le cœur sera blessé émotionnellement et ne guérira jamais, car l'une des choses les plus difficiles à faire est d'abandonner ses rêves et ses objectifs parce qu'on a peur.

C'est douloureux lorsque vous ne pouvez plus poursuivre votre rêve, non pas parce que vous êtes arrêté par quelqu'un ou quelque chose, mais l'incapacité de suivre votre vision et vos objectifs à cause de la peur est l'une des choses les plus tragiques qui puissent arriver. C'est difficile lorsque vous êtes arrêté par des choses hors de votre contrôle, plus difficile à accepter lorsque vous êtes la raison pour laquelle vous n'allez pas plus loin.

La peur dans votre cœur ne vous permettra pas de faire quoi que ce soit; Dieu ne vous a pas donné un esprit de peur. Ainsi, la Bible dit dans le 2ème Timothée 1:7, "Car Dieu ne nous a pas donné un esprit de crainte, mais de PUISSANCE, d'AMOUR et d'ESPRIT SÛR.

Ceci est très puissant car cela vous montre les domaines que la peur dans le cœur affectera. Elle vous affaiblira, tuera votre amour et troublera votre esprit.

Elle vous affaiblira pour ne pas marcher et poursuivre ce que Dieu a préparé pour vous. Elle affaiblira votre ambition, votre désir et votre motivation, tuant essentiellement tout élan que vous aviez pour grandir et réaliser vos rêves. La peur affaiblira souvent votre passion pour la prière ou la recherche de la face de Dieu, réduisant votre démarche spirituelle à néant. Elle sapera votre relation avec Dieu et votre relation avec les autres. Vous ne pouvez pas laisser la peur vous affaiblir, car elle vous entraînera dans une spirale descendante dont vous ne pourrez souvent pas sortir.

Ce n'est qu'à travers une relation avec Jésus et le Saint-Esprit que vous pourrez surmonter cette peur et vaincre la faiblesse qu'elle entraîne. En vous imprégnant de la parole, vous gagnerez en force pour combattre ce virus qu'est la peur. En continuant à chercher sa face, vous serez en mesure de renforcer votre Esprit et votre résolution de ne pas abandonner mais de continuer à avancer et à vous battre.

La peur tuera votre AMOUR, pour Dieu, votre famille et vos amis, ainsi que vos rêves et vos objectifs. Si vous laissez la peur détruire votre amour pour les choses de Dieu, vous devenez froid et insensible à ces choses de l'Esprit. Si votre passion pour les choses de Dieu meurt, vous connaîtrez une sécheresse dans votre vie qui ne peut être remplie par personne ou par quoi que ce soit.

La peur détruira également la passion et l'amour pour vos rêves et vos objectifs. Malheureusement, c'est là que beaucoup de gens abandonnent souvent. Ils deviennent frustrés et ont tendance à blâmer les autres pour leur manque d'action-un mécanisme pour cacher les véritables émotions que leur AMOUR pour la poursuite des rêves et des objectifs est abandonné.

Lorsque l'amour disparaît, la frustration s'installe et le jeu des reproches commence. Cependant, vous ne pouvez pas laisser la peur tuer votre passion; vous ne pouvez pas laisser la peur entraver votre amour à cause de quelques contrariétés que vous pouvez rencontrer dans la vie. Des moments difficiles viendront, des pertes se produiront, mais ce n'est pas une raison suffisante pour permettre à votre amour pour Dieu de s'étioler jusqu'au néant.

Vous ne pouvez pas permettre aux frustrations de tuer votre élan; votre course n'est pas un sprint mais un marathon, et votre amour pour non seulement Dieu mais les choses de Dieu et vos objectifs et rêves personnels de mourir. Tout est mis en péril lorsque vous permettez à la peur de tuer votre amour, et tout s'effondrera lorsque vous permettez à la peur de détruire votre amour.

La peur s'attaquera également à votre esprit, contrôlant votre façon de parler, d'agir et de réagir. Si votre esprit est contrôlé par la peur, vous ne prendrez pas de décisions correctes; elle entravera votre capacité à générer de nouvelles idées et rendra vos actions mortes.

Si votre esprit est affecté par la peur, vous verrez les résultats se manifester dans votre discours, et les preuves de la peur seront visibles dans vos actions. La peur dans votre esprit détruira la capacité de penser correctement, mettant en péril les décisions critiques; votre anxiété se traduira par des décisions qui modifieront le cours de votre marche. La peur dans l'esprit est dangereuse parce que votre esprit est un champ de bataille avec un million et une pensée qui le traverse chaque jour.

Psaumes 27:3 "Quand une armée camperait contre moi, mon cœur ne craindrait pas; quand une guerre s'élèverait contre moi, je serais confiant."

Il enverra des signaux au cœur que vous avez peur, et votre capacité à fonctionner est maintenant remise en question. Aujourd'hui, nous n'avons peut-être pas une armée campée autour de nous physiquement parlant, mais l'ennemi vous fait la guerre pour affecter votre esprit et votre cœur.

Cette guerre est féroce et désordonnée; elle vous fera perdre le sommeil, la faim et d'autres choses encore. C'est une guerre dont vous n'êtes pas exempt, mais c'est une guerre que vous devez affronter de front. Une bataille que vous DEVEZ gagner, et j'insiste sur le terme DEVEZ car si vous commencez à marcher vers votre rêve et à construire votre avenir, vous ne pouvez pas vous offrir le luxe d'abandonner ou de baisser les bras.

La Bible dit dans le 2ème Corinthiens 10:4, "Les armes de notre combat ne sont pas charnelles, mais puissantes en Dieu pour abattre les forteresses".

Il serait préférable que vous reconnaissiez que votre guerre n'est pas charnelle, votre combat n'est pas physique, mais votre bataille et votre guerre ont des implications spirituelles de proportions épiques. Mais il vous a donné des armes suffisamment fortes pour vous permettre de vous battre et de gagner!

Il a dit que vos armes sont PUISSANTES EN DIEU-c'est la clé car elles sont puissantes non pas à cause de vous ou parce qu'elles sont entre vos mains, mais elles sont puissantes en DIEU et en Dieu seul.

Jacques 4:7 dit: "Soumettez-vous donc à Dieu. Résistez au diable, et il fuira loin de vous."

La soumission à Dieu est votre première ligne de défense. Elle vous permet de soumettre vos rêves et vos objectifs à Dieu; elle vous permettra de tuer votre orgueil et vous permettra de poursuivre la réalisation de vos rêves et de vos objectifs.

La soumission à Dieu maintiendra en vie votre amour pour Lui, et elle maintiendra également le désir d'aller de l'avant et de se battre avec de nouvelles forces et la détermination de réussir. Votre soumission à Dieu vous permettra de vous battre et de résister aux œuvres de l'ennemi qu'il a complotées contre vous.

La parole dit aussi, RESISTER à l'ennemi; c'est là que vous devez activer votre Foi, et la parole doit être active et vivante dans votre esprit, votre cœur et votre bouche. Pour être capable de prononcer la parole de Dieu dans votre situation, et vous verrez la puissance qu'elle a pour changer l'atmosphère et modifier le cours de votre marche. Si la parole est vivante en vous, vous serez capable de repousser les attaques sur votre esprit et votre cœur. La parole de Dieu vous permet d'avoir la colonne vertébrale spirituelle pour résister à l'ennemi et à ses attaques.

Lorsque vous soumettez à Dieu vos rêves, vos objectifs et vos visions, vous y incluez Dieu, et si Dieu y est inclus, alors l'échec n'est jamais une option, mais vous obtiendrez d'énormes succès et victoires. Le problème avec beaucoup de gens est qu'ils font des plans sans inclure Dieu; ils essaient de faire de GRANDES choses sans avoir Dieu dans ces discussions ou projets.

La bible dit de ne pas s'appuyer sur son intelligence; en d'autres termes, n'essayez pas de faire des choses sans Dieu car cela échouera sûrement. Maintenant vous pouvez dire, beaucoup de gens réussissent sans avoir Dieu dans leurs plans; ils sont païens, et Dieu est loin de leurs conversations, pourtant ils continuent à prospérer; comment est-ce possible?

Il y a toujours un prix à payer; quelle que soit la décision que vous prenez, ou le chemin que vous choisissez de parcourir, vous paierez un prix pour cette décision. Pour perdre du poids, vous devez payer le prix, dont certains sont le sacrifice, la discipline et la maîtrise de soi. Le sacrifice et l'investissement en temps à la salle de sport, la discipline pour maintenir le cap de votre entraînement et de votre régime, et la maîtrise de soi pour résister à la tentation de ne pas manger ce que vous ne devriez pas manger.

Le prix à payer pour être utilisé par Dieu est d'investir du temps dans la prière, l'humilité, la patience, et bien d'autres choses encore. Pour tout ce que nous choisissons, nous devons payer ce prix. Rien n'est gratuit, rien qui compte, du moins.

Esaïe 35:4 "Dis à ceux qui ont le cœur inquiet:" Fortifiez-vous, ne craignez rien! Voici que votre Dieu vient avec la vengeance, avec la rétribution de Dieu. Il viendra et vous sauvera."

Vous ne pouvez pas vivre dans un état de peur toute votre vie; vous devez être capable d'être fort et de ne pas avoir peur! On peut dire que c'est plus facile à dire qu'à faire, mais en réalité, lorsque vous soumettez vos objectifs, vos rêves et vos visions au Seigneur, c'est alors que votre cœur sera effectivement libéré de la peur.

Ce qui est le plus excitant dans ce verset, c'est qu'Ésaïe dit que votre Dieu viendra avec vengeance, avec la récompense de Dieu. Il viendra et vous sauvera.

Non seulement Dieu vient avec une vengeance, mais aussi avec une récompense! Avec une vengeance pour tes ennemis mais en même temps avec une compensation pour toi! Quand ton cœur prend la parole, la croit et l'applique, alors ton cœur se reposera et sera libre de la peur qui l'étrangle.

Quand tu seras libéré de la peur dans le cœur, tu activeras ta Foi dans une plus grande dimension. Une fois que votre cœur est libre, alors vous serez en mesure de libérer votre Esprit pour être utilisé par Dieu dans une plus grande capacité, en vous rapprochant de votre destinée, et un esprit d'excellence s'empare de vous.

LE POUVOIR D'AVOIR UN ESPRIT D'EXCELLENCE

N'importe qui peut accomplir n'importe quelle tâche qui lui est confiée. Tout le monde peut faire des choses avec la formation et les conseils appropriés, mais ce qui sépare ces personnes de la réalisation de leur destinée est l'esprit d'excellence qu'elles possèdent.

C'est ce qui sépare la moyenne de l'excellence, le médiocre de l'impressionnant, et le nul de l'impressionnant. Pour réaliser votre destinée, vous devez avoir un esprit d'excellence, ou plutôt, vous engager à avoir un esprit d'excellence lorsque vous faites les choses que Dieu vous a appelées à faire.

Dans Matthieu 25, la bible nous raconte une histoire assez puissante; elle dit au verset 14: "Encore une fois, ce sera comme un homme qui part en voyage, qui appelle ses serviteurs et leur confie ses richesses.

Le verset 15 dit: "Il donna à l'un cinq talents, à un autre deux, à un autre un, à chacun selon sa capacité; et aussitôt il partit en voyage.

Arrêtez-vous ici un instant.

Il a donné à chacun selon ses capacités!

Dieu ne vous donnera jamais un fardeau que vous ne pouvez pas porter,

1e Corinthiens 10:13 Il ne vous est survenu aucune tentation, si ce n'est celle qui est commune à l'homme; mais Dieu est fidèle, il ne permettra pas que vous soyez tentés au delà de vos forces, mais il ouvrira avec la tentation un chemin d'évasion, afin que vous puissiez la supporter.

Il vous donnera toujours quelque chose que vous pouvez supporter; il peut sembler que vous ne pouvez pas et que vous serez écrasé par la charge, mais Dieu vous a rendu assez fort pour la porter, la gérer et persévérer quoi qu'il arrive.

Votre destin est aussi grand que vous le voulez et aussi petit que vous le voulez. Dieu sera avec vous, quelle que soit la route que vous choisirez d'emprunter; le choix vous appartient absolument. Dieu a une grande destinée pour chacun, mais tout le monde n'accepte pas cette destinée.

Votre destin dépend de certains facteurs tels que votre foi, votre désir de l'atteindre, votre détermination à continuer quelles que soient les circonstances, votre dynamisme et enfin, votre désir d'atteindre l'excellence.

La bible dit qu'il a donné à chacun des talents, mais ce qui a fait la différence, ce n'est pas le talent mais ce que chaque personne a décidé de faire.

Matthieu 25:16-18 dit Alors celui qui avait reçu les cinq talents alla échanger avec eux, et fit cinq autres talents. De même, celui qui en avait reçu deux en gagna deux autres. Mais celui qui en avait reçu un alla creuser dans la terre et cacha l'argent de son maître.

Et c'est là que réside le problème: il a pris ce que son maître lui a donné, n'a pas prêté attention aux autres et l'a enterré. Il n'avait aucune vision, aucun désir, aucun élan, rien, sauf le fait qu'il a enterré ce que son maître lui a donné.

Combien de fois les gens, vous, enterrent-ils ce que Dieu vous a donné? Par peur, ou par manque de foi, vous enterrez ce don que Dieu vous a fait et vous enterrez votre destin avec.

Les deux autres avaient une vision; les deux autres avaient saisi ce qu'on leur avait donné et ont produit davantage. Un esprit d'excellence vous propulsera toujours à faire beaucoup plus pour le royaume; il ne vous permettra jamais de ne rien faire avec ce que Dieu vous a donné.

Ils ont pris ce qui leur a été donné et ont atteint la grandeur avec ce qui leur a été donné. L'autre n'a rien fait, et pourtant il pensait faire quelque chose. Vous ne pouvez pas faire l'erreur de prendre ce que Dieu vous a donné et de ne rien faire avec.

La bible dit dans Matthieu 7:16, vous les reconnaîtrez à leurs fruits!

Ce que vous faites de ce que Dieu vous donne déterminera le résultat de votre vie. Ce que vous faites des dons et des talents qu'il vous a confiés déterminera votre bonheur et votre taux de réussite dans la réalisation de vos objectifs et de vos rêves.

Il a enterré les talents que son maître lui avait donnés; en d'autres termes, il était paresseux, il a abandonné, il ne voulait pas s'en occuper. Combien de fois sommes-nous comme cet homme? Nous abandonnons parce que nous avons entendu des gens dire que nous ne pouvions pas le faire, nous démissionnons parce que nous blâmons l'éducation que nous avons reçue dans notre enfance, et cela ne veut pas dire que ce ne sont pas des évaluations justes de votre vie, mais aussi justes qu'elles puissent paraître, elles ne devraient jamais être suffisantes pour vous faire abandonner ou arrêter la poursuite de vos rêves.

Lorsque je n'étais encore qu'un jeune garçon, je me souviens avoir entendu mes parents parler de donner à Dieu le meilleur de ce que nous étions et de maximiser les dons et les talents qu'il a donnés à chacun d'entre nous. J'étais jeune et je n'avais pas encore découvert la véritable signification de ce que mon père disait. J'étais plus intéressé à jouer et à faire ce que les enfants font le mieux.

Donner à Dieu ce qu'il y a de mieux ne signifie pas lui donner la perfection, car cela est impossible en soi, mais donner à Dieu ce qu'il y a de mieux signifie d'abord et avant tout lui donner votre cœur. Ensuite, après l'avoir fait, vous vous donnez à 110 % dans tout ce qu'il vous propose.

À l'époque, je ne savais pas jouer du piano, mais je voulais devenir le responsable de la louange à l'église. Mon père était un grand claviériste et avait enregistré quelques cassettes à l'époque, mais avec son emploi du temps et ses responsabilités à l'église, le voir rentrer à la maison et aller directement au lit me faisait mal au cœur, sachant la pression qu'il subissait. Je n'ai pas pu trouver la force d'aller lui demander de m'apprendre à jouer quand j'ai appris à quel point il était fatigué.

Je sais que si je le lui avais demandé, je sais pertinemment qu'il aurait pris 5 minutes pour me montrer quelque chose chaque soir. J'ai donc décidé de prendre sur moi d'apprendre le clavier. Je me tenais à côté du claviériste de l'époque et le regardais jouer, et après chaque service, alors que tout le monde était en communion, on trouvait un jeune garçon dans le sanctuaire qui essayait de se souvenir de ce que j'avais vu et de le rejouer.

Mon frère et moi rentrions à la maison, et pendant notre temps libre, nous mettions une cassette, des CD qui n'existaient pas à l'époque, et nous suivions sur un clavier que mon père nous avait acheté. Chaque jour avançait, chaque jour était plein d'erreurs, et on continuait, mais on n'abandonnait jamais!

Plus on se plantait, plus on voulait essayer de comprendre et de perfectionner ce que la chanson essayait de nous apprendre. Mais nous n'avons jamais abandonné, nous n'avons pas cédé, nous ne nous sommes pas arrêtés et nous n'avons pas abandonné; c'est ce que signifie avoir un esprit d'excellence-vouloir être meilleur qu'hier!

Sommes-nous satisfaits du laisser-aller et de la paresse? Sommes-nous heureux d'avoir abandonné? C'est facile de le faire, mais sommes-nous mieux lotis? Mon père avait une règle qui disait: "Sois le premier à l'église et le dernier à en sortir".

Vous ne pourrez jamais atteindre votre destin avec une attitude paresseuse et une mentalité de lâcheur. Dieu mérite le meilleur de vous, le meilleur de votre temps, de vos efforts, de votre volonté, de votre dynamisme, de votre passion et de vos compétences. Alors donnez à Dieu le meilleur de vous-même et regardez son meilleur pour vous toujours en action.

La marche par la foi n'est pas censée être facile, mais elle est censée vous faire comprendre que si vous faites votre part en lui faisant confiance, alors Dieu ne vous décevra jamais. La lampe de poche de votre téléphone ne vous donne pas beaucoup plus de lumière que deux ou trois pieds devant vous, mais vous avez confiance que la lumière que vous voyez, même si elle brille juste assez pour que vous puissiez marcher, vous aidera à naviguer sur la route sur laquelle vous êtes.

La foi fonctionne de la même manière; la foi ne vous permet de voir que quelques pas en avant et rien de plus, le but de la foi n'est pas de rendre les choses faciles comme je l'ai dit plus tôt, le but de la foi est de créer en vous une dépendance à Dieu, que vous ne savez peut-être pas ce qui vous attend. Cependant, vous Lui faites suffisamment confiance pour continuer à marcher.

Je le répète, vous ne pouvez pas enterrer ce que Dieu vous a donné, mais vous devez l'embrasser avec tout ce que vous avez. Il ne s'agit pas d'une compétition avec quelqu'un d'autre, mais plutôt avec vous-même. Alors, comment pouvez-vous faire mieux et être meilleur que ce que vous étiez hier? La foi en action.

Un esprit d'excellence naît lorsque vous réalisez que vous pouvez et devez faire mieux pour Dieu. Un esprit d'excellence est atteint lorsque vous savez que les talents et les dons que Dieu vous a donnés ne peuvent pas être enterrés mais activés. Un esprit d'excellence naît lorsque vous décidez que ce que vous avez fait pour Dieu et le royaume peut être meilleur!

Un meilleur mari, père, frère, oncle, prédicateur, fils, fille, meilleur qu'hier, meilleur que votre ancienne version de vous.

Matthieu 25:19 dit: "Longtemps après, le maître de ces serviteurs vint régler ses comptes avec eux". "Vous ne devez jamais oublier que le Seigneur exigera toujours un rapport sur les comptes de votre vie et sur ce que vous avez fait de ce qu'il vous a donné ici-bas.

Le verset 20 dit: "Celui qui avait reçu cinq talents vint et en apporta cinq autres, en disant: "Seigneur, tu m'as remis cinq talents; regarde, j'ai gagné cinq autres talents en plus"." Il a été récompensé par un double à celui qui a investi et activé cet Esprit d'excellence!

Il y a toujours une récompense pour vos efforts et votre travail dans le royaume-toujours! Jamais en vain, mais cela donnera toujours une récompense.

Le verset 21 dit: "Son maître lui dit: "C'est bien, bon et fidèle serviteur; tu as été fidèle pour peu de choses, je te ferai dominer sur beaucoup de choses. Entre dans la joie de ton maître."

Bon et fidèle serviteur ces mots sont dignes de confiance et puissants, Bon non pas à cause de qui il était, mais bon à cause de son éthique de travail, sa discipline et son intelligence. Il n'a pas seulement reçu une récompense, mais il a été marqué d'une étiquette qui ne pouvait lui être retirée à vie. Il est passé du statut de serviteur à celui de RÈGLEUR sur de nombreuses choses!

Tout cela parce qu'il a choisi de faire quelque chose, il avait cet esprit d'excellence qui le poussait à agir pour améliorer le royaume et son maître. Il a atteint sa destinée en prenant simplement l'initiative et en surpassant tous les autres, et soudain il n'était plus un serviteur mais un souverain.

Matthieu 25:22-23 dit: "Celui qui avait reçu deux talents s'approcha et dit: Seigneur, tu m'as remis deux talents; voici que j'en ai gagné deux autres. Son maître lui dit: "C'est bien, bon et fidèle serviteur; tu as été fidèle pour peu de choses, je te ferai dominer sur beaucoup de choses. Entre dans la joie de ton maître."

Ce serviteur, lui aussi, était intelligent et il avait doublé ce qui lui avait été donné, et à cause de cela, il a été récompensé, et sa vie a changé à ce moment précis. Maintenant, ce serviteur ne s'est pas plaint parce qu'il n'a reçu que deux talents, et les cinq premiers, non, il a maximisé ce qui lui a été donné.

Arrêtez de regarder autour de vous qui a plus que vous, qui est meilleur que vous, qui a plus de talents et de compétences que vous; ce qui compte, c'est ce que vous faites de ce que Dieu vous a donné à ce moment-là. Il n'a donc pas pleurniché parce que l'autre avait plus que lui, il a fait abstraction de tout cela et a couru sa course, est resté dans son couloir et a fait de son mieux avec ce que Dieu lui avait donné, et à la fin, il s'est avéré être un gagnant.

Regardons devant nous; les versets 24 et 25 disent: "Celui qui avait reçu un talent s'approcha et dit: "Seigneur, je t'ai connu comme un homme dur, moissonnant là où tu n'as pas semé, et recueillant là où tu n'as pas répandu la semence. J'ai eu peur et je suis allé cacher ton talent dans la terre. Regarde, tu as là ce qui t'appartient".

Sa réponse semblait pleine de connaissance et de raison, mais elle était superficielle et vide à l'intérieur en réalité. Donc, d'abord, vous découvrez qu'il était handicapé par la peur, ce qui le rendait inutile. Ensuite, on découvre qu'il a fait ce que personne d'autre n'a fait et qu'il a essayé de le justifier par son raisonnement.

Il est allé l'enterrer; puis il a dû le déterrer et le rendre à son maître-ce qui a demandé du travail. Il a fallu du temps, de l'énergie, de la volonté et du dynamisme pour que quelqu'un prenne son talent et l'enterre. Mais, imaginez s'il avait utilisé ces mêmes principes dans la bonne direction? Imaginez quels auraient été les résultats qu'il aurait eus?

Combien de fois utilisons-nous l'énergie que Dieu nous a donnée, le talent, la compétence, la passion, et bien plus encore, dans la bonne direction? Ou est-ce que nous utilisons toutes ces choses et rendons notre vie pire?

Le verset 26 de Matthieu 25 dit: "Mais son maître lui répondit: Serviteur méchant et paresseux, tu savais que je moissonne où je n'ai pas semé, et que j'amasse où je n'ai pas répandu la semence."

Deux mots me sautent aux yeux dans ce texte: ce sont Méchant et paresseux. Selon le dictionnaire, méchant est Mauvais ou moralement incorrect. Mauvais pour avoir enterré le talent? un peu dur, diriez-vous? Bien au contraire, celui qui ne fait rien est mauvais et moralement incorrect.

Vous devez faire quelque chose; vous devez agir, et vous ne pouvez pas rester tranquille ou paresseux; vous devez essayer et ne pas abandonner-paresseux signifie ne pas vouloir travailler ou utiliser son énergie.

Il n'y a rien de plus horrible qu'une personne paresseuse dans la vie. Je ne sais pas pour vous, mais côtoyer une personne paresseuse est tellement frustrant et exaspérant que cela me fait bouillir de l'intérieur. Une personne paresseuse peut rapidement infecter les autres, et elle les ruinera très vite si on ne s'en occupe pas rapidement.

Regardez ce que l'Écriture dit ensuite; le verset 30 de Matthieu 25 dit: "Et jetez le serviteur inutile dans les ténèbres du dehors. Il y aura des pleurs et des grincements de dents."

Quelle fin pour ce serviteur: non seulement ce qu'il avait a été pris et donné à celui qui avait dix talents, mais il a été jeté dans les ténèbres du dehors! Une triste fin pour un homme qui avait commencé au même niveau que les autres.

Nous commençons tous au même niveau dans cette vie, mais nos choix commencent rapidement à créer une division et une séparation entre vous et les autres, et c'est là que vous voyez certains réussir et d'autres pas. Nous sommes tous confrontés à l'adversité dans la vie; nous le sommes tous, mais ce que nous faisons face à l'adversité est ce qui compte.

Ne vous méprenez pas, oui, certaines choses arrivent qui sont hors de notre contrôle, certaines choses viennent nous briser et nous réduire en bouillie, mais une chose est sûre, la bible dit dans 1 Jean 4:4 "Vous êtes de Dieu, petits enfants, et vous les avez vaincus; car celui qui est en vous est plus grand que celui qui est dans le monde".

Lorsque vous réaliserez la grandeur du Dieu que nous servons et sa puissance, alors à ce moment-là, vous commencerez à changer vos paroles et à changer vos actions. Bien sûr, comme je l'ai dit plus tôt, des défis viendront, mais c'est l'occasion pour vous de vous saisir de la vérité de la parole de Dieu et de l'appliquer à votre vie.

Ne laissez rien vous vaincre, et si quelqu'un vous bat, alors que ce soit vous qui vous battiez! Vainquez votre ancien vous, rempli d'excuses et de plaintes. Battez votre ancien vous, rempli de peurs et d'insécurités, battez votre ancien vous en vous rapprochant de Dieu et en décidant qu'un revers ne signifie pas que vous avez échoué, mais que vous devez plutôt l'utiliser comme un tremplin pour aller plus haut.

Un esprit d'excellence ne se contente pas de l'ordinaire, il ne se conforme pas à la moyenne et ne se contente pas du minimum. Au contraire, cela signifie donner à Dieu le meilleur "produit" ou sacrifice possible. Il ne s'agit pas de rivaliser avec le dynamisme ou la passion de quelqu'un d'autre, mais de faire sa course et de rester dans sa voie.

L'erreur que vous pouvez rapidement commettre est de comparer votre course et votre sacrifice avec ceux des autres; vous ne pouvez pas permettre à l'ennemi de vous attirer dans cette arène. C'est une arène dans laquelle vous perdrez définitivement le combat. Vous devez donc rester concentré sur votre appel, et si d'autres vous dépassent, ainsi soit-il, et si d'autres font mieux que vous, ainsi soit-il, mais vous devez vous concentrer sur vous-même, et VOUS devez être capable de donner à Dieu le meilleur de VOUS.

Votre succès ne dépend pas des autres et de ce qu'ils peuvent penser de vous; non, il dépend en quelque sorte de l'activation de votre foi, de votre confiance en Dieu, de votre course, de l'ascension de votre montagne, de la défaite de vos géants et de l'achèvement de votre tâche.

Le mont Everest est la plus grande montagne de la planète, culminant à 29 032 pieds. Les personnes qui escaladent cette montagne sont considérées comme uniques, et pour le faire, vous êtes en effet fantastique pour le faire. Mais laissez-moi vous parler d'une petite colline près de chez moi. En été, je me mets chaque fois au défi de la gravir trois fois en courant aussi vite que possible. Cette petite colline est mon mont Everest; cette petite colline représente un défi chaque année; cette petite colline doit être conquise chaque fois que je décide de la monter en courant.

Je dis cela parce que nous devons tous faire face à notre petit mont Everest, mais mon mont Everest peut être différent du vôtre, et ce n'est pas parce que ma colline est plus importante ou vice versa qu'elle n'en est pas moins significative.

Vous devez décider de vous mettre au défi avec un esprit de détermination, avec un cœur d'excellence et de résolution, que vous ne serez pas refusé ou dissuadé; vous n'abandonnerez pas et ne baisserez pas les bras. Mais d'abord, vous devez vous montrer à la hauteur de l'événement, courir jusqu'au sommet de la colline et, quand vous y parvenez, courir jusqu'à la montagne et atteindre le sommet-célébrez-le et ne regardez pas le sommet des autres ou leurs célébrations.

Célébrez vos accomplissements, célébrez vos réalisations, et ne comparez jamais votre victoire à celles de quelqu'un d'autre. Paul l'a bien dit dans 2e Timothée 4:7-8 "J'ai combattu le bon combat, j'ai achevé la course, j'ai gardé la foi. Enfin, il m'est réservé la couronne de justice, que le Seigneur, le juste Juge, me donnera en ce jour-là, et non pas à moi seulement, mais à tous ceux qui auront aimé son apparition.

Avec un esprit d'excellence, décidez une fois pour toutes que vous vous lèverez, que vous serez meilleurs, et surtout, donnez à Dieu le meilleur de ce que vous êtes.

CHAPITRE 3

VOTRE DESTINÉE MAINTENANT PRÉPARATION ET DISCIPLINE

Pour qu'une chose soit grande, elle doit être bien préparée; il faut se préparer à accomplir cet objectif pour atteindre la grandeur. Par conséquent, la préparation et la discipline sont essentielles à l'excellence de votre avenir. Aussi dévoué que vous puissiez être, sans préparation et discipline, l'exécution desdits objectifs et rêves ne se réalisera jamais.

Jérémie 29:11 Je connais les pensées que je forme à votre égard, dit le Seigneur, des pensées de paix et non de malheur, pour vous donner un avenir et une espérance.

Pour chaque pensée, il doit y avoir un plan qui doit suivre, car s'il n'y a pas de plan qui suit, cette pensée mourra et ne se réalisera pas. Ainsi, chaque rêve a besoin d'un plan d'action; chaque projet nécessite une discipline pour l'exécuter. Il y aura des géants et des adversités qui viendront défier vos rêves et vos objectifs. Ils viendront tuer votre foi et s'assurer que votre vision ne verra jamais la lumière du jour.

Vos ennemis essaieront de vous salir, vous et votre foi; vous aurez de nombreuses occasions d'abandonner et de renoncer. On vous encouragera à arrêter de construire vers votre rêve, on vous incitera à arrêter de courir vers la ligne d'arrivée, mais quand leurs cris pour que vous arrêtiez deviennent plus forts, c'est là que vous devez pousser plus fort, courir plus vite et surtout, ne pas abandonner!

Vous feriez mieux de remercier Dieu, car vos ennemis ont fait plus pour vous que tous vos amis n'ont jamais fait. Si tu vois les choses du point de vue de la foi, tu sauras qu'ils te pousseront à persévérer; si ton ennemi avait su ce qu'il faisait pour toi quand il te le faisait, il t'aurait laissé tranquille.

Il ne se serait jamais frotté à vous; c'est pourquoi la Bible dit de prier pour vos ennemis. Matthieu 5:44 dit: "Mais moi, je vous dis: Aimez vos ennemis, bénissez ceux qui vous maudissent, faites du bien à ceux qui vous haïssent, et priez pour ceux qui vous maltraitent et vous persécutent...". Par exemple, la New International Version dit: "Mais moi, je vous dis d'aimer vos ennemis et de prier pour ceux qui vous persécutent".

Mes ennemis me font tomber sur la tête; ils me font dire: Dieu, j'ai besoin de toi maintenant plus que jamais. Ils me forcent à jeûner, à prier, à croire et à continuer à marcher. Vous pouvez laisser vos ennemis vous abattre et vous tenir à l'écart, ou vous pouvez laisser vos ennemis vous pousser plus près de Dieu et plus près de vos rêves et de vos visions.

Il y a une chose fascinante à propos des funérailles: lorsqu'on sort le cercueil, il y a généralement six personnes qui le portent. Pourtant, dans la vie, lorsque vous travaillez à la réalisation de vos rêves et de vos objectifs, vous vous retrouvez souvent seul. Où sont ces six personnes lorsqu'il fait le plus sombre avant que la lumière ne vienne? Où sont ces six personnes lorsque vous vous sentez tous vaincus?

Dans ces moments-là, vous devez vous appuyer sur le Dieu éternel qui ne manque jamais d'être là quand personne d'autre ne l'est. Il a dit dans sa parole en Hébreux 13:5, "...Car il a dit: "Je ne te quitterai jamais, je ne t'abandonnerai jamais.""

Vous devez être un fauteur de troubles à la paresse; vous devez être un fauteur de troubles à la conformité; vous devez être un fauteur de troubles à votre doute, donner plus de maux de tête à l'ennemi que l'ennemi ne vous donne de maux de tête. Jetons un coup d'œil à cette histoire;

Actes 17:6 dit, Mais comme ils ne les trouvaient pas, ils traînèrent Jason et quelques autres croyants devant les fonctionnaires de la ville, en criant: "Ces hommes qui ont semé le trouble dans le monde entier sont maintenant venus ici,

Je crois fermement qu'être un fauteur de troubles, spirituellement et prophétiquement, c'est inverser le scénario et le remuer; vous devez vous lever et déclarer la guerre à votre incrédulité et à votre doute. Mais, pour obtenir la victoire, il doit y avoir un prix à payer. Peut-être que la douleur que vous ressentez est le prix à payer pour donner naissance à votre miracle.

Peut-être que la douleur que tu ressens est le prix à payer pour donner naissance à ce que Dieu veut faire PAR toi, il y a toujours un prix à payer, et dans ta détresse, Dieu t'élargira.

Lorsque vous réalisez que Dieu fait tout, il le fait exprès, avec un but et pour un but. Et vous vous demandez pourquoi personne n'y a pensé? Peut-être qu'il y a une poignée de buts uniquement pour vous.

Il y a une raison pour laquelle Dieu fait ce qu'il fait, et il y a une raison pour laquelle Dieu permet aux choses de se produire et d'avoir lieu; la Bible dit dans

Isaiah 55: 8-9, "Car mes pensées ne sont pas vos pensées, Et vos voies ne sont pas mes voies, dit le Seigneur. Car, comme les cieux sont plus élevés que la terre, Mes voies sont plus élevées que vos voies, Et Mes pensées plus que vos pensées.

Nous ne pourrons jamais, et nous ne comprendrons jamais les voies et les pensées de Dieu, nous ne serons jamais capables de comprendre son raisonnement, nous ne serons jamais capables de comprendre comment Dieu pense. Pourtant, dans le monde de la Foi, la compréhension n'est pas nécessaire, la compréhension n'est pas nécessaire, la vraie Foi n'est pas quand vous comprenez tout; vous ne savez rien et choisissez quand même d'avancer.

La vraie foi, c'est lorsque vous êtes entouré de doutes et d'incrédulité, mais que vous choisissez quand même de croire en la parole de Dieu. Les sentiments suivent la concentration; si je me concentre sur la paix et sur le remède et le processus, je me sens confiant.

Lorsque je suis confiant, je me sens paisible et joyeux, mais si je me concentre sur le problème, je suis anxieux et j'ai peur. Si je me concentre sur ce qui ne va pas, je me sens nerveux. Si je me concentre sur ce que j'ai perdu au lieu de ce qu'il me reste, mes rêves sont en danger.

Quand je réalise que si Dieu crée un miracle dans votre vie, ce ne sera souvent pas avec ce que vous avez perdu; au contraire, il utilisera ce qu'il vous reste.

Jésus a pris les restes de poisson et de pain et a nourri les cinq mille personnes, laissez-moi vous rappeler que Dieu peut prendre tout ce qui vous reste et le transformer en un miracle surnaturel.

Vous pouvez être brisé parce que personne n'a cru ou ne croit en vous et en vos rêves, mais Dieu prendra ce qu'il vous reste et vous bénira avec. Il vous bénira avec ce que le monde pense et croit être insignifiant; il l'utilisera pour "montrer" sa puissance et sa gloire à travers vos actes de Foi.

Dieu ne fera jamais ce que vous devez faire; votre préparation est essentielle, votre discipline est cruciale et votre Foi doit être implacable.

La vraie question que vous devez vous poser est la suivante: voyez-vous ce qu'il vous reste? Lui accordez-vous de la valeur? Croyez-vous que Dieu peut s'en servir pour renverser la situation? Bien sûr, la réponse à toutes ces questions doit être un Oui retentissant!

2 Rois 4 nous parle d'une femme étonnante et de ses actes de confiance et de foi dans la parole qui sortait de la bouche du prophète.

Son mari était mort, et elle avait de lourdes dettes, à tel point qu'on venait prendre ses deux garçons comme serviteurs pour payer la dette. Alors qu'elle pensait que tout était fini, qu'il n'y avait plus rien à faire, Dieu est apparu par l'intermédiaire du prophète.

Tout ce qui lui restait était une jarre d'huile; Elisée lui dit: "Que puis-je faire pour toi? Dis-moi, qu'as-tu dans la maison?" Elle répondit: "Ta servante n'a rien dans la maison, si ce n'est une jarre d'huile." 2 Rois 4:3

D'une jarre d'huile allait sortir un grand miracle; de quelque chose de si petit et insignifiant allait sortir une percée pour elle et sa famille. Il ne lui a donc pas demandé ce qu'elle avait perdu, même s'il savait qu'elle avait tout perdu, il lui a demandé ce qu'elle avait dans sa maison?

La foi regardera toujours ce qui vous reste et jamais ce que vous avez perdu. La foi ne verra jamais la tasse à moitié vide, elle la verra plutôt à moitié pleine. Pour obtenir la force de passer à l'étape suivante, vous devrez faire preuve de beaucoup de patience et de discipline pour que les choses commencent à se produire dans votre vie.

Le prophète lui demande ensuite de faire quelque chose de très inhabituel: il lui demande de rassembler de nombreux pots et de remplir les jarres vides avec l'huile qui lui reste. Cet ordre aurait pu sembler sans aucune logique à l'esprit naturel, mais les gens de la Foi n'avaient pas besoin d'explication; seule la Foi était nécessaire. La vraie foi n'exige pas de compréhension, elle n'exige pas de raison, mais elle exige une patience et une discipline non conventionnelles.

Au milieu d'un moment de crise, on lui a ordonné de travailler pour son miracle. Au milieu de ses épreuves, elle a été appelée à prendre ses deux fils et à se mettre au travail. L'homme de Dieu aurait pu facilement prier, et le miracle aurait pu se produire sur-le-champ, mais au lieu de cela, on lui a ordonné de se mettre au travail.

Pourquoi n'a-t-il pas prié? Parce que la prière sans action est nulle. Un miracle sans travail effectué créera en vous une mentalité d'enfant gâté. Remarquez que la femme ne s'est pas plainte ou n'a pas remis en question ce qu'on lui disait de faire; elle n'a pas levé les mains en l'air et abandonné; elle a retroussé ses manches avec ses deux garçons et s'est mise au travail.

Vos rêves, vos visions et vos objectifs vous amèneront toujours à travailler pour les atteindre. Elle et ses garçons étaient prêts à travailler, ce qui exigeait de la discipline. Ils ont adhéré au plan; ils étaient déterminés à se sortir du pétrin dans lequel ils se trouvaient. Vous devez être prêts et disciplinés pour faire un effort supplémentaire, peu importe ce que Dieu vous demande.

J'ai souvent dit à l'église que si Dieu disait: "Je vous donne un million de dollars et tout ce que vous avez à faire, c'est de faire dix fois le tour du pâté de maisons en courant, combien d'entre vous resteraient à leur place? Je peux presque garantir que très peu de personnes resteraient assises à leur place.

Celles qui resteraient seraient celles qui refuseraient de faire ce qu'on leur demande et qui se plaindraient en disant: "Pourquoi courir? Pourquoi Dieu ne me donne-t-il pas le million sans courir autour du pâté de maisons?

Comme je l'ai dit plus haut, les vrais miracles ne seront jamais accomplis pour vous si vous êtes dans un état d'esprit paresseux. Si vous voulez vraiment une bénédiction, vous devez être prêt à vous lever, à vous habiller et à faire ce qu'on vous demande. Si la femme décide de rester dans son état d'esprit négatif, elle aura perdu ses garçons et n'aura jamais vu les miracles devant ses yeux.

Si elle s'était plainte ou avait demandé une explication, son miracle serait mort, et l'histoire se serait terminée différemment. Pourtant, elle a choisi de ne pas remettre en question l'instruction, mais elle a montré sa préparation et sa détermination à faire tout ce qu'il faut pour que le travail soit fait. Si elle décide de s'en aller, son miracle aussi.

Si vous décidez d'abandonner la poursuite de vos rêves et de vos objectifs simplement parce que vous n'aimez pas les instructions qui vous sont données, que vous n'êtes pas d'accord avec la méthode ou que vous pensez que ce que l'on vous demande n'est pas raisonnable. Alors, vous pouvez dire adieu à vos rêves et à vos objectifs, car à partir du moment où vous décidez d'adopter cette attitude, vous n'atteindrez jamais votre destin.

Il serait utile que vous soyez préparé et discipliné pour être mentalement, émotionnellement et spirituellement prêt à recevoir la parole ou l'instruction, puis que vous trouviez en vous la force de vous lever et de poursuivre votre route vers la grandeur.

Vous devez, et j'insiste, être prêt à faire ce que Dieu vous a appelé à faire à un moment donné. Si vous vous asseyez et vous plaignez, alors ne vous plaignez pas quand les choses meurent, vous êtes appelé à la grandeur, et donc vous devez, à tout prix, continuer et ne jamais vous arrêter. Avec de la préparation et de la discipline, vous débloquerez de grandes choses pour vous-même et activerez votre Foi. Lorsque cela se produira, vous commencerez à voir des miracles surnaturels se produire, pas seulement des bénédictions mais des dons surnaturels.

PRENDRE DE L'ÉLAN

Lorsque vous lancez une fronde, vous devez d'abord tirer en arrière pour libérer la pierre; plus vous tirez en arrière, plus la pierre se déplace loin.

Dans notre quête de la réalisation de nos rêves et de nos objectifs, nous passons souvent par un processus de recul. Ce sentiment ne semble pas toujours agréable et accepté, mais il est nécessaire. Lorsqu'on vous tire en arrière, c'est comme si on vous empêchait d'aller plus loin.

Vous faites un pas en avant et trois pas en arrière; c'est un sentiment déprimant, et à moins que vous ne soyez prêt à remettre vos objectifs et vos rêves entre les mains de Dieu, vous ne comprendrez jamais ce processus. Enfin, vous vous cambrez en arrière pour prendre de l'élan et vous lancez votre bras en avant pour obtenir la distance maximale, même pour lancer une pierre à main nue.

Vous ne devez pas vous décourager.

La fronde est le processus que Dieu utilisera souvent pour vous propulser en avant à une vitesse maximale. Même si nous ne comprenons pas ce qui se passe lorsque nous sommes tirés en arrière, si nous avons l'impression de reculer et non d'avancer, nous devons savoir que nous prendrons de l'élan grâce à ce processus, nous lançant vers notre destinée.

Ici, au Canada, nous savons une chose ou deux sur l'enlisement dans la neige, et nous connaissons le mal de tête de l'enlisement. Vous faites patiner les pneus en appuyant sur l'accélérateur, mais vous n'allez nulle part. Vous tordez les pneus à gauche et à droite, et tout est encore plus compliqué si vous êtes vous-même.

Mais heureusement que nous sommes Canadiens, que tôt ou tard, quelqu'un passera et vous proposera de vous donner un coup de main. J'ai donc été des deux côtés de ce scénario, et les deux sont formidables parce que d'un côté, vous pouvez aider quelqu'un en détresse, et de l'autre, vous êtes soutenu dans votre période de deuil.

Maintenant, cela tient pour exact; vous commencez par essayer de vous sortir du pétrin à la pelle; ensuite, vous commencez à balancer la voiture d'avant en arrière pour vous donner une certaine traction. Lorsque vous commencez à balancer la voiture d'avant en arrière, vous créez un élan pour vous sortir du pétrin dans lequel vous êtes.

Vous vous balancez d'avant en arrière jusqu'à ce que finalement, vous soyez libre, et que vous ayez la traction pour aller de l'avant. Mais, encore une fois, le retour en arrière était nécessaire pour vous permettre d'avancer.

Ne vous laissez jamais décourager par l'idée que vous devez aller "en arrière" ou par l'idée que vous êtes tiré en arrière. Dieu manifeste sa puissance la plus extraordinaire sur une idée qui peut ne pas avoir de sens pour vous à ce moment-là.

L'histoire de Daniel est intéressante: tout allait bien jusqu'à ce qu'il soit condamné à la fosse aux lions. Ce n'est qu'au verset 25 de Daniel chapitre 6 que nous trouvons le pouvoir de rédemption.

La Bible dit dans Daniel 6:25: "Alors le roi Darius écrivit à toutes les nations et à tous les peuples de toutes langues, sur toute la terre: "Puissiez-vous prospérer grandement! "Je publie un décret selon lequel, dans toutes les parties de mon royaume, les gens doivent craindre et révérer le Dieu de Daniel. "Car il est le Dieu vivant, et il subsiste à jamais; son règne ne sera pas détruit, sa domination ne prendra jamais fin. Il sauve, et il sauve; il accomplit des signes et des prodiges.

Il a été envoyé à la mort, mais Dieu avait un plan différent; vous pouvez vous trouver dans un moment de crise, en reculant au lieu d'avancer. Vous devez faire confiance à Dieu et à son plan parfait et omniscient pour votre vie. Souvent, être tiré en arrière est la meilleure chose qui puisse vous arriver, car Dieu voit ce que vous ne pouvez pas voir, et le fait qu'il vous tire en arrière a pour but de vous propulser en avant et de vous donner l'élan que vous recherchez.

Lorsque nous ne comprenons pas que Dieu est aux commandes, nous sommes frustrés et en colère à l'idée de revenir en arrière. Nous ne pouvons pas contrôler ce qui nous arrive, mais nous pouvons contrôler la façon dont nous réagissons à ces choses. L'élan va souvent en arrière, mais seulement pour vous propulser en avant.

Daniel a fait face à une mort imminente en étant envoyé dans la fosse aux lions; son avenir était certain, la mort était assurée, mais ils ont oublié que Daniel avait un Dieu qu'il priait constamment. Il semblait devoir faire marche arrière, et c'était le cas de certaines façons, mais Dieu était sur le point de se manifester puissamment.

Il serait préférable que vous n'oubliiez jamais que le Dieu de la Bible est un Dieu vivant, et qu'il n'a encore jamais perdu une bataille. Par conséquent, le fait de prendre de l'élan ne peut être attribué qu'à Dieu, car c'est lui qui vous permet d'exceller, de croître et de vous développer.

La Bible dit dans le Corinthiens 3:6: "J'ai planté, Apollos a arrosé, mais Dieu a donné l'accroissement."

La clé ici est que Dieu donne l'accroissement! À ce stade, nous ne pouvons pas oublier que c'est Dieu qui vous donne la croissance et l'élan. La Bible dit aussi dans Apocalypse 3:8: "Je connais tes oeuvres. Voici, j'ai mis devant toi une porte ouverte, et personne ne pourra la fermer; car tu as un peu de force, tu as gardé ma parole, et tu n'as pas renié mon nom."

Lorsque Dieu vous donne de l'élan, cela vous accélère vers des endroits que vous pensiez n'être qu'un rêve. Des choses qui devraient prendre des mois et des années à réaliser sont réalisées en quelques jours et quelques heures. L'élan en Dieu augmente la faveur dans votre vie; il fait en sorte que les bénédictions soient mises devant vous, il provoque un changement dans la poursuite de vos rêves et de vos objectifs.

Psaumes 23:5 dit: "Tu dresses devant moi une table en présence de mes ennemis; Tu oins d'huile ma tête; Ma coupe déborde".

C'est un verset puissant à considérer; Un, Tu prépares une table devant moi en présence de mes ennemis. Cela me ramène à la grâce et à la faveur que Dieu met sur ta vie, des choses qui ne devraient pas arriver-arrivent, et tes ennemis te font être en paix, et ils ne peuvent que témoigner de ce que Dieu fait pour toi et à travers toi.

Cela signifie que lorsque vos ennemis veulent vous combattre, Dieu dit NON-et il commence à vous bénir en présence de ceux qui peuvent ne pas vous aimer ou ne pas être pour vous.

Deuxièmement, il dit: "Tu oins ma tête d'huile. L'huile qui éloigne les moustiques, l'huile qui fait de toi un répulsif pour les choses qui pourraient venir te faire du mal. Il t'oint d'une huile précieuse, te donnant un arôme doux qui attire les gens et la bénédiction dans ta vie. Ne vous méprenez pas; je ne dis pas que l'ennemi ne viendra pas vous attaquer, mais ce que je dis, c'est qu'il ira contre vous mais ne prévaudra pas contre vous.

La Bible dit Psaumes 91:7 "Mille peuvent tomber à ton côté et dix mille à ta droite, Mais ils ne viendront pas contre toi."

C'est ce que fait l'huile; elle vous donne une couverture autour de vous dans laquelle vos ennemis ne peuvent pas pénétrer. Cette huile ne vient que par votre recherche de Dieu; plus vous le cherchez, plus il vous oint d'huile.

Troisièmement et enfin, il dit: "Ma coupe déborde". Il parle ici d'abondance et de ce que j'aime appeler l'élan. Ici au Canada, nous avons un endroit formidable que j'aime visiter: Les chutes Niagra.

Niagra Falls, en Ontario, est une ville canadienne où se trouve la célèbre chute d'eau du même nom, reliée aux États-Unis par le pont Rainbow. On dit que les chutes de Niagra ont le débit le plus élevé du monde. Environ vingt-huit millions de litres ou environ 700 000 gallons d'eau descendent les chutes de Niagra chaque seconde.

C'est beaucoup d'eau qui coule, et la Bible dit que votre coupe déborde! Tout à coup, vous avez tellement de bénédictions qui viennent vers vous que vous ne pouvez pas l'expliquer avec une explication humaine, seulement donner la gloire à Dieu.

Votre coupe déborde, ce qui signifie que vous avez tellement d'élan, et que vous êtes sur une telle lancée que vous vous développez d'une manière que vous pensiez ne jamais pouvoir atteindre. Vous commencez à faire d'énormes progrès, des sauts et des bonds, à tel point que vous ne pouvez pas expliquer ce qui se passe à ce moment-là, mais seulement dire que Dieu est derrière ce qui se passe.

Votre premier lieu de gain est sur vos genoux en prière; c'est là que tout commence, sur vos genoux. La prière vous permet d'avoir non seulement une relation avec Dieu, mais elle vous permet de voler haut et de gagner beaucoup de distance dans la poursuite de la vision et des objectifs que vous pouvez avoir.

La prière vous permet de courir plus vite, de voler plus haut, de grimper plus haut et de ne jamais abandonner dans la poursuite de ce que vous essayez d'atteindre.

LA DERNIÈRE LIGNE DROITE

J'adore voir les courses de relais en ligne car j'analyse constamment pourquoi ils ont mis ce coureur dans cette position de course. Pourtant, l'expérience la plus exaltante est cette dernière ligne droite qui mène à la ligne d'arrivée. Chaque coureur est soigneusement choisi et stratégiquement placé pour donner à l'équipe un avantage pendant la course.

En 2015, aux Jeux olympiques de Pékin, les Jamaïcains ont remporté la course finale du relais 4x100m. Regarder Usain Bolt s'élancer sur les derniers 100 mètres était si excitant qu'il faut le regarder encore et encore. Chaque position est importante, chaque seconde compte, les remises doivent être parfaites pour que l'équipe réussisse.

Dans votre voyage vers la ligne d'arrivée, vous devez vous rappeler que chaque association que vous avez compte; chaque fois que vous investissez du temps dans quelqu'un ou quelque chose compte, et cet investissement produira des effets négatifs ou positifs dans votre vie.

Vous voyez la ligne d'arrivée, la fin est proche, mais la partie la plus difficile ne fait que commencer; il est essentiel de franchir la ligne d'arrivée, et généralement, les batailles les plus complexes sont laissées jusqu'à la toute fin.

J'ai souvent parlé du pouvoir de l'association, et lorsque vous voyez la ligne d'arrivée, cela devient encore plus important que jamais. Je crois fermement qu'il faut être gentil avec tout le monde, quelle que soit leur attitude à votre égard. Je sais que cela peut sembler plus facile à dire qu'à faire, mais c'est la vérité, soyez gentil avec tout le monde.

Soyez gentil avec les gens à tous les niveaux, car une relation ou une association peut changer du jour au lendemain. Cette relation ou association peut souvent faire la différence entre franchir la ligne de la victoire ou ne pas la franchir du tout.

Le succès est toujours lié au mouvement; vous devez vous mettre en mouvement; ce sont les vrais principes de la grandeur; le travail, une bonne attitude, l'amour et la gentillesse.

Vous devez être la personne qui travaille le plus dans la pièce; personne ne peut vous surpasser. Le dynamisme que vous devez avoir doit être copié sur celui de tous les autres; vous devez être le premier arrivé et le dernier parti. Votre éthique de travail doit être de premier ordre; une éthique de travail de second ordre ne permettra jamais d'atteindre la grandeur.

Les gens doivent se nourrir de votre passion et de votre dynamisme, mais ils ne peuvent pas vous inspirer la grandeur; lorsque c'est votre rêve, vous devez être au volant et aux commandes de votre navire.

Votre attitude doit être confiante en Dieu, et non arrogante, et il y a une différence entre les deux. La Bible dit dans Jacques 4:6: "Mais il donne plus de grâce. C'est pourquoi elle dit: "Dieu résiste aux orgueilleux, Mais il fait grâce aux humbles.""

La grâce vous donne de l'assurance et de la prestance; c'est une force silencieuse qui entoure puissamment votre vie. La grâce est ce que les autres voient en vous, mais que vous ne voyez pas vous-même. La grâce ouvre des portes que l'argent ne peut souvent pas ouvrir; elle vous met en présence de personnes qui ne le pourraient pas dans d'autres circonstances.

La grâce couvre vos erreurs, rend vos défauts imperceptibles, vous donne un éclat lorsque vous parlez et fait que vos ennemis sont en paix avec vous.

Par contre, l'orgueil est le contraire de la grâce; c'est un excellent diviseur, qui ferme les portes partout où vous allez. L'orgueil est offensant et passe pour désagréable. Si Dieu lui-même résiste aux orgueilleux et ne supporte pas une personne orgueilleuse, cela se produit aussi naturellement.

L'orgueil tue la bonne volonté que les autres peuvent ressentir à votre égard; il tue la volonté d'aider quelqu'un, il offense les autres, blesse, coupe et souvent brûle des ponts qui ne pourront jamais être réparés. Mais, d'un autre côté, la fierté peut venir des réalisations et des progrès que vous faites, et c'est là que vous devez faire attention à ne pas détruire tout ce sur quoi vous avez travaillé dur car, en un instant, tout peut être ruiné.

Proverbes 11:12 "Quand vient l'orgueil, alors vient la disgrâce, mais avec les humbles est la sagesse."

1 Pierre 5:5: De même, vous qui êtes plus jeunes, soyez soumis aux aînés. Revêtez-vous tous d'humilité les uns envers les autres, car "Dieu s'oppose aux orgueilleux, mais il fait grâce aux humbles."

L'humilité est souvent caractérisée par une véritable gratitude et un manque d'arrogance, une vision modeste de soi-même. Cependant, la définition biblique de l'humilité va au-delà de cela. L'humilité est un aspect essentiel et permanent de la piété dans la Bible, car nous sommes appelés à être d'humbles disciples du Christ et à faire confiance à la sagesse et au salut de Dieu. Par conséquent, soyons humbles devant notre créateur pour le don de la vie qui nous a été fait.

L'humilité biblique est fondée sur Dieu. Le Père descend pour aider les pauvres et les affligés; le Fils incarné manifeste son humilité depuis sa naissance jusqu'à sa crucifixion. L'utilisation conjointe de "doux" et "humble de cœur" dans Matthieu 11:29 souligne l'humilité du Christ devant l'humanité, qu'il est venu servir, et sa soumission devant Dieu. L'humilité et la douceur sont souvent liées car toutes deux sont des traits de caractère justes pour faire la volonté de Dieu.

"Fais confiance à l'Éternel de tout ton cœur et ne t'appuie pas sur ton intelligence", Proverbes 3:5.

L'importance de l'humilité est directement liée aux conséquences mortelles de l'orgueil. L'orgueil nous sépare de Dieu car nous ne reconnaissons pas et n'apprécions pas la souveraineté éternelle de notre Seigneur. Par conséquent, l'importance de l'humilité se manifeste dans la profonde gratitude que nous éprouvons en reconnaissant comme il se doit la divinité de Dieu et son amour pour nous. L'importance de l'humilité se trouve également dans la reconnaissance de notre nature imparfaite en tant qu'humains sur terre et de notre susceptibilité au péché si nous ne sommes pas vigilants face à la tentation.

"Soyez sobres d'esprit, soyez vigilants. Votre adversaire, le diable, rôde comme un lion rugissant, cherchant quelqu'un à dévorer." ~ 1 Pierre 5:8

Pendant la dernière ligne droite, vous devez veiller à ne pas laisser l'orgueil obscurcir votre jugement et à ne pas laisser les réalisations ou les accolades que vous pourriez recevoir ruiner tout ce que vous avez accompli jusqu'à présent.

Rester humble, c'est reconnaître que c'est Dieu qui vous a donné le pouvoir de vous rendre jusqu'ici et réaliser que sans Lui, rien ne serait possible, et que grâce à Lui, tout est possible.

Jean 15:5 dit: "Je suis la vigne, vous êtes les sarments. Celui qui demeure en moi, et moi en lui, porte beaucoup de fruit; car sans moi vous ne pouvez rien faire."

2ème Timothée 4:7-8 dit, "J'ai combattu le bon combat, j'ai achevé la course, j'ai gardé la Foi. Enfin, il m'est réservé la couronne de justice que le Seigneur, le juste Juge, me donnera en ce jour-là, et non seulement à moi, mais encore à tous ceux qui auront aimé son apparition."

La course n'est pas terminée tant que vous n'avez pas réussi, vous devez continuer à travailler dur, à garder la tête baissée, à reconnaître Dieu dans toutes vos voies et à presser à travers, à presser dedans, car vous êtes trop près pour que tout s'écroule.

Il sera très tentant de dévier, bien sûr, à cause de vos réalisations, sans effort de perdre votre concentration à cause des accolades que vous recevez, et tout cela se produit juste quand vous êtes près d'atteindre vos objectifs.

Il y a une bataille pour arriver là où vous allez, mais n'oubliez jamais qu'il y aura une bataille pour rester là où vous allez. La lutte ne s'arrête pas parce que vous avez réussi; vous devez reconnaître que vous avez réussi mais que la guerre ne fait que commencer. Pendant cette dernière ligne droite, lorsque vous voyez la fin en vue, ce n'est pas la fin, c'est le début de quelque chose de nouveau. Un nouveau chapitre de votre vie est sur le point de commencer, et c'est là que vous ne devez pas ralentir et vous reposer sur vos lauriers; c'est là que vous vous préparez, que vous trouvez cette nouvelle force et que vous vous battez encore plus fort.

Tout ce que vous avez fait de bien vous a conduit à ce stade de votre vie, et ce n'est pas le moment de céder. Je me souviens de l'hiver 1997, lorsque j'ai franchi les portes du 212 Murray St pour la toute première fois et que j'ai dit à mon père, "c'est l'endroit, papa."

Je pensais que nous avions réussi; c'était le moment le plus important de l'église; nous étions sur le point de construire notre tout premier bâtiment. Il était vide, mais je pouvais déjà voir les gens, sale, mais tout ce que je pouvais voir était une beauté; c'était un chef-d'œuvre qui attendait de se produire.

Alors que nous faisions le tour du bâtiment, j'étais un peu comme un enfant dans un magasin de bonbons, excité par ce qui allait se passer, excité par le début de ce nouveau chapitre. Je me souviens avoir dit à ma mère combien c'était excitant, combien ce serait génial; ma mère a souri et a accepté de garder sa joie à l'intérieur pendant que l'agent immobilier nous faisait visiter l'endroit.

Nous avions réussi, pensais-je, ce sur quoi mon père avait prêché pendant tant d'années se révélait enfin, ce dont on avait parlé et rêvé voyait enfin la lumière du jour. Il ne restait plus qu'à mettre les points sur les "T" et les "I", et le rêve était réalisé. L'était-il, cependant?

Mon esprit était passé du sale au beau et avait sauté tout ce qui se trouvait entre les deux. J'étais passé du vide au plein et j'avais contourné tout ce qui était nécessaire pour y arriver. Je pensais que mon résultat se manifesterait instantanément en un claquement de doigts, et je me suis trompé.

Nous sommes souvent pris dans les images du produit fini et nous oublions qu'il y a un processus pour y arriver, et il n'est pas toujours joli.

Le bâtiment était sens dessus dessous et à l'envers, mais mon cadeau n'a rien vu de tout cela; tout ce que j'ai vu, c'est le produit fini poli. Il serait donc préférable de s'enthousiasmer pour le produit fini, mais de ne jamais se décourager en regardant le processus pour y arriver.

L'achat du bâtiment n'était que le début, mais pour moi, c'était la fin, sans me rendre compte que le chemin de la grandeur dans la réalisation de vos objectifs et de vos rêves n'est jamais terminé; il est constamment en croissance et en expansion.

Nous sommes sur le point de célébrer 25 ans de ministère au 212 Murray St, ici même dans la capitale nationale, et je peux sincèrement dire que nous n'avons pas atteint le but final, loin de là. Nous avons connu de multiples rénovations, des réparations et des modifications importantes, et il reste encore beaucoup à faire.

Des milliers de dollars ont été dépensés pour améliorer et s'adapter à l'époque au fil des ans, et nous n'avons toujours pas terminé. Des choses qui étaient autrefois géniales sont devenues obsolètes, mais nous ne nous laissons pas abattre à la pensée des sommes d'argent qui ont été dépensées; nous réalisons que c'était le prix à payer sur cette route que nous appelons le ministère.

Vous ne pouvez pas regarder en arrière et vous abattre sur les décisions que vous auriez dû prendre ou sur la route que vous auriez dû emprunter; quelle que soit la décision que vous avez prise ou la route que vous avez décidé de suivre, elle vous a amené à ce point ici et maintenant. Nous ne pouvons pas changer le passé, mais nous pouvons influencer notre avenir.

Si nous nous arrêtons un instant et réalisons que nous devrions être reconnaissants de ne pas être morts ou pire en enfer, alors nous devrions être reconnaissants d'avoir la possibilité de changer notre avenir maintenant, dans le présent. Regarder en arrière avec regret ne fait de bien à personne; qu'auriez-vous pu être? Et tant d'autres questions sont absurdes et constituent une perte totale de temps et d'énergie.

Au moment où vous pensez avoir réussi et avoir atteint la ligne d'arrivée, prenez un peu de recul, respirez et réalisez que vous avez atteint la fin d'une étape importante, mais qu'une autre est sur le point de commencer.

La dernière ligne droite est souvent la plus difficile car elle est remplie d'excitation et d'illusions. Excitation parce que vous avez sincèrement cru que vous aviez réussi, mais illusion parce que la route continue. Alors pourquoi l'appelle-t-on la dernière ligne droite?

Chaque étape a une "dernière ligne droite". Chaque fois que vous atteignez la fin de l'étape de croissance dans votre vie, vous entrez dans cette zone où beaucoup échouent. Puis, finalement, vous arrivez à ce point où vous pensez et croyez que vous avez réussi, et soudain vous jetez vos mains en l'air et célébrez, mais seulement pour réaliser que la prochaine étape est sur le point de commencer.

Beaucoup se découragent parce que, comme moi, ils se précipitent sur le résultat final, alors qu'ils ne voient pas que l'atteinte de leur objectif est en perpétuel changement et évolution, et que nous n'avons jamais fini. Je le répète, vous ne pouvez pas vous décourager à l'idée que ce que vous pensiez être le "but" n'est que le début de la réalisation de vos rêves et de vos objectifs.

Lorsqu'un avion se déplace d'un point A à un point B, des "marqueurs" spécifiques doivent passer sur leur route vers leur destination. Ces marqueurs permettent aux pilotes de savoir qu'ils sont sur le bon chemin vers leur destination. Le pilote ne célèbre pas le marqueur; il célèbre jusqu'à ce qu'il ait atteint sa destination.

Chaque marqueur doit être célébré dans la vie car il représente notre croissance en maturité, en connaissance, en confiance, en obéissance et en relation avec Dieu. Nous observons que chaque jour nous apprenons et grandissons à travers les expériences que nous pouvons traverser. Chaque adversité et chaque épreuve auxquelles nous sommes confrontés sont une opportunité si nous les laissons s'améliorer et devenir une meilleure personne alors que nous nous efforçons d'atteindre notre but.

Une fois que vous aurez accepté le fait que notre véritable objectif est le ciel et que les objectifs terrestres sont nécessaires mais secondaires par rapport à notre objectif éternel, nous serons alors en paix lorsque nous atteindrons ces étapes qui semblaient être la fin mais qui, en réalité, ne sont que le lieu de naissance de votre prochain niveau.

LA NAISSANCE DU NOUVEAU VOUS!

C'EST ICI QUE LE NOUVEAU VOUS COMMENCE

2ème Corinthiens 5:17 "Ainsi donc, si quelqu'un est en Christ, il est une création nouvelle; les choses anciennes ont disparu; voici, toutes choses sont devenues nouvelles."

Il y a toujours un niveau supérieur, et chaque niveau supérieur nécessite un plus grand vous. Vous êtes venus jusqu'ici pour ne pas revenir en arrière, mais vous avez atteint et franchi le point de non-retour.

De nombreux panneaux vous indiquent ce que vous pouvez ou ne pouvez pas emporter lorsque vous voyagez et que vous êtes sur le point de passer le contrôle de sécurité. Quelle que soit votre destination ou la raison de votre voyage, tout le monde doit passer par ce contrôle de sécurité. Si vous transportez quelque chose que vous n'êtes pas censé avoir, l'entrée vous sera refusée.

Plus votre quête de grandeur est élevée, plus elle exigera des changements spécifiques dans votre vie qui ne cadreront pas avec l'endroit où Dieu veut vous emmener. Certaines choses qui ont pu fonctionner pour vous dans le passé ne fonctionneront peut-être pas avec vous à l'avenir. Les méthodes, les plans et les stratégies qui ont pu vous aider auparavant ne signifient pas qu'ils fonctionneront dans cette nouvelle saison ou ce nouveau niveau que vous êtes sur le point d'atteindre.

L'une des plus grandes erreurs que vous pouvez commettre est de vivre une nouvelle saison avec une ancienne mentalité. La parole dit: "toutes choses sont faites nouvelles", pas certaines, mais toutes les choses sont faites nouvelles.

Chaque personne poursuivra ses propres objectifs et rêves, et aucun n'est meilleur que l'autre, mais vous ne devez pas regarder la vision de vos amis ou des membres de votre famille et comparer la vôtre à la leur; vous devez atteindre vos rêves et vos objectifs.

Atteignez ce rêve, priez pour ce rêve, jeûnez et semez pour lui, car en faisant cela, vous activerez votre Foi, et Dieu répondra. Ne vous arrêtez pas avant d'avoir atteint votre objectif, et lorsque vous l'aurez atteint, trouvez en vous la force d'exceller et de passer à la saison suivante.

Puisqu'il y a un nouveau vous, il y aura de nouveaux défis, de nouveaux géants à affronter, de nouvelles adversités sur votre chemin, mais rappelez-vous que la Bible dit, dans 1 Jean 4:4, "Vous êtes de Dieu, petits enfants, et vous les avez vaincus; car celui qui est en vous est plus grand que celui qui est dans le monde".

Dieu sera toujours plus grand que ces choses, y compris les personnes qui se dresseront contre vous. Vous devez croire que vous êtes digne de cette bénédiction que vous poursuivez. Vous ne pouvez permettre à personne de vous dire que vous êtes indigne de vos objectifs et de vos rêves à cause de votre passé.

Votre passé ne vous disqualifie pas de toutes les bonnes choses, mais par le sang de Jésus, nous sommes une nouvelle création, l'ancien vous est lavé et de nouveau, toutes les choses sont rendues fraîches, y compris vous.

Souvent, les gens abandonnent la poursuite de leurs rêves et de leurs objectifs parce que les autres leur disent qu'ils sont fous ou farfelus. Ce sont des phrases indirectes qui vous disent que vous n'en valez pas la peine. Cette négativité est un tel poison qu'elle paralyse la personne en lui faisant croire qu'elle ne mérite pas un rêve ou un objectif aussi fou.

Vos rêves, vos objectifs, vos aspirations et vos visions devraient être énormes. Cependant, il serait préférable de se rappeler que les rêves, les buts, les aspirations et les idées plus modestes doivent être réalisés au préalable pour arriver au produit fini. Réaliser ces choses à la fin vous permettra d'atteindre ce produit fini.

La construction d'une voiture commence toujours par un rendu de la voiture, des modifications sont apportées, des dessins en 3D sont réalisés et, après plusieurs rendus, le fabricant décide du produit fini.

Une fois les rendus approuvés, la voiture est construite; d'abord, la coque du véhicule est fabriquée, suivie de tous les autres composants, et après plusieurs semaines, la voiture sort et arrive chez le concessionnaire, prête à être achetée par ses nouveaux propriétaires.

Il y avait un processus pour créer la voiture; maintenant, le concepteur ne se décourage pas parce que le véhicule n'est pas apparu instantanément ou n'est pas frustré parce qu'il a dû faire des révisions; non, il savait qu'il y avait un processus. Lorsque vous comprenez le processus, la frustration n'a plus sa place dans votre vie.

Je le répète, chaque nouveau niveau exige un nouveau vous, une nouvelle façon de penser, de parler, de s'engager et de s'adapter. On dit qu'on ne peut pas apprendre à un vieux chien de nouveaux tours, oh, mais on peut!

Lorsque vous faites un rêve, il vous est souvent chuchoté; Dieu ne crie pas, il vous chuchote. Plus tu es proche de Dieu, plus sa voix devient douce. Dieu doit être ta source d'inspiration; lorsqu'il devient ta source d'inspiration, tu commenceras à recevoir la sagesse et la compréhension dans toutes les choses que tu fais et que tu veux faire.

N'abandonnez jamais; sans engagement, vous ne commencerez jamais rien; sans constance, vous ne finirez jamais; ce n'est pas facile; si ça l'était, l'histoire serait différente. Donc, au lieu de cela, vous devez continuer à travailler sur le nouveau vous, tomber sept fois mais vous relever huit fois, vous battre pour reconnaître que l'ancien vous ne peut pas vous porter au-delà de points spécifiques de votre vie.

1 Corinthiens 13:11 dit: "Quand j'étais enfant, je parlais comme un enfant, je comprenais comme un enfant, je pensais comme un enfant; mais quand je suis devenu homme, je me suis débarrassé des choses enfantines."

Vous devez grandir chaque jour, chercher Dieu, grandir en maturité, en connaissance, en obéissance, en soumission et en respect. Grandir dans l'appréciation des autres, grandir dans votre amour pour la parole de Dieu, grandir dans le désir d'être proche de Dieu et d'entendre sa voix.

L'un des facteurs les plus importants qui me motivent à poursuivre ce voyage est le doute et l'incrédulité que les autres peuvent avoir en moi ou en mes rêves. Le fait qu'ils doutent de moi me pousse à aller plus loin, à mieux servir, à viser le plus haut et à surpasser tout le monde dans la pièce.

Le nouveau vous devra laisser beaucoup de choses derrière lui, s'adapter à de nouveaux environnements et, surtout, continuer à poursuivre la grandeur pour laquelle Dieu vous a appelé. Bien sûr, l'ancien vous s'accrochera et luttera pour ne pas lâcher prise, mais il est impératif que vous démissionniez de votre ancien vous et que vous acceptiez le nouveau vous pour lequel Dieu vous a appelé.

Le nouveau vous doit accepter que des défis plus importants vont se présenter, et donc votre vocabulaire doit changer, les mots qui sortent de votre bouche doivent être alignés avec la parole de Dieu. Par conséquent, il est crucial pour le nouveau vous d'entrer dans la parole de Dieu, de la mémoriser, de l'étudier, de la déclarer et de vivre par elle.

La Bible dit dans la 2ème Corinthiens 5:7, "Car nous marchons par la foi, et non par la vue."

Votre vieux vous veut marcher en fonction de ce que vous voyez et entendez, en fonction d'une expérience qui vous aide à continuer à marcher. Le vieux toi a besoin de preuves pour croire, a besoin de choses qui sont ressenties pour marcher. Le nouveau toi n'a besoin de rien de naturel; il n'a pas besoin de ce qui est entendu, senti et vu pour marcher; notre confiance est dans le Seigneur Dieu, et c'est l'énergie dont nous avons besoin pour marcher.

Le nouveau vous n'a pas besoin que la motivation ou l'encouragement vienne de quelqu'un d'autre; vous le trouvez dans le Seigneur. Ainsi, 1er Samuel 30:6 dit, "...mais David s'encourageait dans le Seigneur son Dieu.

Trouvez l'encouragement et la motivation en sachant que tout est possible avec Dieu, et que rien n'est possible sans Dieu. Car si vous n'acceptez pas ce fait, alors quand verrez-vous la gloire de Dieu se manifester dans votre vie?

Le moment est venu pour le nouveau vous de renaître de ses cendres et d'enterrer votre ancien vous. Lâcher ces choses qui ne vous ont servi qu'à vous bloquer, vous libérer de la culpabilité, de la honte et de votre passé, et accepter qu'aujourd'hui Dieu vous a appelé pour quelque chose de plus grand.

Chaque jour, mois, année, heure et seconde qui passe à vivre dans l'ancien vous, plein de déceptions et d'échecs, de culpabilité et de honte, est un moment qui ne nous reviendra jamais. Bien sûr, il ne nous reviendra jamais lorsque le temps aura passé, mais la graine que nous avons plantée à ce moment-là donnera des fruits dans notre lendemain. Qu'elles soient bonnes ou mauvaises, ces graines vous aideront à grandir ou vous maintiendront dans les fosses du désespoir.

Car c'est le moment, c'est le moment où vous devez décider de vous lever et de vous prendre en charge avant tout. Devenez une nouvelle version de vous-même, redéfinissez qui vous êtes, mettez-vous au défi d'être meilleur; c'est le moment. La Bible dit, dans Ecclésiaste 3:1, "Il y a un temps pour tout et une saison pour toute activité sous les cieux."

Car c'est la saison où Dieu veut faire de grandes choses avec vous, par vous et pour vous!

SI CE N'EST PAS MAINTENANT, QUAND?

Quel est le bon moment pour faire quoi que ce soit? Devons-nous attendre de ne plus avoir de problèmes? Ou jusqu'à ce que nous ayons tout l'argent nécessaire? Quand est-ce le bon moment pour agir?

Si nous attendons que tout s'aligne, nous risquons de rester ici quelque temps. Si Pierre avait attendu que les eaux se calment, il n'aurait peut-être jamais marché sur l'eau; si Daniel avait attendu qu'il n'y ait pas de décret, il n'aurait jamais vu les merveilles de Dieu dans la fosse aux lions.

Si David avait attendu d'être plus grand et plus fort, Goliath n'aurait pas été vaincu. Si ces hommes, parmi d'autres, avaient attendu pour agir, nous aurions une histoire différente à lire dans la Bible.

Si nous attendons que les choses soient parfaites pour agir, nous ne travaillerons jamais car rien ne sera jamais parfait. La Bible dit, Proverbes 3:5-6, "Il y a un temps pour tout, et une saison pour toute activité sous les cieux."

Pierre a dû faire confiance à Dieu, et il a marché sur l'eau; Daniel a dû être fidèle à sa prière, et Dieu a envoyé la délivrance; David a dû croire en lui-même, et son Dieu et Goliath sont tombés.

Vous ne pouvez pas vous asseoir et espérer que les choses s'arrangent d'elles-mêmes, parfois elles le font, mais vous devez retrousser vos manches et vous mettre au travail quand ce n'est pas le cas. Espérer que Dieu fasse tout est une perte totale de temps et d'énergie. Dieu ne fera jamais ce que vous êtes censé faire, il fait ce que vous ne pouvez pas faire, mais il attend que vous fassiez ce qu'il vous a donné la capacité de faire.

Il n'y a pas de moment parfait pour faire quoi que ce soit; il n'y a pas de scénario correct pour commencer, vous devez le décider et c'est à vous de vous dire, c'est mon heure! La foi n'attend pas le bon moment; la foi crée le moment d'agir. La foi n'attend pas que les étoiles s'alignent; la foi est audacieuse et active, la foi provoque le mouvement.

Les excuses vous disent que vous devez attendre le bon moment, et oui, comme je l'ai dit plus tôt, il y a un temps et une saison pour tout sous le soleil, mais vous devez agir quand il s'agit de votre Foi.

La Bible dit, Jacques 2:14, "Que sert-il, mes frères, si quelqu'un dit qu'il a la foi et n'a pas d'oeuvres? La foi peut-elle le sauver?

Le verset 18 dit: "Mais quelqu'un dira: "Tu as la foi, et moi j'ai les œuvres." Montre-moi ta foi sans tes œuvres, et je te montrerai ma foi par mes œuvres".

C'est un verset puissant, surtout à la fin, quand il dit: "Je te montrerai ma foi par mes œuvres! ".

Vos œuvres résultent directement de votre Foi et vice versa, votre manque d'œuvres résulte directement de votre manque de confiance. Ainsi, dire que vous attendez le "bon" moment, c'est simplement masquer le fait que vous avez des raisons pour lesquelles vous ne voulez pas commencer.

Il peut s'agir de raisons justifiables ou de points de vue valables, mais la réalité est que si vous ne décidez jamais de commencer, vous ne le ferez jamais. Quand est-ce que ce sera le bon moment? Quel que soit le bon moment, il y aura toujours des choses qui ne seront pas parfaites, et si vous vous concentrez sur les choses qui ne vont pas, elles serviront à vous bloquer avant même que vous ne commenciez.

Les excuses se font souvent passer pour des choses légitimes, et comprenez-moi bien, elles peuvent très bien l'être. Cependant, j'essaie de faire comprendre que si vous laissez toujours ces choses vous arrêter, quand allez-vous réussir à faire quelque chose?

Esther était une femme audacieuse, confiante dans sa vocation, saine d'esprit, mais son timing n'était pas le meilleur. Il n'était pas possible de s'approcher du roi sans être convoqué; cela signifiait une mort certaine. Elle avait le dos au mur; l'ennemi était tout autour, les restrictions hors de son contrôle, mais elle savait ce qu'elle devait faire.

Connaissant la loi et la sanction concernant l'approche du roi à l'improviste, elle a décidé de faire l'impensable. D'une seule phrase, elle a scellé son destin et s'en est remise à Dieu en disant dans Esther 4:16: "Allez, rassemblez tous les Juifs qui se trouvent à Suse, et jeûnez pour moi; ne mangez ni ne buvez pendant trois jours, ni nuit ni jour. Moi aussi, et mes jeunes filles, nous jeûnerons de même. Et c'est ainsi que je me rendrai auprès du roi, ce qui n'est pas conforme à la loi; et si je péris, je péris."

Elle ne pouvait pas attendre le bon moment ou être appelée par le roi; elle devait activer sa Foi et agir selon sa Foi et ce qui devait être fait. Il y a des moments où vous devez attendre que certaines choses se produisent pour que vous puissiez agir, mais il y a aussi des moments où vous devez agir avant que le bon moment soit venu.

Les deux points de vue sont essentiels, mais si vous vous obstinez à toujours attendre le bon moment, la bonne heure ou les bonnes circonstances pour agir, alors le moment peut ne jamais se présenter à vous. Au cours de votre quête pour accomplir ce que Dieu vous a appelé à faire, vous rencontrerez des moments qui vous obligeront à attendre qu'une fenêtre s'ouvre; ces moments nécessitent de la patience, des conseils et des directives.

La patience pour voir la fenêtre s'ouvrir suffisamment pour que vous puissiez saisir votre chance, recevoir des conseils pour savoir si vous devez agir ou non, et être guidé par ceux qui sont passés par là pour que des erreurs similaires ne se reproduisent pas.

Puis il y a ces moments où la Foi en action est requise. Encore une fois, Pierre, pour marcher sur les eaux, n'a pas demandé le vote des autres disciples; il n'a pas vérifié ce qu'ils pensaient de lui marchant sur l'eau. Pierre n'a pas non plus attendu qu'il n'y ait pas de tempête et que la mer soit calme. Pierre a réagi par la foi, a profité de l'instant et a marché sur les eaux.

Il y aura des jours où vous devrez prendre du recul et analyser la situation, mais il y aura aussi des jours où vous devrez agir et voir les merveilles que Dieu a pour vous.

Esther a dit, c'est bien, si je péris, je péris! Néanmoins, elle était prête à risquer sa propre vie pour voir un miracle se produire.

Daniel 3:16-18 dit: Schadrac, Méschac et Abed-Nego prirent la parole et dirent au roi: O Nebucadnetsar, nous n'avons pas l'attention de te répondre dans cette affaire. S'il en est ainsi, notre Dieu que nous servons peut nous délivrer de la fournaise ardente, et il nous délivrera de ta main, ô roi. Sinon, sache, ô roi, que nous ne servirons pas tes dieux et que nous n'adorerons pas la statue d'or que tu as dressée.

Sinon, sache, ô roi, que nous ne servirons pas tes dieux et que nous n'adorerons pas la statue d'or que tu as dressée. Comme on dit, ils ont tracé une ligne dans le sable, et ils ont tenu bon.

Face à une fournaise ardente, face à la mort, ils ont tenu bon, et ils ont déclaré avec audace leur foi en Dieu. Cette déclaration audacieuse les a fait agir de manière "provocante" devant le roi, mais c'était la seule issue possible.

Face à la perspective de la mort, ils ont choisi de défendre hardiment ce en quoi ils croyaient au lieu de céder pour sauver leur propre vie. Qu'êtes-vous prêt à faire maintenant? Êtes-vous prêt à céder ou à rester debout?

Vous, et vous seul, pouvez prendre cette décision; vous devez vous approprier cette décision et vous y tenir, quoi qu'il arrive. Vous devez chasser la peur de votre esprit, de votre cœur et de vos paroles. Vous devez être capable de vous lever et de dire,

"Que devons-nous donc répondre à ces choses? Si Dieu est pour nous, qui peut être contre nous? Romains 8:31

Ce "qui" peut symboliser une personne ou une chose, ce "qui" doit être vaincu dans votre vie, même si ce "qui" est vous-même.

Nous sommes dans une saison qui est si imprévisible, tant de variables se produisent autour de nous, et les choses changent à chaque minute. Ainsi, la parole de Dieu dit, dans le 2ème Timothée 1:7, "Car Dieu ne nous a pas donné un esprit de crainte, mais de puissance, d'amour et de sagesse".

La peur ne peut pas avoir une place dans vos pensées et vos paroles. La peur ne peut pas avoir une place pour vivre dans votre esprit; la peur ne peut pas avoir une place dans la façon dont vous vivez; vous devez être libre de tout libre.

La seule façon de se libérer de la peur est de s'entourer et de s'immerger dans la présence de Dieu. Ensuite, vous êtes libéré de cette peur lorsque vous le faites, et vous pouvez prendre des décisions claires et directes concernant votre avenir.

Vous ferez des erreurs dans votre prise de décision, vous vous tromperez, vous prendrez le mauvais virage, et parfois vous prendrez des décisions horribles que vous regretterez plus tard. Mais rappelez-vous: "Quant à vous, vous avez voulu faire le mal contre moi; mais Dieu a voulu le bien, en faisant qu'il en soit ainsi aujourd'hui, pour sauver beaucoup de gens. Genèse 50:20"

Vous vous tromperez parfois, mais Dieu, dans sa sagesse infinie, dans sa grande grâce, retournera les choses pour vous de la manière dont Lui seul sait le faire.

Pierre aurait pu facilement penser, lorsqu'il se noyait, "c'était une erreur de ma part". Combien de fois avez-vous dit ces mots? Je peux vous dire que j'ai dit ces mots de nombreuses fois au cours de ma vie. Pourtant, à travers toutes mes erreurs, j'ai conclu que la miséricorde de Dieu est tellement immense et très spéciale qu'il nous donne la grâce et la compassion même lorsque nous devrions recevoir un jugement.

Dans les moments où nous sommes coupables, il nous accorde un pardon, c'est cela le grand amour de Dieu. Nous ne serons peut-être jamais capables de le comprendre ou de l'appréhender, mais la réalité est que si nous faisons confiance au Seigneur de tout notre cœur, alors nous pouvons être assurés que sa miséricorde ne nous fera jamais défaut.

Vous avez peut-être raison, mais Dieu est absolu, vous avez peut-être une perspective, Dieu voit tout, nous avons peut-être une idée, Dieu a le chemin; car sans Dieu, nous ne pouvons rien faire.

C'est ma prière sincère que votre vie ait été édifiée et mise au défi de faire l'impensable à travers ce livre. Je prie pour que vous vous leviez aujourd'hui et que vous poursuiviez le rêve, le but ou la vision que Dieu a mis sur votre cœur et que vous le voyiez se réaliser.

Car c'est la saison, le moment que Dieu a attendu, le moment où vous décidez de vous lever, de vous dépoussiérer et d'être ce que Dieu vous a appelé à être.

Vos problèmes sont aussi grands que vous leur donnez du crédit, et Dieu peut être aussi grand que votre foi le laisse être. Ainsi donc, vous pouvez vous lever aujourd'hui et accomplir ce que vous vous êtes fixé.

Soyez le Daniel qui n'a pas cessé de prier, soyez l'intrépide Déborah, soyez le David qui a terrassé un géant et sauvé une nation, soyez l'Esther qui s'est levée face à l'incertitude, soyez le Pierre qui a marché sur l'eau.

La Bible est pleine de héros de la foi et nul autre que notre Seigneur et Sauveur Jésus-Christ.

Encore une fois, le monde est plein de héros, mais le moment est venu d'écrire un nouveau chapitre et de faire émerger un nouveau héros, et ce héros doit être vous!

Soyez le héros de votre famille, le héros de vos amis, le héros de vous-même. Reconnaissez que Dieu est de votre côté, et qu'il ne vous quittera jamais ni ne vous abandonnera.

C'est votre moment et votre heure, saisissez-le, conquérez-le, levez-vous, levez-vous et criez-le du haut de la montagne;

J'AI ÉTÉ DESTINÉ À LA GRANDEUR!

Printed in the United States
by Baker & Taylor Publisher Services